Mountain Biking
Wisconsin

by

Colby Thor Waller

FALCON®

HELENA, MONTANA

AFALCONGUIDE®

Falcon® Publishing is continually expanding its list of recreation guidebooks. All books include detailed descriptions, accurate maps, and all the information necessary for enjoyable trips. You can order extra copies of this book and get information and prices for other Falcon guidebooks by writing Falcon, P.O. Box 1718, Helena, MT 59624 or calling toll free 1-800-582-2665. Also, please ask for a free copy of our current catalog. Visit our web site at http://www.falconguide.com

All photos by the author unless otherwise noted.
Cover photo by Cathy and Gordon Illg.

Library of Congress Cataloging-in-Publication Data
Waller, Colby Thor, 1971-
     Mountain biking Wisconsin / by Colby Thor Waller.
        p.   cm.
     "A FalconGuide"—T.p. verso.
     Includes bibliographical references (p.) and index.
     ISBN 1-56044-666-8 (pbk.)
     1. All terrain cycling—Wisconsin—Guidebooks. 2. Bicycle trails—Wisconsin—Guidebooks. 3. Wisconsin—Guidebooks I. Title.
    GV1045.5.W6W35 1998
    917.7504'43—dc21
                                         98-16773
                                                CIP

♻ Text pages printed on recycled paper.

CAUTION

Outdoor recreational activities are by their very nature potentially hazardous. All participants in such activities must assume the responsibility for their own actions and safety. The information contained in this guidebook cannot replace sound judgment and good decision-making skills, which help reduce risk exposure, nor does the scope of this book allow for disclosure of all the potential hazards and risks involved in such activities.

Learn as much as possible about the outdoor recreational activities in which you participate, prepare for the unexpected, and be cautious. The reward will be a safer and more enjoyable experience.

This book is dedicated to the memory of Sumner Matteson,
Wisconsin's first fat-tire rider.

Contents

Acknowledgments

Thanks are due to Scott Frey, Ron Bergin, and all the fellow riders and friends who have helped make this project fun throughout the course of 1997.

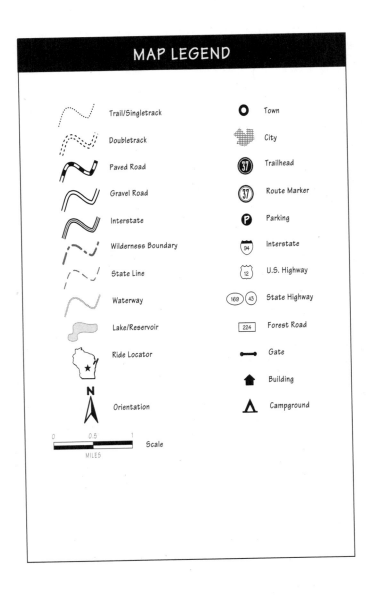

Wisconsin

DULUTH, MN

Iron Mountain, MI

TO MINNEAPOLIS

Eau Claire

Wausau

Green Bay

Tomah

Sheboygan

La Crosse

Prairie du Chien

Portage

Madison

MILWAUKEE

Dubuque, IA

Beloit

TO CHICAGO

Preface

It's right . . . that we should have to pay for beautiful things.
And being here in this spot, now, is worth travelling a thousand miles for, and for all that that has cost us. Maybe we have
lived only to be here now.

—Rockwell Kent, *N by E*

My first bike, given to me when I was six, was spray-painted orange and
had solid rubber tires. I rode all over our family farm on it, exploring every
corner. I rode it until the spokes were too bent to fit between the forks and
the mechanics of the bike were beyond repair. My father soon noticed this
and bought me my first true off-road bike—a BMX Mongoose Supergoose. I
used it to push past the stone and barbed-wire fence line of our farm to the
quarries nearby and the neighboring county forest. I was driven to see every inch of the surrounding land, to make it a part of my memory. I began to
daydream while I rode of traveling faster and faster over the land, though I
couldn't achieve these speeds at my young age. I thought of eating up earth
under my tires, covering miles and miles of terrain, seeing more and more
of the world. As I outgrew BMX I thought that perhaps I had outgrown
bicycling altogether, but the thought of covering so much ground remained
with me.

Years later, working for a local bike wholesaler, I saw my first mountain
bike. I bought the simplest, cheapest machine I could find and began to ride
again. I moved out from the forests and quarries in my hometown. I learned
the trails in Milwaukee and the Kettle Moraine like the back of my hand. I
made friends with bikers in Madison and learned their trails. I traveled
north to St. Germaine, Rhinelander, Cable, and a dozen other towns until I
had covered the state of Wisconsin and truly felt like it was my own.

Wisconsin and mountain biking are a natural mix—a match made in
heaven. Approximately 12,000 years ago a mass of ice slowly made its way
down through Canada into Wisconsin, carrying a payload of rock and soil
with it. As the earth's climate slowly moderated, the ice melted and the
glacial lakes receded, leaving behind the terrain we have today. The French
encountered this terrain when they first visited the state in 1634, led by
Jean Nicolet. Indians navigated the countryside 7,000 years before Nicolet,
traveling here originally to bury their dead by the shore of Lake Michigan.
The Indians traveled by foot, horseback, and canoe. As bikers we are the
next generation to travel the diverse state of Wisconsin. In this era we still
move under our own power, not on horseback but instead on a modern
machine. There are places in this world that are still sparsely inhabited,
where you are offered the chance to see nature untamed and untouched.
Much of Wisconsin is just this sort of place.

I have lived in Wisconsin all my life. The northern portion of the state
has been a sacred place to me since I was a small child, and traveled the
area for the first time in the middle of a snowy night. Some of my first

A sweeping corner at a central intersection in the Emma Carlin Cluster.

memories are of these travels with my father on the lonesome highways of the north country. In this part of the world, the pine forests sprawl in either direction as far as the eye can see and on a clear winter night the stars are the only things that outnumber the trees.

I hope you take the information in this book to heart and take it upon yourself to explore the far corners of the state. This book was written with the intention of sharing the experience of viewing Wisconsin from the saddle of a mountain bike. As the ground whips by beneath your bike and the trees at the edges of the trail begin to blur, it should become obvious that mountain biking is able to deliver on the daydreams of a six-year-old child, able to eat up more and more ground on a shiny metal machine. Have fun and explore your own frontiers.

The author descending through the hardwoods and ferns on the John Minix Trail.
LAURA HUTCHINS PHOTO

Introduction

THE LAND

Any discussion regarding the geography of Wisconsin will eventually turn to the subject of glaciation. The last of the glaciers that pushed their way south through the state approximately 12,000 years ago made a profound impact on the terrain that is so well-suited for mountain biking today. This varied terrain can basically be broken into three segments: the glaciated north; the terminal moraine in the central part of the state where the glacier came to a stop; and the driftless area of southwest Wisconsin, which had no direct contact with the ice but was instead covered by a glacial lake.

The Wisconsin Glacier, as it came to be known because of its final resting spot, was a massive sheet of ice more than 400 feet thick in some places. Glaciers form when more snow falls in the winter than can melt in the summer for a period of many years. As the snow accumulates, its own weight crushes the bottom layers and freezes them into ice. Then the ice begins to move. The heat of the earth itself causes the bottom of the glacier to melt, forming a slippery base on which it moves forward. Considering the enormity of the Wisconsin Glacier, which covered the entire state as well as the bulk of Canada, it is no surprise that mountains were sheered off, lakes dug out, and the entire terrain compressed into rolling hills.

The northern half of Wisconsin was formed primarily by the weight of the glaciers and by the remnants left when they retreated. Many of the depressions that formed in this way filled with water, becoming lakes connected by a vast system of rivers and streams. While exploring the state by mountain bike, it quickly becomes apparent that this is a land of lakes. The Winnebago Indians named the land known today as Wisconsin *Mekousing* meaning, "where the waters gather"—in reference to the Mississippi, the Great Lakes, and hundreds of smaller lakes and rivers. Many of the formations in the land found between the lakes were created as the glaciers melted and receded. As temperatures rose the glaciers broke down, cracking and breaking apart. The sediment that had collected in the ice was washed out by streams of melt water running down the cracks and out onto the earth. The sediment collected in these stream beds formed eskers, long thin strips of land that run like a spine across the ground, and kames, rounded hills left behind as debris washed down through holes in the ice.

The terminal moraine, or terminus, where the glacier came to a halt, is one of the most interesting features on which to mountain bike in Wisconsin. The terminus of the glacier is marked today by a winding path of rock and diverse geographic features running from southeast Wisconsin near Milwaukee in a northwesterly direction toward Eau Claire and out to the Mississippi River. The area was formed as the glaciers pushed a pile of rock, vegetation, and soil downward through the state. The pile remained after the glaciers retreated and is today among the most rugged terrain in the state.

Of its more eclectic remnants, erratics or "hitchhikers" are the most peculiar. These rocks traveled in the ice from Canada down into southern Wisconsin, only to be left behind after the melt, in many cases balanced in the most precarious of positions. Devil's Lake near Baraboo is an excellent place to see these odd formations. The Kettle Moraine, which is found in the terminus, actually takes its name from two different types of formations. A kettle is a depression in the earth created where a block of ice wedged into the ground and later melted away. A moraine is a rock pile formed when glaciers pushed debris forward, retreated momentarily, and then pushed forward again, scraping over the pile and smoothing it.

As all this destruction happened in the north, southwestern Wisconsin remained clear. Most of its features are remnants from its past as the floor of glacial Lake Wisconsin. The ancient lake formed as the glaciers melted and flowed out toward the Mississippi. The sandstone formations and tall turret-like bluffs found today are a testament to this aquatic history. During the ice age, the area also served as a refuge for wildlife while the rest of the state was in a deep freeze. After the glaciers were gone, life returned to the rest of the state, having been preserved for the most part in the southwestern corner of Wisconsin.

THE SEASONS AND SAFETY

It is understandably difficult for those not native to Wisconsin to prepare for its climate. The weather here is diverse, to say the least, and notoriously harsh. From brutal snow-filled winters to sweltering, humid summers, Wisconsin demands that its inhabitants be hearty. Knowing the seasons and the appropriate gear for those seasons is of the utmost importance in getting enjoyment out of each and every ride.

Winter: The first and most infamous Wisconsin season to discuss is winter. When winter comes to the northern counties, the snow flies as early as October and stays around well into May. Temperatures duck down into single digits, with wind chills well below 0 degrees. This isn't to say that winter need be a dormant time for mountain bikers. While road riders crank away on indoor trainers, mountain bikers are able to explore the winter landscape on sturdy, well-treaded fat-tire bikes. I always find that the added adversity of winter brings out the essence of riding, even on the most mundane city streets or seldom-ridden trails. It should be noted that many of the trails in this book will be closed during winter to grant use to cross-country skiers; but then again, the roads are tough enough when piled high with snow and ice.

Preparing to ride in such tough arctic conditions is not as difficult as it may seem and, amazingly, riders often overdress for winter conditions. Keep in mind that while you are riding you are heating up. Let your body's circulation work for you. When layering clothes make certain not to restrict the flow of blood to extremities. A single pair of socks that allow a bit of movement will be much warmer than two pairs that barely fit into cycling shoes.

Use your judgment as you dress. Take wind speed, precipitation, and your own physical condition into consideration as you prepare.

A helpful hint for those a bit more ambitious is to build a set of studded tires for better traction in snow and ice. Using a pair of old knobby tires, insert 0.5-inch-long machine bolts (not sharp-ended woodworking screws) through the treads every two inches on alternating sides. Secure these bolts with washers and nuts. Running an old inner tube along the inside of the tire helps to protect the actual inner tube from the sharp edges of the bolt heads. A fine set of spikes offers excellent traction in all sorts of extreme conditions, whether ice, snow, or mud.

One last tip for winter riding is the importance of proper hydration. Be sure you continue to consume fluids even in cold weather. Though this type of riding isn't as taxing or dehydrating as summer riding, water is still essential to staying on top of your game and keeping your body in prime working order.

Spring: Spring is the next most difficult season to ride. The nature of the season is particularly inviting as birds return to the state, sweeping in from the south in flocks along migration corridors. Plants come to life again, and the landscape returns to green instead of the monotonous white that has dominated the previous four months. Spring is an unpredictable time when trying to prepare for riding. Snow can easily stick around until April or May. As the snow melts, the rivers overrun their banks and normally dry fields turn to mud. Many trails are closed to avoid the massive erosion

Water crossing (note spiked tires). Laura Hutchins Photo

common to this transition period, while some less-maintained trails begin to open. The riding is tough on bikes, and parts begin to fail as they are pushed past their limits in the mud.

Temperatures will vary as winter turns to summer and, while one day will be in the 60s or 70s, the next may be back down to freezing. It is important during this time of year to dress appropriately to avoid catching a cold in the cool, damp weather. Breathable rain gear is excellent for this, allowing condensation to escape while repelling water from puddles and spring rainstorms. Because of the predominantly wet weather, it is a good idea before riding to phone trail officials and check trail conditions and closings. A little patience in the spring will lead to better trails in the summer.

Summer: Summer is of course one of the best times of year to be out riding. The whole world seems to be alive, audibly alive in the evenings on the edges of forests and marshes as the plethora of crickets, frogs, and birds call back and forth to each other in a cacophony of chirps and hums. The sun returns and the trails are dry and ready for bikers. All the riding through winter and spring under piles of adversity pays off as the most difficult of obstacles are once again conquerable. After riding the same slippery, snow-covered obstacles all winter, it is a great feeling to come out on the first day of summer and glide over them with grace, utilizing the great traction summer trails have to offer.

Fall: Fall is the last season that needs to be mentioned, and also happens to be my personal favorite for biking. In the fall, temperatures dip back to tolerable levels, normally into the 50s or 60s. Cooler nights kill off the bugs that can make summer a trying time, and the growth on the trail edges begins to recede in the colder weather, making it easier to thrash through the trails already packed hard and fast by a summer's worth of riding. The humidity finally leaves the air, too, allowing riders to fill their lungs to capacity with the clear, crisp air.

The trees in Wisconsin are plentiful and when autumn hits, their colors burst into life, making each ride a unique tour. The weather also begins to turn and, as winter approaches, rain turns to sleet and then to snow as the weeks go by. As with spring and winter, it is important to gauge the conditions of each day on an individual basis in order to stay warm and dry throughout each ride. A word of warning: October and November mark the beginning of various hunting seasons for fowl, small game, and big game; take precautions when exploring the wilderness. Don't give hunters a target. Deer are not bright orange, nor do they have flashing amber lights strapped to their posteriors, so use these clues to make yourself look more like a biker and less like a trophy buck.

The bottom line is that Wisconsin experiences the full gamut of seasons. Each has its own distinct characteristics, some good and some bad. All the seasons are good for riding, some just take more ingenuity to conquer. The trails in this book are primarily meant for the summer and fall months, especially since the majority of the trails are restricted in the winter months to cross-country skiers. Spring is often too sloppy, with erosion being a real problem, and trail closures are common. In these seasons when the trails are closed, road riding can be equally fun, especially in the larger cities where there are a limitless number of back alleys and side streets to explore. In the off-season, the logging roads of the north are normally rideable as well, allowing riders to explore the wilderness after the trails have closed.

Heat, Humidity, and Insects: Summer has drawbacks in two forms: bugs and humidity. I normally know summer has arrived on the first ride when I have to make the decision whether to swallow a bug that has slammed into the back of my throat, or to go through the disgusting process of hacking it up. I tend to swallow the bug and try to forget the event happened altogether. A helmet visor is very helpful for taking the brunt of swarms found on the trail and protects equally well against the elements. Bug spray that repels blackflies, horse flies, and mosquitos is a must throughout the warmer months. Ticks can also be a problem; a check for the parasites after each forest ride is a good idea.

Summer weather in Wisconsin has its extremes and is no different than winter in this regard. Temperatures in July and August soar to 95 degrees and above, with high humidity. The humidity is the killer. In Wisconsin's hot, humid conditions, sweat pours off the body and hydration is the key to survival on the trail. For the purpose of safety it is important to stay within your individual limits while riding in the heat. Stay in tune with your body and realize that if you stop producing sweat, it is well past the time that you should stop riding. Find shade and rehydrate.

Water Consumption: Twenty ounces of water before, 40 ounces during, and 20 ounces after is the minimum on a hot day. Try not to start a ride dehydrated. Instead, make it a point to continuously drink water during the summer months, and consider starting to increase your ingestion of water the day of or night before a ride to help your body stow the proper amount. A Hydrapak is a possible solution if you are not getting enough water from bottles. Hydrapaks allow you to carry up to 90 ounces of water on your back and make it easier to continue drinking throughout the ride, leaving your hands on the bars while your mouth does the work, gulping water from a tube. Be particularly aware of proper hydration on longer trips in more desolate areas.

First Aid and Fuel: While we're on the subject of safety measures, in addition to water make certain to have a medical kit back at your car or base camp for emergencies. Also, take some food along to eat on the trail, especially on longer rides where you are burning a lot of energy. Pudding-like carbo mix has been hailed as the new style for sustaining energy in the saddle because of its ease of digestion. Energy bars, trail mix, and fruit are also good choices and can fight off the infamous "bonk," the point where your blood sugar drops, and your body basically gives out on you. Try to stay ahead of your body by keeping it properly fueled and your performance throughout the course of your ride should remain steady.

FLORA AND FAUNA

Wisconsin is teeming with life in the warmer seasons of spring, summer, and fall, audibly alive when you take a moment to listen. In winter, however, when this life is blanketed with snow and ice, the animals that don't migrate or hibernate are faced with an ongoing struggle to find food in the barren landscape. Most plants go dormant, waiting to return to life in the spring. The pines alone maintain their appearance throughout the year, becoming turret-like crystal mounds in the winter, ready to shake off their snowy coat in the wind. Unlike many U.S. states, the plant and animal life is similar throughout Wisconsin, getting more abundant the farther you travel north and away from the population centers.

Fauna: From Lake Superior to the Illinois border, Wisconsin is a rugged wilderness spawning large animals in all forms. The fish in the bottoms of lakes and streams grow to monstrous proportions. The famed Brule River in the northwest quadrant of the state produces some of the most beautiful rainbow and brown trout you can shake a fly at. The deep cold waters of the northwoods hide the elusive muskellunge, an enormous member of the pickerel family and a true trophy at an average 30 to 40 pounds.

From the central part of the state north to Superior, raptors are visible from many of the bluffs and open plains where hunting is good for these keen-eyed predators. Bald eagles rip the tips off pines in the northern portion of the state to establish nests, most often along the banks of area rivers and lakes. An unforgettable image is that of an eagle coming in close over a stream, slapping the water with exposed claws and rising up with a northern pike in its grip. On the bluffs surrounding Devil's Lake or the Levis and Trow Mounds, red-tailed hawks soar on air currents for hours, gazing into fields to detect the movement of small mammals that don't stand a chance when spotted. In marshes and ponds throughout the state, the graceful crane pauses to rest its mammoth wings. To see one lift off is an amazing sight, conjuring up images of prehistoric pterodactyls taking flight.

Throughout Wisconsin and particularly in the north, the mammals are among the most exciting to view in all of North America. In the northwest, sitting by the campfire at night, the howl of coyotes and wolves haunts the night. Wolves have been reintroduced into northern Minnesota for the last decade and have made their way back into many of their original hunting grounds in Wisconsin. Red foxes are visible in the daytime and also audible at night—their sound is a yelp, not a howl, and is easy to distinguish from those of the coyotes and wolves. Also in the north is the black bear, rare but potentially dangerous. As you approach the Upper Peninsula border, begin to think of keeping your food in airtight containers, out of reach of predators and preferably not in your tent where unwanted visitors may come to snack.

The author climbing over wide grass paths at the Point Beach State Forest Trails.
LAURA HUTCHINS PHOTO

The most common large mammal to be seen in the state is the white-tailed deer. These deer are abundant throughout the state, and in the more remote areas several may be seen on each ride. The deer use mountain bike trails as short cuts through the woods and occasionally will run alongside bikers before they realize their mistake and spring away into the forest. Whitetails are always present. In fall during the rut you often can hear them in the distance, raking their antlers together in struggles over territory and mating rights.

No listing of the animal life of Wisconsin would be complete without the badger. The badger is the state animal, and the mascot of the University of Wisconsin. This small mammal rides low to the ground and is striped brown and white down its back. It has nasty claws, but don't worry—it's as rare to see as a bear, and probably as elusive as the Ho-dag, the mythical fanged creature that northerners have claimed to have seen roaming the woods for decades.

Flora: Wisconsin is green throughout, from the Illinois border to the shore of Lake Superior. Forests consisting of oak, sugar maple, birch, aspen, willow, and alder fill the land. Wherever cities or farmlands don't exist, trees do. The pines of the north woods are vast, thickly aromatic, and hearty. Wildflowers of a thousand varieties mixed with prairie grass lead up to the forests in the rolling prairies. Flowers from the blue stem to the upland plover are native to the land and sprinkle the golden fields with color. Many southern areas of the state are undergoing a process of restoration, returning the native plants to the soils that for years have been used as farmlands and now are being converted back to their original state. Lapham Peak in the southeast corner of the state is a prime example of this replanting effort. Programs like this help to sustain other life forms that depend on this natural vegetation.

THE PEOPLE

Because of the geography of Wisconsin, the history of the people who have settled here is very interesting. To past cultures the land was truly God's country and an obvious choice for settlement with its rich soil, expansive water routes, and access not only to the Atlantic through the Great Lakes, but also to the Gulf of Mexico by the Mississippi River.

The first to come here were the mound builders. These prehistoric Indians came to the state in what must have been a mystical journey. The Indians came to bury their dead by the shores of the great waters of Lake Michigan. They lived among the bluffs and the prairies, leaving more than fifteen thousand mounds to help us interpret their existence. While many of the mounds were for burial purposes, many more were ceremonial, pointing to their deep-rooted religion based in the powers of nature and the soul of the human. Many of the mounds captured the things in nature that they held in reverence, such as the hawk and the bear. The civilization that was established here became an extension of the prehistoric metropolis of Cahokia in southern Illinois, another group of mound builders who constructed monuments second only to Mexico's in size on the North American continent.

As these early cultures developed, they fragmented and new nomadic groups introduced themselves to the mix. The tribes known as the Winnebago, Menominee, Sioux, Chippewa, and Fox, names familiar as cities and land formations to Wisconsinites, established their territories in the state. The Indians inherited many of the farmlands left behind by previous cultures and themselves became accomplished farmers and hunters in the abundant land. The Chippewa nation controlled much of the upper Northwest with the Menominee to the east and the Winnebago to the south. Many of the tribes claimed the islands surrounding Door County and the southern portion of Lake Superior near present-day Ashland to improve their fortitude and bolster their position on trade routes. It is amazing to think of simple bark canoes crossing the rough waters from Door County out to Washington Island, a passage that has claimed numerous modern vessels.

In the mid 17th-century the French arrived on the western shores of Lake Michigan, still in search of the shortcut to Asia that had brought Columbus to America in the first place. When Jean Nicolet first set foot in Wisconsin in 1634, he greeted the Indians in Chinese silk robes, firing pistols into the air to impress them, with hopes that they would lead him to Asia. In 1673, Father Jacques Marquette discovered the Fox portage, a route used to connect the Great Lakes to the Mississippi via the Fox River. The route stirred the fur trade in Wisconsin into a frenzy, with Indian tribes reporting to the French, trading furs for trinkets in an all-out onslaught on the small mammals of the region.

As time passed and the United States government established itself, the Indians were corralled and finally asked to sign treaties turning over America to the new settlers in exchange for hunting and fishing reservations in the northern part of the state. Though many Indians refused to go quietly, in the

Tough climbs on hard packed earth are numerous at New Fane. LAURA HUTCHINS PHOTO

end they retreated to the thick forests of the north to hunt and farm the land. Many are still there today.

At the end of the 19th century as the Industrial Revolution came to fruition, the rich land of Wisconsin drew immigrants straight from Ellis Island to farm the land and work in the industrial cities along the shore of Lake Michigan in southeast Wisconsin. Germans, Italians, Irish, and Polish flocked to the state in search of work knowing that Milwaukee and its satellite cities were a good bet for employment at the time. Through the generations, these original immigrants have populated the state, giving us the diverse mix we have today.

An interesting figure who came to the state during this era was Sumner Matteson, a bicycle salesman and photographer from Colorado. Already with thousands of miles in the bicycle saddle under his belt, Matteson turned his camera on Milwaukee, telling the story of life at the turn of the century in the budding industrial center. It could be said that Matteson was Wisconsin's first fat-tire rider, exploring the terrain much as we do on his one-speed safety bicycle. Though his stay in Milwaukee only spanned a decade, bikers can feel a tie to the man as a similar individual making his way through a different place and time. Matteson died at a young age while climbing mountains in South America.

The people of the state appreciate this sort of adventurous spirit and tireless pursuit of nature. In present-day Wisconsin you will be greeted with friendly smiles by most everyone. The small towns are charming and the people more so, happy to see new faces passing by on their way to the wilderness. As it is anywhere in the world, pull into a small mom and pop restaurant for a meal to get a real feel for the town. While rubbing elbows with the locals, you'll find the essence of the place and take with you a sense of what the state is all about.

CAMPING

Many of the rides in this book are in areas not necessarily accessible to what most of us consider civilization. For this reason it is often the best idea to couple biking trips with camping trips. Doing this often places you trailside so you can be ready to ride as the sun comes up and don't have to pack up early to return home. Finding out what works best is basically a process of trial and error. Hopefully, with help from this text, a few of the most common mistakes can be avoided.

I normally set up a base camp that I use as my hub for a number of days. Normally a clear, level area with room for a fire and tent will suffice. State and National Forest Campgrounds are often your best bet. For $5 to $8 dollars a day you can settle down in incredibly scenic spots in the forest, with most sites equipped with their own fire pit and table. Throughout the book I offer suggestions of nearby sites in the text accompanying each ride. Contacting the Department of Natural Resources to receive their packet on state parks is a must for locating some of the lesser known parks.

As for equipment, a good 3- or 4-season tent is necessary to be comfortable. Often these are double-wall tents that are weatherproof and hold heat well. In spring and fall temperatures drop considerably, more so in the far north than in the southern regions. It is not unusual to wake up to frost on the top of the tent in late April and even early May. I would suggest packing warm on all counts—tents, sleeping bags, and clothing. It is good to remember that the farther north you are the closer you are to the shores of Lake Superior, where cold air blows in off its waters.

If you are setting up a stationary camp, one you plan to ride out from and return to each night, you may as well prepare your firewood at home and bring it with you. This way you aren't forced to forage and chop wood after a long day in the saddle. If you keep the wood in your vehicle, it will stay dry until you need it. I've enjoyed fires during rainstorms by using the dry wood out of my truck to build a fire under the protection of tall trees (emphasis on the word "tall"). Citronella candles are also a must for enjoying a campfire and a starry night. Add some bug spray and you should be able to survive the hordes of mosquitoes and biting flies that Wisconsin is famous for in summer.

For food, it is hard to beat non-perishables. Nothing will ruin a trip quicker than a run-in with potato salad or ham that has been sitting in a cooler full of lukewarm water for two days. Think of items found in cupboards instead of refrigerators for camping sustenance. Pasta, canned vegetables, fruits, breads, power bars and plenty of liquids (don't forget coffee) are all great for rebuilding energy and staying fresh on extended trips.

Depending on the space available, I usually bring a small tool kit and definitely a knife and ax. Having the right tools separates us from cavemen wandering around with rocks as hammers and teeth as can openers. A hammer for pounding tent stakes is an easy one to forget, and the extra tools are always handy for nighttime bicycle maintenance around the fire.

The main thing to take along, however, is a sense of adventure. Camping and biking are what it is all about. Being in the outdoors, 24 hours a day for an extended period, away from traffic and TVs, can change a person's outlook. I've heard it said that there are no frontiers left on this planet. In my mind, a frontier is a place I haven't been, and until I've set up camp and spent some time, it will still be out there waiting for me.

EQUIPMENT

Mountain biking is to a large extent an equipment-driven sport. The tools and equipment put to use on the trail will prove very important to the enjoyment of mountain biking. This doesn't necessarily mean that to participate in the sport you need to run out and buy the newest, most technically advanced bike. Quite the contrary. It simply means that with an adequately equipped and rugged bike, along with the proper tools in case of emergency, it is possible to complete each ride without a great deal of difficulty. Here are a few tips that should help you to prepare.

The Bike: When buying a mountain bike the most important step is to start with a good base in the form of a strong frame and fork. Frames can be manufactured from a wide variety of materials from tried-and-true steel to titanium, aluminum, or carbon-fiber. Whatever frame you choose, it should be designed for off-road riding, not trail riding more suited to hybrid bikes. Many of the off-road trails described in this book will literally eat a hybrid bike on the first ride because of its weaker materials and improper design.

A true mountain bike has a beefier frame, fork, and rim set for riding over obstacles without sustaining damage. It is also designed with geometry that puts the rider's weight in the proper position for technical trail riding.

The second step is to look at the bike's components, which include the brakes, hubs, derailleurs, shifters, bottom bracket, and all the other parts that form the mechanical workings of the bike. I recommend buying bikes with metal components. Normally reserved for higher-end bicycles designed for true off-road conditions, metal components will perform better under stress, for instance when clogged with mud, and last longer in harsh conditions. When shopping for a bike, you'll find that many of the best bikes are often the simplest, having only the necessary accessories.

One upgrade that can make a world of difference is a shock absorption fork. Some of the more technical trails described in this book take a toll on the upper body if the bike isn't helping to take the brunt of the blows. A front fork shock is not necessary but will help to improve comfort and handling. For instance, the front end will track along the ground, holding tight to terrain with a shock fork. A rigid fork, while very solid and fast, will cause the front end to bounce off obstacles and makes cutting hard corners a bit trickier. Suspension is available for the front fork, stem, and rear end of the bike. Rear suspension is, for the most part, only necessary for high-speed descending over obstacles and is not as popular in Wisconsin as it is out west in more mountainous states.

There are two pieces of equipment I suggest for Wisconsin riding that are relatively cheap, easy to install, and can save a lot of headaches. The first is known as a rock ring. This simple metal disk bolts onto the cranks alongside the largest chain ring. By providing an extra half-inch of height around the largest chain ring, the rock ring takes any blows from underneath the bike that would normally chip teeth off the big sprocket. This also helps eliminate having to dismount to walk around large fallen trees and rocks on the trail. With the rock ring in place it is possible to clear almost anything without fear of doing extensive damage to the drive train.

The second add-on piece I suggest is a derailleur guard. This small metal accessory bolts on over the rear derailleur to protect it from rocks it may come in contact with in a bad fall or tight passage. The metal loop bolts onto the frame just above the derailleur and for a mere $5 can save a vital component that can cost anywhere from $30 to $100 to replace.

Tools: The most important repair item to have on the trail is a multi-tool. Most of these compact tool sets contain metric allen wrenches, metric socket wrenches, and a phillips and flat screwdriver. Multi-tools help in making minor repairs to components that fail and in tightening parts that shake loose along the way. For riding in desolate areas, carrying this tool is an absolutely necessary precaution. With it you can adjust or fix just about any component that becomes inoperable while riding and pedal home instead of walking.

A good reason to have a tool kit.

A chain tool and a few extra links of chain are also a must to have. In the event that the chain or derailleur break, the rider can reattach the links to ride home. Do this by using what is left of your chain to create a 1-speed drive system. Loop the chain around the middle chain ring in front and the small ring in back, bypassing the rear derailleur entirely. Reconnect the chain using the chain tool and enjoy the ride home, remembering not to shift.

The next items on the list of necessities are a patch kit and pump. I ride with as many as 10 patches on each tube before replacing them, which illustrates how often I repair blow-outs. Motorcycle patches work particularly well, as they cover more tire and stay affixed better than the skimpy patches available at most bike shops. Tire levers used to separate the tire from the rim when repairing a blow-out are helpful but optional. In a pinch, the flat end of a quick-release can be used by inserting it under the tire and sliding it around the rim, the same as with a tire lever.

This kind of basic knowledge and a few tools can save the heartache of wasting a beautiful day carrying your bike home. While the items listed above may sound cumbersome, they can actually fit compactly onto your bike. Most pumps manufactured today will easily fit inside the triangle of the frame, attaching to the top or down tube with velcro straps. The rest of the tools all should fit into a hip sack or a pack underneath the seat.

RIDING TIPS

Just about the time I started to think I knew everything about riding style, I was invited out to an afternoon of riding at Kettle Moraine South with a triathlete friend of mine. He proceeded to lead me around the trail for hours, never straining and always in the right position to take on a hill, descent, or extended flat area. I was standing the entire time, trying, to no avail, to keep up through furious pumping. Now that I've learned my lesson, here are a few basic tips I can pass along to improve riding performance and add to the general enjoyment of mountain biking.

To start, remain seated for long stretches of flat land. Aerodynamics are improved and the muscles of the legs, instead of body weight, are used to propel the bike. A smooth pedal stroke while seated will work the legs without straining them and makes the most of the effort. Standing is only necessary on tough climbs and sections of technical riding. On climbs, when energy resources are dwindling, jump back and forth from side to side letting weight instead of muscle push the pedals down.

For technical riding, sitting and standing are equally important stances. On downhill sections or tough ledges it is most often a standing position that will prevail. Getting behind the seat for steep sections will position weight in such a way that the rider is not thrown over the bars. In the same sense, sitting on tough climbs, especially when the tread beneath is loose, will keep weight on the back tire and improve traction. The most important aspect of any technical riding is not to give in. It is a pleasant surprise to find out what can be cleared, be it a stump, ledge, or climb, when the rider sticks to the task and pushes the envelope to make it through. Most sections simply take concentration, finesse and experience. Clear a few huge obstacles and soon it doesn't seem overwhelming to come across a tree or stump lying in the trail.

Choosing a good line is also very important. Don't look down at the front wheel. For technical riding it is best to be looking out 5 to 10 feet ahead of the bike to dodge out and around obstacles. For descents and climbs it is best to watch 10 to 25 feet in front of the bike to plan for any changes in direction that are beneficial. On clear straightaways, look as far ahead as possible to anticipate major adjustments in direction that must be made. Normally the high side of the trail will have the best line, most of the debris having washed down to the lower side during rainstorms.

A final point that I can't stress enough is the importance of stretching. Stretching helps to reduce the risk of injury, brings out better performance, and promotes muscle growth. It is hard for me to feel a ride is complete without stretching at the end. Find a varied group of stretches that relaxes sore muscles without straining them: touching toes from a seated position with one leg tucked in, leaning back in a hurdler's pose, trunk rotations, neck rolls, and windmills with the arms all help to work the whole body. Realize that it is important to take stretching on physically and mentally and to take the time to relax during the process. It is necessary to use the mind to concentrate on the muscles being stretched and mentally relax them. The object isn't to strain the muscles but instead to gradually let them release. Letting this happen is more a mental than a physical process.

Three Falcon Principles of Leave No Trace

- *Leave with everything you brought in.*
- *Leave no sign of your visit.*
- *Leave the landscape as you found it.*

IMBA Rules of the Trail

The International Mountain Bicycling Association (IMBA) has established a set of rules to help guide mountain bikers' actions along the trails. The rules are intended to place in our minds the ideals of behavior while riding, all of which point to the idea of leaving the trail and surrounding areas as they were found, without human trace. If riders will take it upon themselves to care for the trails and leave them in better condition than they were found, land officials will return the favor with additional acres of access and fellow riders will be able to immerse themselves in the outdoor experience without the reminder that 10,000 others have traveled the trail before them.

While the rules may seem basic and a bit strict, each has its importance in allowing thousands of riders to cover the same ground without it ending up looking like a freeway. It is amazing at times to see the rules at work. A mid-1997 race in southeast Wisconsin had a portion of trail that ran right down the middle of an area of protected ferns. Area land management was worried that the race would widen the path and trample the plant life. The word spread through the crowd at the starting line and throughout the race, riders were conscientious of the leave-no-trace clause of the IMBA rules. After the race was completed, only the thin ribbon of trail that was there to start with was visible and the land management officials were able to see how non-invasive mountain biking can be to the land.

Thousands of miles of dirt trails have been closed to mountain bicyclists. The irresponsible riding habits of a few riders have been a factor. Do your part to maintain trail access by observing the following rules of the trail, formulated by IMBA. The IMBA mission is to promote environmentally sound and socially responsible mountain biking.

1. **Ride on open trails only.** Respect trail and road closures (ask if not sure), avoid possible trespass on private land, obtain permits and authorization as may be required. Federal and state wilderness areas are closed to cycling. The way you ride will influence trail management decisions and policies.

2. **Leave no trace.** Be sensitive to the dirt beneath you. Even on open (legal) trails, you should not ride under conditions in which you will leave evidence of your passing, such as on certain soils after a rain. Recognize different types of soil and trail construction; Practice low-impact cycling. This also means staying on existing trails and not creating any new ones. Be sure to pack out at least as much as you pack in.

3. **Control your bicycle!** Inattention for even a second can cause problems. Obey all bicycle speed regulations and recommendations.

4. **Always yield trail.** Make known your approach well in advance. A friendly greeting (or bell) is considerate and works well; don't startle others. Show your respect when passing by slowing to a walking pace or stopping. Anticipate other trail users at corners and blind spots.

5. **Never spook animals.** All animals are startled by an unannounced approach, a sudden movement, or a loud noise. This can be dangerous for you, others, and the animals themselves. Give animals extra room and time to adjust to you. When passing horses use special care and follow directions from the horseback riders (dismount and ask if uncertain). Running cattle and disturbing wildlife is a serious offense. Leave gates as you found them, or as marked.

6. Plan ahead. Know your equipment, your ability, and the area in which you are riding, and prepare accordingly. Be self-sufficient at all times, keep your equipment in good repair, and carry necessary supplies for changes in weather or other conditions. A well-executed trip is a satisfaction to you and not a burden or offense to others.

Keep trails open by setting a good example of environmentally sound and socially responsible off-road cycling.

How to Use This Guide

Mountain Biking Wisconsin describes forty-two mountain bike rides in their entirety. The majority of the rides are loops, beginning and ending in the same spot. Many of these loops are located within clusters of loops, departing from a single trailhead. A handful are of the out-and-back variety, and some are just plain mazes.

To make navigating this book easy, each trail description is divided into three sections. The first covers the overview of the area, the trail conditions, and what it is that makes the whole thing tick. Following this is a series of categories covering everything from the location to the hazards. Lastly, the highlights of each ride are covered, and an outline of each route is given. Use the map in conjunction with this last section to trace the ride before physically doing it. If you are unfamiliar with the trails in this book, try them first as described here. The directions follow the path of least resistance (which does not necessarily mean easy). After you've been over the terrain once, you can determine whether different routes might be more fun.

Portions of some rides follow gravel or paved roads. Purists may wince at road rides in a book about mountain biking, but these are special rides offering the chance to explore areas of immense beauty. Some of the road rides described in this book cover rather difficult terrain. Others that are less difficult can in some instances be used by hard-core riders on active rest days or when weather makes trails unrideable.

This book does not include elevation charts. While climbing is no stranger to Wisconsin riders, it most often comes in short spurts—short and frequent spurts to be more specific, thanks to the state's glaciated terrain. The numerous 10- to 30-foot hills that do not show on topographic maps throw the scale off by a long shot, making tough rides seem rather easy at a glance. Instead of charts, a more accurate statement of what to expect is made in the "elevation change" listing of each ride description. Each listing paints an accurate overview of the climbing conditions and points out the monster uphills you will be facing.

Each ride description in this book follows the same format, listed here:

Number and name of the ride: Rides are cross-referenced by name throughout this book. For the names of rides I relied on official names of trails, roads, and natural features as shown on national forest and U.S. Geological Survey maps. In some cases newly named trails are still known by the moniker given by area riders.

Technical Difficulty: The level of bike-handling skills needed to complete the ride upright and in one piece. Technical difficulty is rated on a scale from 1 to 5, with 1 being the easiest and 5 the hardest (see the explanation of the rating systems on page 23).

Aerobic Level: The level of physical effort required to complete the ride: easy, moderate, or strenuous.

Tread: The description of what the tires ride on when they are rubber-side down.

Length: Total mileage of trail/trails described.

Overview: Brief introduction to the area described.

General location: The general whereabouts of the ride, distance and direction from the nearest population center.

Elevation change: A basic overview of the rise and fall of the trail, with major climbs noted.

Camping: A list of area campgrounds and directions from the trailhead to them. In most cases the number of sites found at a given camping area are listed as well as any amenities that weary travelers can expect to find.

Season: The dates for which each trail or group of trails is open to the public, along with a synopsis of the best times of year to ride.

Fees: Any fees that must be paid for trail passes or parking are listed here.

Services: This listing helps to point out services such as toilets and water that may be available at the trailhead or on the trail itself. Sources of equipment and necessities, usually found in nearby population centers, are also listed.

Hazards: A list of dangers that may be encountered on a ride, including traffic, weather, trail obstacles and conditions, risky stream crossings, obscure trails, and other perils. Remember: conditions may change at any time. Be alert for storms, new fences, tree falls, missing trail signs, and mechanical failure. Fatigue, heat, cold, and/or dehydration may impair judgment. Always wear a helmet and other safety equipment.

Rescue: Suggestions for how to seek help in case of emergency. In more desolate areas, it is advisable to ride in a group and carry medical equipment.

Land status: A list of managing agencies or land owners. Most of the rides in this book are on state property, but many of the rides also cross portions of private, state, or municipal lands. Respect the land, regardless of who owns it. See Appendix A for a list of local addresses for land-managing agencies.

Maps: A list of available maps, both from agencies and at the trailhead. Specific USGS topographic maps in the 7.5-minute quad series are also listed and provide a close-up look at terrain. USGS maps are available at public libraries.

Finding the trail: How to find the trailhead or the start of the ride.

The ride: An overview of the trail taking riders through the highlights and a description of each route. Using the map and the text it should be easy to trace the route before laying tires to the trail. Trail markings throughout each ride are noted and used to direct riders from point to point. It should be mentioned that terrain, riding technique, and even tire pressure can affect odometer readings, so treat all mileages as estimates.

The information presented here is as accurate and up-to-date as possible, but there are no guarantees out in the forest. You alone are responsible for your safety and for the choices you make on the trail.

If you do find an error or omission in this book, or a new and noteworthy change in the field, I'd like to hear from you. Please write to Colby Waller, c/o Falcon Publishing, P.O. Box 1718, Helena, MT 59624.

Rating the Rides

Finding a rating system for mountain bike trails that will accommodate riders of all skill levels is a challenging task. Riders of all types will use this guide and, therefore, an attempt has been made to rate each ride as an intermediate rider would on a good day. Take into consideration when setting out onto the trail your personal physical condition, experience, and even how you feel at the time—we all have off days.

FalconGuides rate each ride on two types of difficulty: the physical effort required to pedal the distance, and the level of bike-handling skills needed to stay upright and make it home in one piece. We call these "Aerobic Level" and "Technical Difficulty."

Aerobic Level Ratings

The aerobic level rating at the top of each trail description measures the amount of physical effort it will take to make it through each ride. Mountain biking is one of the more challenging sports in terms of aerobic conditioning, and years of heavy riding are necessary before huge lung capacity is attained. For many riders, the longer and more technical rides described in this book will take a physical toll on the cardiovascular system. The best advice I have is to ease into the regimen. Physical conditioning is a long and continuous process. By staying within your personal limits while riding, you will allow your body to build, your lungs to expand, and your heart to strengthen at a healthy rate.

To help give you an idea of the physical demands of each ride, this guide uses a standardization of sorts that measures the difficulty level of each ride. Here's how the exertion level for terrain covered in this book is rated:

Easy: Flat or gently rolling terrain. No steep or prolonged climbs.

Moderate: Some hills. Climbs may be short and fairly steep or long and gradual.

Strenuous: Frequent or prolonged climbs steep enough to require riding in the lowest gear requires a high level of aerobic fitness, power, and endurance (typically acquired through many hours of riding and proper training). Less fit riders may need to walk.

Many of the strenuous sections demand every ounce of power found in the entire body to make it through. Not only the legs but also the upper body are needed for some of the tougher climbs. Proper body English and riding style are necessary for some of the more technical sections, and at times the athletic grace that only comes from being in excellent physical condition can be all that guides your riding. Even in easy flat sections, it is important to concentrate on your actions and properly use your body to propel the bike.

Some of the riding covered in this book will be too much for those just starting, and it will be necessary to walk or carry the bike around tricky sections or steep climbs. Don't be afraid to do this when necessary. To start, carrying a 20- to 30-pound hunk of metal up a steep rocky hill is no small task and beats melting into a couch for a workout. In addition, a smart rider is in tune with his body and knows that pushing past physical limits often leads to injury or excessive fatigue. It's better to work into the experience of mountain biking slowly. With time, you'll be the one blazing down the trails making others think, "Well, that looks easy!"

Technical Difficulty Ratings

The sport of mountain biking evolved from the fact that while road riding is scenic and healthy, it gets downright boring. Logs, rocks, roots and mud all prove to be necessary ingredients for biking once you've hopped a few hazards and slung some mud. The trails within this book will provide many opportunities for practice. Technical terrain takes concentration and a knowledge that only comes from practice and multiple failed attempts.

Crashing is an integral part of the technical ride and can only be eliminated to an extent by expertise. Those who avoid the endos and bail-outs common to technical riding only do so by never attempting to succeed.

They settle for walking out and around the rocks, staying clean, and missing the fun. The rest of us wedge our tire in between the rocks, flip upright, pausing for an eerily long moment, and plant our chin in the mud a lot. Then the learning curve kicks in and we begin to plant our tire to the side of the rock, gliding through. One day we do that while someone carrying their bike around the rock watches and we realize the new level of skill that has been attained. And that is a satisfying feeling.

Technical riding is more physical than any other biking activity and, therefore, we use a system of standard ratings. We rate technical difficulty on a scale from 1 to 5 (1 being easiest). We tried to make the ratings as objective as possible by considering the type and frequency of the rides' obstacles. The same standards were applied consistently through all the rides in this book.

We've also added plus (+) and minus (-) symbols to cover gray areas between given levels of difficulty: a 4+ obstacle is harder than a 4, but easier than a 5-. A trail rated as 5+ would be unridable by all but the most skilled (or luckiest) riders.

Here are the 5 levels defined:

Level 1: Smooth tread, road, or doubletrack; no obstacles, ruts, or steeps. Requires basic bike riding skills.
Level 2: Mostly smooth tread; wide, well-groomed singletrack or road/doubletrack with minor ruts or loose gravel or sand.
Level 3: Irregular tread with some rough sections; single or doubletrack with obvious route choices; some steep sections; occasional obstacles may include small rocks, roots, water bars, ruts, loose gravel or sand, and sharp turns or broad, open switchbacks.
Level 4: Rough tread with few smooth places; singletrack or rough doubletrack with limited route choices; steep sections, some with obstacles; obstacles are numerous and varied, including rocks, roots, branches, ruts, sidehills, narrow tread, loose gravel or sand, and switchbacks.
Level 5: Continuously broken, rocky, root-infested, or trenched tread; singletrack or extremely rough doubletrack with few route choices; frequent, sudden, and severe changes in gradient; some slopes so steep that wheels lift off ground; obstacles are nearly continuous and may include boulders, logs, water, large holes, deep ruts, ledges, piles of loose gravel, steep sidehills, encroaching trees, and tight switchbacks.

Most of the rides in this book cover varied terrain, with an ever-changing degree of technical difficulty. Some trails run smooth with only occasional obstacles, and other trails are seemingly all obstacle. The path of least resistance, or line, is where you find it. In general, most obstacles are more challenging if you encounter them while climbing than while descending. On the other hand, in heavy surf (e.g., boulder fields, tangles of downfall, cliffs), fear plays a larger role when facing downhill.

Realize, too, that different riders have different strengths and weaknesses. Some folks can scramble over logs and boulders without a grunt, but they crash head over heels on every switchback turn. Some fly off the steepest drops and others freeze. The key to overcoming "technical difficulties" is practice: keep trying.

About WORBA

The Wisconsin Off Road Bicycle Association (WORBA) serves as the main trail advocacy group for the state. The significance of organizations such as this cannot be overstated: through the use of education combined with manual labor, they create and protect the singletrack we ride on. By implementing erosion control systems and optimum routing, the trails WORBA creates make for some of the best riding in the state.

Members of WORBA take part on all levels. Many roll up their sleeves and pitch in to clean, maintain, and create new trails in their area. WORBA newsletters keep members up to date on the Wisconsin mountain biking scene. In many cases, the organization uses its collective political muscle to help convince land managers that mountain biking is a viable use of their land. This is important: the more bikers who sign up with WORBA, the more clout they have when negotiating with legislative bodies to preserve our right to bike on current trails and get new trails opened to biking. WORBA has chapters taking care of trails throughout the state—local people working to preserve their own riding areas.

The yearly membership fee is a mere $20. This includes some fringe benefits as well: in the past, members have enjoyed discounts of 10 to 15 percent at some bike stores around the state, a 10 percent discount at participating bed and breakfasts, and free issues of various biking magazines. Members are also invited to attend the annual WORBA banquet and membership meeting.

For more information on WORBA, visit their website at www.worba.org, or write to WORBA, P.O. Box 1681, Madison, WI, 53701-1681.

Author's Favorites

As a technical rider I'm a bit biased in picking my favorite Wisconsin rides. The Kettle Moraine is my home and when I'm on these trails I'm dialed into each and every rut in the path. I've ridden in a lot of places and these are by far my favorite trails for letting loose. The technical nature coupled with excellent trail conditions and markings makes for great riding from the very start.

Farther away from home, The Quarry in Madison and the Levis and Trow Mounds north of Black River Falls are also sources of technical excitement, The Quarry being quite simply insane and Levis and Trow being a little slice of singletrack-purist heaven. The views from the tops of the mounds are wonderful, and are about the only thing that could make you take pause in the midst of such challenging routes.

For camping and biking combined, the CAMBA Trails (Chequamegon Area Mountain Bike Association) win out. The national park camping within CAMBA's lands is second to none, as are the trails. CAMBA is the place to be in the warmer months and, depending on a rider's ability or energy level, there is always a trail that suits the rider.

The truth, however, is that if I were king, I would ask that the readers of this book take it upon themselves to ride all the trails and make their own call. They all have something to offer and the more terrain you cover, the more well-rounded you become. Enjoy.

Technical Rides (most challenging listed first)
The Quarry
Greenbush Trails
Levis/Trow Mounds Trails
John Muir Trails
Nine Mile State Forest
The Farm

Camping and Riding Combined
Devil's Lake State Park Trails
Black River—Smrekar and Wildcat
Copper Falls State Park Trails
Pines and Mines Trails
Chequamegon Area Mountain Bike Association Trails

Scenery (they are all beautiful)
Levis/Trow Mounds Trails
Wyalusing State Park
Governor Dodge State Park
Perrot State Park
High Cliff State Park Trails
Perry Creek Trail
Peninsula State Park
Standing Rock Trails
Chequamegon Area Mountain Bike Association Trails

Beginners (easiest to most difficult)
Blue Mound State Park
Hartman Creek State Park Trails
Lowes Creek Trails
Newport State Park Trails
Mirror Lake Trails
Lapham Peak Trails
Potawatomi State Park
Point Beach State Forest Trails
LumberJack Trail
Escanaba Trail

Kettle Moraine Forest

The Kettle Moraine Forest in southeastern Wisconsin is one of the most diverse landscapes in the state and offers the most technically challenging mountain biking around. The terrain really lends itself to off-road riding, constantly throwing changes at riders, with enough action to keep those who've been addicted to video games since birth completely enthralled. The forest is divided into two sections: a 30,000-acre plot referred to as the Northern Unit, surrounding the towns of Kewaskum, New Fane, and Greenbush; and a 20,000-acre Southern Unit, surrounding the towns of Eagle and Palmyra. Besides being flush with trees, the area displays nearly every type of glacial formation, having been drastically impacted by the glaciers that moved through the state during the Ice Age. Huge kettle valleys form basins at the base of eskers and lengths of piled rock, softened by vegetation and old age, climbing and winding amongst the trees. The hills are filled with rocks and debris that were pushed to the kettle moraine on the front end of the glacier. The area lies on the terminus of the glacier, the point where the ice stopped its movement and began receding, leaving behind a long river of stone laid out across the state. Erratic boulders, ranging in size from softballs to small cars, are strewn throughout the landscape.

The Kettle Moraine is one of the most heavily ridden areas in the state because of its close proximity to Milwaukee. The John Muir Trails in the Southern Unit of the forest receive more than 100,000 riders per year and, amazingly, with the care of trail activists, stay in excellent shape throughout the season. The clusters are extremely well marked, the newest in erosion control devices have been used to insure years of riding, and, though they are safe for anyone to ride, they are some of the most challenging courses in the entire state. For many racers both from Wisconsin and northern Illinois, the Kettle Moraine is the home course for racing and training.

Five rides in this area are covered in this section of the book: 2 to the north, 2 to the south, and 1 in between. Greenbush is the trail system found farthest north and is one of the more technically advanced. The dense forest and remote location make this one of the better bets for getting away from the crowds. The second trail system in the Northern Unit is the New Fane, tucked into the forest at the edge of area farmlands. The New Fane Trails are very fast and, where they lack technical qualities, they excel in sweeping corners and all-out, rock-strewn descents through the rolling hills. The Northern Unit is the lesser known of the 2 sections of forest, but every bit as valuable to area mountain bikers.

The John Muir Trail lies farthest south in the Kettle Moraine, and is by far the most well-known and well-ridden trail in the state. Technical and endurance skills will be pushed to the brink in a setting of dense pine forest far from any major civilization. Just to the north and joined by a must-ride connector trail is the Emma Carlin Cluster.

In the middle of them all, Lapham Peak resides just west of Waukesha. The trails found at this park are the tamest of the bunch but also among the most scenic. The park prides itself on its prairies, and the wandering off-road trail makes its way across an extensive plain, with golden, swaying grass spread out evenly to the forest rim.

In all, the trails of southeastern Wisconsin offer some of the most involved riding to be found anywhere, lacking only the huge mileage of the treks found to the north. Riders training on the John Muir, Emma Carlin, and Greenbush trails will find themselves well-prepared physically and mentally for what lies ahead in the remainder of the state.

Lapham Peak Trails

Lapham Peak has drawn people to its summit for years to view the surrounding countryside from its many lookouts. The peak itself is the highest point in Waukesha County and offers beautiful views of rolling farm fields and forest in all directions. Lapham Peak Park was named after Increase Lapham, a 19th-century meteorological pioneer who practiced his science on this very hill. It was here that one of the first National Weather Service stations was built and received weather reports from Pikes Peak in Colorado.

The mountain bike trails currently open in the park were relocated, in the fall of 1997, to a set of farm fields across from the main park grounds on County Highway C, to protect the park's hiking paths from erosion. The new, wide paths run through grassy meadows on single- and doubletrack paths with several areas of gravel mixed in for good measure. The area is open to hikers, bikers, and, in some places, horseback riders, so care must be taken in traversing the trail network. The trails form a single loop, with three cutoff paths thrown in to offer some different choices of routing and keep things fresh.

An intermediate rider should be able to tackle this in 30 to 35 minutes and probably will want to pedal multiple laps. This is the sort of trail riding that can be quite addictive on a summer afternoon, especially for those looking to get a solid, balanced leg workout. There are not a lot of obstacles to concentrate on missing or tough cutbacks to break the bike's momentum. Instead, the course rolls along through fields with long straightaways and

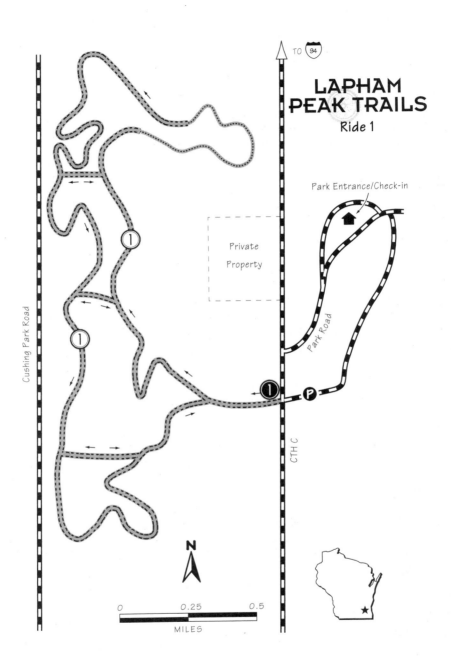

LAPHAM
PEAK TRAILS
Ride 1

Park Entrance/Check-in

Private
Property

Cushing Park Road

Park Road

CTH C

TO 94

P

N

0   0.25   0.5

MILES

sweeping corners. It is easy to get dialed into the riding and spin fast loops, concentrating only on a good pedal stroke and a good line over the smoothest section of the path. The ability to see the details of the terrain ahead and stay on the most even and solid parts can make this a very rewarding ride.

The surrounding countryside is pure Wisconsin—forest and field interspersed, with barns and farmhouses both modern and old dotting the landscape. The well-glaciated and hilly terrain is common to the terminal moraine. Luckily for riders wanting to make good time on the course, the majority of larger rocks have long since been plowed from the fields and piled at the far corners to form rock walls separating properties.

General location: Lapham Peak is located just outside the city of Waukesha, approximately 12 miles west on Interstate 94 and 1 mile south of Delafield.

Technical Difficulty: Level 2.

Aerobic Level: Moderate.

Tread: Single and doubletrack.

Length: 4.2 miles.

Elevation change: The terrain is rolling, with a few 20- to 30-foot climbs, but for the most part the riding is very level.

Camping: There is no camping within the park itself or in the immediate vicinity.

Season: This trail unit is monitored quite heavily for erosion because of its many uses. The trails will be closed anytime they are wet; therefore during spring and fall accessibility could be sporadic. Late spring through early fall are the best times to go. Once the snow flies Lapham becomes a mecca for cross-country skiers.

Fees: A trail pass and vehicle admission sticker are required and can be purchased at the main gate. Daily and annual passes are available.

Services: The parking lot offers vending machines and toilet facilities. Food is available in Delafield, bicycle repair is offered in Oconomowoc, 3.5 miles west off I-94.

Hazards: The trails are very safe and free of debris. Watch out while crossing the street to get to the main loop, as traffic is traveling at 45 mph.

Rescue: Park rangers are nearly always present in the park and the town of Delafield is located just two miles north on the opposite side of I-94.

Land status: Lapham Peak, Kettle Moraine State Forest.

Maps: The trail area is shown on the USGS 7.5-minute quad for Oconomowoc East. Maps are available from the Wisconsin Department of Natural Resources and at the entrance to the park.

Finding the trail: Travel west out of Milwaukee on Interstate 94 and take Delafield Exit 285. Head south on County Highway C for 1 mile to the Lapham Peak Park entrance on the left (east).

Sources of more information: See Appendix A, in particular the Delafield Chamber of Commerce, Wisconsin Department of Tourism, and WORBA.

The author climbing in the converted farm fields at Lapham Peak.
LAURA HUTCHINS PHOTO

THE RIDE

The trail leaves the west side of the parking lot and immediately crosses over County Highway C. Continue across the field to the first intersection, 0.13 mile in. The path forks and directs bikers to the right, horses to the left. The bike path snakes back and forth across the meadow through rolling hills and up to a small knoll that looks out over the picturesque Wisconsin landscape.

Continue on the trail to the north. You will pass one cutoff within 0.5 mile, heading to the left. Stay on the main trail. The path cuts in and out of the forest and at the far north end winds back and forth over the rolling hills before turning back to the south. You can use the cutoff at the north end to avoid the 0.75-mile turnaround section. Heading south the trail picks up speed along a hardwood tree line and passes the same cutoff paths seen on the way out.

The path cruises along to the south, parallel to Cushing Park Road, until it again turns back on itself, following a 0.75-mile turnaround back to the starting intersection. The trail is short and fast enough that multiple loops are possible. Watch for private property along the eastern edge of the trail, being careful to stay on the trail through these particular sections.

New Fane Trail

The New Fane Trail is one of a handful of mountain bike–approved areas within the bounds of the Kettle Moraine State Forest. The trail covers a mix of beginner to advanced terrain allowing riders to warm up on easier trails before tackling the more demanding rides. Four intertwined loops ranging from 0.7 mile to 3.1 miles are offered. What these trails appear to lack in terms of distance is more than made up for in terrain changes and tricky technical sections.

Intermediate riders should be able to traverse the 3.1-mile yellow loop from beginning to end within 30 minutes. At several points along the way, riders have the option of shortening the chosen trail by switching loops and circling in a bit early. Acclimating to the area with a few shorter warm-up laps is a good way to get used to the ever-changing terrain and to help sharpen vision for choosing good lines. After a couple of laps the loops become quite familiar and easier to navigate thanks to a well-marked and maintained system of color markers.

The terrain encountered in the Kettle Moraine is famous for its diversity. The rolling hills left behind by the glaciers never seem to let up as you make your way through the various loops. More advanced riders, able to play off their momentum, are treated to a roller coaster ride up and down the rapid descents. The trail has a mix of bases from grass to sand, with the majority over hard-packed dirt strewn with small rocks and roots. The descents on some of the more advanced loops can be a bit unstable and require advanced technical prowess.

As you ride, be sure to look around and take in the wonderful Wisconsin scenery. Rolling meadows and dense forest are the main attractions. The forest is home to white-tailed deer and the occasional roving hawk, waiting to swoop down on unsuspecting field mice.

General location: The New Fane Trail is located within the Northern Unit of the Kettle Moraine State Forest, 5 miles northeast of Kewaskum.

Technical difficulty: Level 3.

Aerobic level: Moderate.

Tread: Wide singletrack.

Length: 0.7- to 3.1-mile loops.

Elevation change: The majority of the ride is over flat land with some rolling hills that cover 30 to 40 feet of elevation. Most of the hills can be traversed rather easily by throwing the momentum of the previous downhill into the climb.

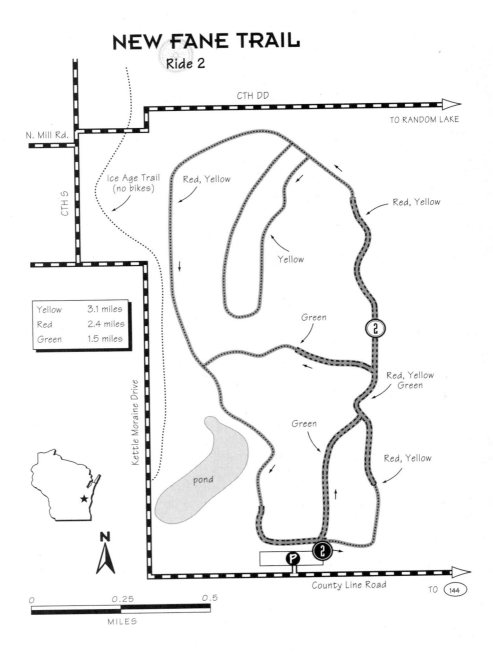

NEW FANE TRAIL
Ride 2

CTH DD

TO RANDOM LAKE

N. Mill Rd.

CTH S

Ice Age Trail
(no bikes)

Red, Yellow

Red, Yellow

Yellow

Green

Red, Yellow
Green

Green

Red, Yellow

Yellow	3.1 miles
Red	2.4 miles
Green	1.5 miles

Kettle Moraine Drive

pond

N

County Line Road

TO 144

0   0.25   0.5

MILES

Camping: Camp Long Lake and Mauthe Lake are both found in the state forest's Northern Unit.

Season: Comfortable temperatures and the lack of mosquitoes make fall and spring the best times to explore this trail. Summer months are also good for riding, though hotter by far and with high levels of humidity. Early April into November are the suggested months for riding. In mid-November hunters return to the area, making it unsafe for bikers.

Fees: A trail pass and vehicle admission sticker are required. Both are available as annual passes from the DNR.

Services: Water is provided via a trailside pump. Restrooms are accessible from the parking lot. As mentioned earlier, the trails are well-marked starting with a color-coded map at the trail head.

Hazards: The 3 longer loops are slightly eroded in some areas, particularly on descents, and therefore contain many rocks and roots which riders must navigate. As always, helmets are a must. In summer months make certain to drink plenty of liquids before, during, and after the ride to fight off dehydration.

Rescue: Park rangers stop quite frequently to check trail passes at the trail head. Emergency personnel are stationed in Kewaskum. The small town of New Fane to the west also can be turned to in the case of an emergency.

Land status: Wisconsin State Forest, Northern Kettle Moraine Unit.

Maps: The trail area is shown on the USGS 7.5 minute quad for Kewaskum. Additional maps are available from the Wisconsin DNR or at the forest headquarters. Maps are also available at the trailhead.

Sources of more information: See Appendix A, in particular the Kewaskum Chamber of Commerce, Wisconsin Department of Tourism, and WORBA.

Finding the trail: From U.S. Highway 45 at Kewaskum take Wisconsin Highway 28 east two blocks to County Highway S and turn left (north). Follow CH S for 2 miles to Kettle Moraine Drive and turn right. After 1.5 miles turn left onto County Line Road, which will take you to the parking lot and trailhead. Signs are visible on County Line Road, directing you to the lot.

THE RIDE

The trail begins with a quick climb out of the parking lot to a field of waist-high meadow grass, where it immediately splits. The Brown Trail (0.7 mile) heads off to the left and makes an arcing oval out to the forest line. This is a scenic yet uneventful beginner ride (not shown on map). The trail to the right takes off with a series of small rolling hills. Within half a mile you'll find yourself at the edge of the forest and begin a short climb on hard-packed soil through the trees. Before exiting this section of the forest you are challenged by a pair of quick descents and one steep ascent, curiously positioned on a sharp curve.

After a fast straight section out of the trees the trail branches once again, allowing riders to change loops. The Green Loop (1.5 miles) branches to the

Well-marked trails lead the way on climbs at New Fane. LAURA HUTCHINS PHOTO

left and starts off across the forest with a bumpy climb to the top of a central ridge. It then winds back and forth through a series of switchbacks before meeting again with the longer loops on the far side of the forest. If you opt to stay to the right you are treated to a rigorous climb which ends in the rewarding cool shade of tree cover in the second forest section. The rider is entertained with a rolling ride through the shaded section which allows for momentum to carry you through most of the hills.

Following a fast and bumpy descent over wide cut grass the trail forks off in two directions. The Yellow Trail to the left contains an extra 0.7 mile long loop featuring a rapid descent culminating in a 90-degree corner on a bed of pine needles. The trail to the right is considered the Red Loop (2.4 miles)and continues on through the forest, gently winding through the fields and allowing the rider to catch his breath.

Before returning to the parking lot all three of the longer loops (Green, Yellow, Red) come together, just in time for the tricky section of descents and climbs that are sure to see your wheels leave the trail as you lift over the crest of each hill. A great after-ride activity that is certain to please tired summertime riders lies 5 miles north off County Highway S. Mauthe Lake is a beautiful motor boat free lake and a wonderful place to cool off in the late afternoon hours.

Greenbush Trails

The Greenbush mountain-biking trails are some of the best in the state. The four loops in this densely wooded section of the Kettle Moraine State Forest are all challenging in their own way. The entire area is heavily glaciated with large open kettles scattered throughout the wilderness. The location is rather desolate and offers a nice escape from some of southeastern Wisconsin's more crowded trails. As with all of the Kettle Moraine Trails, the loops are very well marked and even on the first time through riders can easily find their way through each divergence of the trail. Expect to be stunned by the abundance of wildlife. From hardwood forests to marshes to pine stands the surrounding land is flush with wilderness. Whitetail deer are abundant as are a great variety of songbirds. The Greenbush Trails are a part of the terminal moraine, which provides some of the most erratic mountain biking known to man. The area is basically two ridges with a valley running straight down the middle. Each loop starts high on the south rim, descends into the valley, and climbs back to the north rim. A short ride to the right along the top of the rim heads back to the trail head.

Each of the trails is color-coded and runs over tight single- and doubletrack through thick hardwood forest. The Pink Trail is the shortest of the bunch, logging in at 0.7 mile. Don't be fooled by the soft, cuddly name— the Pink Loop at Greenbush is rated most difficult and lives up to its designation. It should take only about 15 minutes for an intermediate rider to traverse this loop. The trail offers rapid descents with quick cutbacks riders can really lean into. The last quarter of a mile is a winding uphill climb back to the trailhead.

The 2.6-mile Green Loop appears to be mountain biking heaven and indeed it is, as it cuts away from the yellow loop and dives down into the forest floor. Quick descents followed by minor uphills continue the trek downward through the kettles. Then come the climbs which prove a true rule of mountain biking: what goes down must come up. This loop takes about 35 minutes to complete and will challenge even the most advanced rider.

The Red Loop is quite similar to the Green Loop in terms of terrain, but it diverts from the Yellow Loop a bit earlier, making it shorter at only 1.5 miles. This loop takes about 20 minutes for an intermediate rider to complete.

The Yellow Loop is the longest of all the trails, coming in at 5.1 miles, and all the other trails split from it. The loop basically travels along the tops of the two ridges, passing out past Bear Lake and Bear Lake Marsh. Don't be

GREENBUSH TRAILS
Ride 3

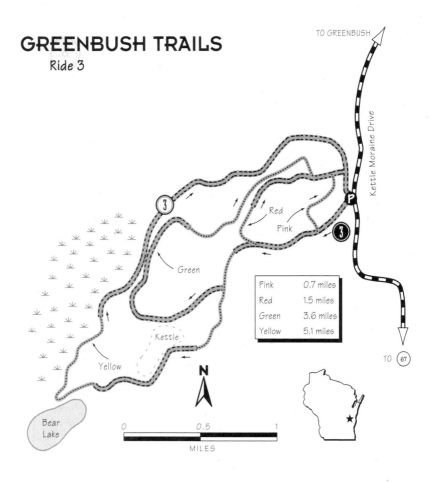

Pink	0.7 miles
Red	1.5 miles
Green	3.6 miles
Yellow	5.1 miles

fooled, however. Although this portion of the trail system runs along the tops of the ridges, this area was seriously dismantled by glaciers and holds its share of surprises.

General location: Approximately 25 miles west of Sheboygan, or 2.5 miles south of Wisconsin 23 in Greenbush, or 6 miles west of Plymouth.

Technical Difficulty: Level 4.

Aerobic Level: Moderate to strenuous.

Tread: Single- and doubletrack.

Length: 0.7- to 5.1-mile loops.

Elevation change: The terrain is rolling throughout with very few flat areas. Steep 40- to 50-foot climbs are found on all of the loops.

Camping: Camp Long Lake and Mauthe Lake are found in the Kettle Moraine Northern Unit.

Season: From spring thaw to first snow fall, April 15 to November 15. The yellow

Loop is closed to biking each year with the beginning of small game season and on through deer hunting season.

Fees: A trail pass and vehicle admission sticker are required. Both are available as annual passes from the DNR.

Services: Water is available both at the parking lot 0.25 miles south of the Greenbush picnic area and off of the brown loop that connects to the picnic area. Restrooms are located at the trailhead directly to the left of the trail map. Restaurants and groceries are available in Greenbush.

Hazards: Many of the descents in this area are extremely steep and littered with roots, rocks and stumps. Inexperienced riders should travel cautiously over these areas. Stay off the front brake as much as possible to avoid going over the handlebars.

Rescue: Greenbush is the closest point of civilization. These trails are well ridden, however, and riders are sure to encounter others rather often.

Land status: Kettle Moraine State Forest, Wisconsin DNR.

Maps: The trail area is shown on the USGS 7.5-minute quad for Elkhart Lake.

Sources of more information: See Appendix A, in particular the Wisconsin Department of Tourism and WORBA.

Finding the trail: Take Wisconsin Highway 23 west 6 miles out of Plymouth. Turn left (south) on County Highway T and enter the village of Greenbush. Follow CH T for 1.25 miles and turn left (south) onto Kettle Moraine Drive. Go another 2 miles farther down this road to the Greenbush picnic area and trailhead, on the right side of the road.

Mountain biker Mike Hudson cutting a good line on the fast descents at Greenbush.

Starting from the Greenbush picnic area the trail heads west in a clockwise direction. The Pink Loop is the first to break away from the main trail at about the 0.25 mile mark, heading off to the right and immediately descending. A series of quick switchbacks and descents keep the rider busy for the first half mile. The last 0.25 mile is all uphill over small roots on a curving path.

Back on the main trail, the Red Loop is the second to cut away, again to the right. The descent here is mainly in the first few seconds of riding. The trail rolls along through the forest and up and down the hills, flattening out and cutting back rather hard at times, until it reaches the main trail on the other ridge.

The Green Loop is the third to diverge from the main trail and does so at about the 1 mile mark. The trail descends quickly through rolling hills, each normally carrying a great deal of momentum as you crest the top of each mound. The challenge comes in the last two miles where the rider is plagued by countless climbs. It's quite challenging and will certainly take its toll on even the best rider's legs and lungs.

The Yellow Loop is the main trail and runs out and around all the others. It is a bit less technical but, being the longest, it strains riders just as well as the others. This is perhaps the most scenic of the trails, leading riders out through the pines and past the shores of tiny Bear Lake and the expanse of Bear Lake Marsh.

4

John Muir Trails

The John Muir Trails, nestled in the heart of the Southern Unit of the Kettle Moraine State Forest, are the gem of Wisconsin mountain bike trails. They are the best kept, most extensively ridden, and all around most enjoyable routes in the state. About 30 miles of singletrack are laid out in a variety of technical paths offering everyone from beginners to experts a loop to ride. In addition to being one of the best, this cluster is also the source of some of the highest traffic. In 1996, eighty thousand day passes were sold at this park, putting the number of riders well over one hundred thousand.

The trail system is named after the legendary environmentalist of the same name who traveled the country around the turn of the century and founded the Sierra Club. While much of Muir's research took place in the West, Wisconsin was a favorite state of his that cropped up often in his writing. Perhaps his book *Steep Trails*, published four years after his death in 1918, was a predecessor of sorts to mountain biking guides.

There are five loops to choose from here. The Red Loop is the shortest (1.5 miles) and easiest, staying close to the parking lot and exploring a small portion of the forest. This is a good warm up with very small climbs and a single fast descent. Intermediate riders can spin this easily in 10 minutes before heading out onto one of the more challenging loops.

The White Loop is a bit longer coming in at 4 miles even. The terrain is a bit more difficult, with switchbacks and a long winding climb midway, but is definitely the next step for those graduating from the Red Loop. For those not prepared for heavy climbing, this route mercifully bypasses the massive climb found on the Orange Loop by breaking off midway and climbing to the north on a much more gradual slope. This portion of the cluster will take riders twenty-five to thirty minutes to complete.

The Orange Loop is next in line and logs in only a bit longer at 5.3 miles in length. This route takes riders to the far edge of the forest and includes three of the more difficult sections encountered in these woods: a very steep and demanding climb of approximately 1 mile, an equally steep descent I refer to as the "frame breaker," and a seemingly endless winding climb to finish things off. Intermediate riders will need thirty-five to forty minutes to make their way around this loop. This is probably the most taxing loop of all in terms of endurance.

The 6.8-mile Green Loop covers a great deal of ground on the north end of the property. This is one of the most technically demanding loops in the cluster, second only to the Blue Loop. The first large climb on the Orange Loop is included, along with its hammering descent and, for good measure, an incredibly steep climb is thrown in at the end to finish riders off. This is a very challenging circuit that will take riders forty to forty-five minutes to navigate.

JOHN MUIR TRAILS
Ride 4

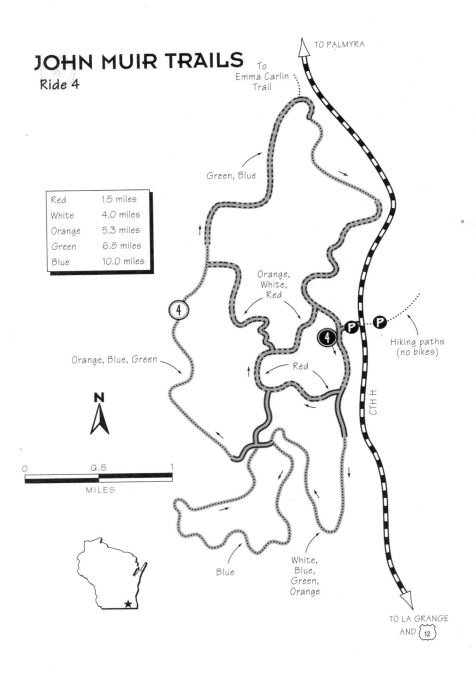

TO PALMYRA

To
Emma Carlin
Trail

Green, Blue

Red	1.5 miles
White	4.0 miles
Orange	5.3 miles
Green	6.8 miles
Blue	10.0 miles

Orange,
White,
Red

4

4   P   P

Hiking paths
(no bikes)

Orange, Blue, Green

Red

CTH H

N

0   0.5   1

MILES

White,
Blue,
Green,
Orange

Blue

TO LA GRANGE
AND 12

The longest loop in the cluster is the Blue Loop, and it includes the best parts of all the routes. Instead of the tough climb at the beginning of the Orange Loop, however, the Blue Loop bypasses this with a 1.75-mile section of switchbacks that gradually covers the elevation change. The tough descent of the Orange Loop is included along with the distance and climbing of the Green Loop.

The Trek Fall Color Festival Race takes place each October and brings in riders from northern Illinois and all of Wisconsin. The sport class consists of two laps on the Blue Loop along with a warm up on the Red Loop. Riders definitely take this area seriously and many call it home. The Blue Loop will take about 60 to 70 minutes to complete.

General Location: 6 miles south of Palmyra within the Kettle Moraine State Forest Southern Unit.

Technical Difficulty: Level 3 to 4.

Aerobic Level: Moderate to strenuous.

Tread: Wide singletrack and doubletrack.

Length: 1.5- to 10-mile loops.

Elevation Change: The riding is mainly done over rolling terrain which falls and rises 20 to 30 feet at a time. A couple of 50- to 60-foot climbs are encountered on the longer loops, with one climb of 100+ feet to make riders work for their fun.

Camping: There are 63 sites at Whitewater Lake Campground, 10 miles south of the trails. Follow County Highway H south to Wisconsin Highway 12. Turn right (west) and follow the road for 2 miles to CH O, then turn left. After 0.75 mile turn right onto Kettle Moraine Drive and follow it to the camp area on the right. Fire pits and toilets are available.

Season: The trails are open from April to November. Erosion is an issue and signs will be posted after heavy rains and early in the spring thaw asking riders to refrain from using the trail. Any season is excellent for riding at John Muir.

Fees: A trail pass and vehicle admission sticker are required. Both are available as annual passes from the DNR.

Services: Water and restrooms are available in the parking lots at the trailhead. The restrooms are located across the street in the hiking trails parking lot. Food can be found in the nearby town of Palmyra, food and gas can be found further along WI 67 in the town of Eagle.

Hazards: Though the trails are well groomed, they are very technical; tough descents and corners are found throughout. Always keep speeds under control. This doesn't mean that you need to ride the brakes throughout the ride, but at all times you must be able to steer and stop effectively. Erosion is well under control and should not cause troubles. For some, it is a new experience to ride on the rubber mats and diversion devices.

Rescue: The trails are very well ridden and finding help on them should not be a problem. In case of injury, use the map in your pocket to pick the quickest route back to the parking lot. Traffic on Wisconsin Highway 67 is fairly steady.

Land status: Wisconsin DNR, Kettle Moraine State Forest.

Maps: The trail area is shown on the USGS 7.5-minute quad for Whitewater. Maps are available at the trailhead.

Sources of more information: See Appendix A, in particular the Palmyra Chamber of Commerce, Wisconsin Department of Tourism, and WORBA.

Finding the trail: From Interstate 94 take the Oconomowoc exit for Wisconsin Highway 67 and drive south for 13 miles to the town of Eagle. Turn right (west) onto County Highway NN and travel 6 miles to Palmyra. Continue through the town of Palmyra (the road turns into CH H). Follow CH H for 3 miles to the trailhead on the right.

THE RIDE

The John Muir Trails depart from the parking lot on the west side of County Highway H on a gravel doubletrack path. The trails head one way, to the south, winding through a series of minor climbs and descents, still on gravel but getting into some hard-packed earth. The first intersection is in 0.5 mile. To the right the Red Loop branches off and takes riders on a beginner route through the woods; to the left the main trail continues on.

The next 1.25 miles on the main trail have some excellent descents and climbs, and a section of switchbacks that is second to none. The path is still rather wide at this point but begins to look more and more like single track as distance goes by. The path through the trees darts back and forth around sharp corners, demanding every bit of the rider's instincts to make it through

The author climbing over gravel and erosion control devices at the John Muir Trails.
MIKE HUDSON PHOTO

unscathed. At the 2.75-mile mark the second intersection approaches, presenting some interesting choices. Going straight takes the rider on a rather steep climb up an erosion control mat to the top of a bluff. Turning left takes the rider onto the Blue Loop (the main trail) and accomplishes the same climb, this time stretched out over a winding set of switchbacks 2 miles long with two exciting descents. Taking a right at the intersection gets riders back on the White Loop, which shares the same end as the red.

Back on top of the bluff on the main trail, riders weave through the forest and through a series of small hills. The trail has turned to singletrack by this time and starts to really pick up momentum. Halfway through this section is the segment I refer to as the "frame breaker," named so for the hammering it gives riders at speed. The trail breaks to the left, back hard to the right, then dives down to the foot of the bluff before entering a gentle "S" curve. This portion of the trail, which includes some rather deep ruts and large rocks, is very exciting but should be taken at a controlled speed.

The trail then breaks out into the sunlight across a meadow and enters a sandy region on doubletrack. The last intersection approaches at the 6.5-mile mark. The path to the right leads onto the orange loop and immediately up what seems to be a never-ending hill. The climb covers 100 + feet in elevation and doubles back on itself 4 times. Unable to see how much longer this steep climb will last, these switchbacks can really take a mental toll on the rider.

Staying on the main trail and heading straight, the path leads into the forest once again and cuts back and forth through the pines. Sand is fairly common and climbing is minimal until the 8-mile mark where the steepest climb of the day awaits. At the base of the climb, the connector trail to the Emma Carlin Trail heads off to the north, a tempting escape route in the face of this monstrous climb. The climb quickly covers 75 to 100 feet of elevation. A perfect balance of weight on the front and back tires will help traction while keeping the front tire from hopping up. After the climb there are 2 miles still ahead before reaching the parking lot. The trail becomes excessively bumpy and strewn with rocks. The last 2 miles are very taxing, and riders interested in riding all the loops in a single afternoon should consider trying this longest loop first, while they still have the energy.

5

Emma Carlin Trails

The Emma Carlin Trails can easily be described as the little brother to the nearby John Muir trails, a little smaller and less established, and hanging on by a shirttail in the form of a 5.5-mile-long connector trail. This small cluster is another in a series of well-marked and maintained Kettle Moraine Forest Mountain Bike Trails. In comparison with John Muir, this set is a little less traveled and the distances are a bit easier to handle for riders not yet ready for 10 miles of technical challenges and climbing. There are three loops here: a 4-mile outer loop designated as Green, a 2.4-mile Orange Loop, and a 2-mile Red Loop. The 5.5-mile connector trail is a two-way path covering some of the most exciting terrain in all of Wisconsin, with switchbacks, rocky descents, and wide-open singletrack. I normally wouldn't mention a connector path other than to say that it exists, but in this instance, the connector comes close to outshining the main trails themselves.

The main cluster of trails will take approximately 1.5 hours to complete for an intermediate rider and includes technical terrain on all loops. The connector is found on the west corner and heads off in a southwesterly direction for the John Muir Trail. The entire length of the connector is two-way and has all the elements necessary for top-notch technical riding. Switchbacks, singletrack, huge climbs and descents, and large fields of rocky debris can all be found along the way. An incomparable afternoon of riding can be put together by riding both systems and the connector back and forth. A ride of this sort is truly an olympian effort and one that will leave even the best of riders thoroughly beat.

The surrounding countryside is a paradise for wildlife. Raptors are visible from the higher lookouts, riding air currents for hours on end and diving into surrounding fields to scoop up small mammals. Deer are also plentiful and often seen springing away through the forest as bikers approach. The trails are set in some of the most beautiful protected forest in all of Wisconsin, with row upon row of pine trees that are both pristine and at times eerie to behold. In the fall, the hardwoods explode into a panorama of autumn colors, while the pines maintain their contrasting green hue.

General location: Three miles east of Palmyra.

Technical Difficulty: Level 2 to 3.

Technical Difficulty for Connector: Level 4 to 5.

Aerobic Level: Moderate to strenuous.

Tread: Wide single- and doubletrack.

Length: 2- to 5.5-mile loops.

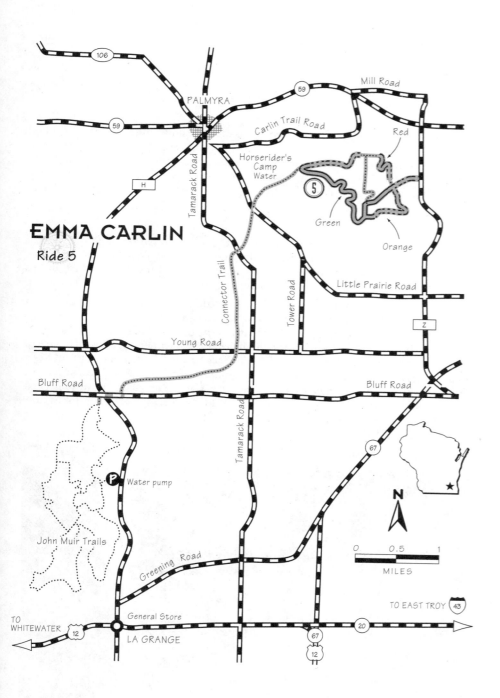

EMMA CARLIN
Ride 5

106

PALMYRA

59

Mill Road

Carlin Trail Road

Red

Horserider's
Camp
Water

S

Green

Orange

59

H

Tamarack Road

Connector Trail

Tower Road

Little Prairie Road

Z

Young Road

Bluff Road

Bluff Road

Tamarack Road

67

P

Water pump

John Muir Trails

Greening Road

N

0   0.5   1
MILES

TO EAST TROY 43

TO
WHITEWATER 12

General Store

LA GRANGE

67

20

12

Elevation change: The terrain is choppy and seldom level. The majority of the climbs are 20 to 30 feet, but several are in the 60+ range. Two in particular are found at the tail end of the connector to John Muir, both at insanely steep pitches. There are several on the south side of the Emma Carlin Loops.

Camping: There are 99 sites north of the trails, including two walk-in sites. Follow Wisconsin Highway 59 across to Eagle, and follow WI 67 north. Ottawa Lake Campground is found at the intersection of CH ZZ and WI 67. Fire pits and toilets are available.

Season: From April to November. Erosion is an issue and riding will be suspended after rain or snow in an effort to maintain the trails. Spring and fall are the best riding times, with cooler temperatures and smaller crowds. Overgrown trails are not a real problem here, so summer is also very good though much hotter. Be sure to take enough water, especially when crossing over to the John Muir Trails and back.

Fees: A trail pass and vehicle admission sticker are required. Both are available as annual passes from the DNR.

Services: A toilet is all that can be found in the trailhead parking lot. The nearest on-trail source of water is at the trailhead to the John Muir Trail. All other services are available in Palmyra to the west or Eagle to the east. Bike retail and repair are located to the south in the town of Whitewater.

Hazards: The normal set of hazards for the Kettle Moraine await riders at Emma Carlin. Roots and rocks are the norm along with loose gravel at the base of many of the descents. Erosion control is used on many of the trails in the form of rubber mats on climbs. It is easy on some of the downhill sections to gather a great deal of speed, so make certain it is always a speed that can be controlled. The connector trail has a great deal more technical terrain to challenge riders, the roots and rocks are larger and looser and demand every second of the rider's attention. There are also several road crossings and a short stretch along Bluff Road to cross over to the John Muir Trail. These roads are secluded and traffic tends to travel at higher speeds, making full stops and traffic checks before crossing a must for bikers.

Rescue: The entire South Kettle Moraine network is rather well ridden and riders

The Emma Carlin Trail is shown on the left, the connector to the John Muir Unit to the right.

are nearly always passing by, able to assist in an emergency. The roads of the forest are also well traveled and are another source of aid. The town of Palmyra is the closest civilization.

Land status: Wisconsin DNR, Kettle Moraine State Forest.

Maps: The trail area is shown on the USGS 7.5-minute quad for Whitewater. Maps are available at the trailhead.

Sources of more information: See Appendix A, in particular the Palmyra Chamber of Commerce, Wisconsin Department of Tourism, and WORBA.

Finding the trail: From Interstate 94 take the Oconomowoc exit for Wisconsin Highway 67 and drive south. Follow WI 67 for 13 miles to the town of Eagle. Turn right onto County Highway NN and travel 3 miles to CH Z. Turn left (south) and the trailhead parking lot shows up on the left within 0.5 mile.

THE RIDE

All three loops start out on the same path. The trail starts out on a wide dirt path that switches back and forth from doubletrack to just plain forest floor. The main loops are found at an intersection 0.25 mile in from the parking lot and all 3 break to the right at this point and continue on through the rolling hills. After 0.75 mile the trails break from each other, the Red and Orange turning to the left and heading out across a ridge through the center of the trail cluster. After 0.5 mile the Red Loop turns sharply in on itself and heads another 0.5 mile back to the lot. The Orange carries on for another quarter mile, cuts back hard on itself and follows the gravel path through some tough hills back to the lot.

The Green Loop carries on from where it breaks from the Red and Orange and continues to the far western edge of the cluster. An intersection at the 1.5-mile mark offers several options. A lookout to the north shows an excellent view of the surrounding state forest and farmlands. The trail to the right that continues on to the southwest is the connector path to the John Muir Trails. This 5.5-mile trail crosses several country roads but never diverges so it is nearly impossible to get lost. At the far end however, it runs into Bluff Road. Turn right on Bluff Road and follow it for 0.25 mile, go across CH H, and within 100 yards turn left onto the dirt path leading into the woods. You'll be on the John Muir Trail within another 100 yards. Follow this in reverse to return to Emma Carlin.

The third option at the Emma Carlin intersection is the path to the left, which continues the Green Loop. The loop gets more difficult in the last miles, and there are several good climbs and descents over loose gravel. At the 3.25-mile mark the trail splits. The left is a cutoff heading directly over to the Red Trail and back to the lot, the right picks up the Orange Loop and follows it back to the lot.

Southwest Wisconsin

The landmass of southwest Wisconsin is the highest portion of the state. It is known as the driftless area because of its lack of contact with any of the glaciers that scoured the Midwest over the last million years. The area instead gets its characteristics from time spent as a lake bottom, a lake formed from the melt water the glacier produced as it receded. Towering sandstone bluffs and mounds are common and, because of the richness of the soil, vegetation grows out of control in natural areas. The driftless area is separated from the rest of the state by the terminal moraine which runs diagonally across the state.

The entire area is a glowing example of the midwestern farmland most people imagine when thinking of Wisconsin. Because they were never rubbed flat by tons of glacial ice, the hills are larger here than in other parts of the state and roll out to the horizon in an endless continuum of geometrically perfect crops. Thin strips of trees divide property lines and crop types. Stone walls at the ends of fields are made up of rocks tumbled from the earth through a century or more of plowing. Turn-of-the-century farmhouses sit next to barns several stories high and filled to capacity with black-and-white Holsteins lumbering out and across the pasture. In some counties the livestock outnumber the people, making it more likely to bump into a Holstein than a fellow biker.

In amazing contrast to the rest of the state, the southwest, being higher and less rutted by glaciation, is almost completely devoid of lakes. In their place, several rivers make their way down out of the highlands on their way either to the Mississippi or across the state to Lake Michigan. Many rivers that flow across the northern part of the state flow through valleys in the southwest on their way to the Mississippi. Across this driftless area one such river, the Wisconsin, makes the final portion of its journey to the Mississippi from its headwaters in the northeastern lake country, gathering speed and volume from the Kickapoo River, its largest tributary.

In this section of the book six trails are covered. Three trails around the state capital of Madison are included, and rightfully so. The city is well known as a biking town and centers around the University of Wisconsin campus, academically one of the best schools in the country. The streets are literally filled with bicycles and, because of this, trails crop up simply out of necessity. Quarry Park off of University Avenue in the heart of the city is the most technically advanced ride covered in this book. The trail is a great confidence builder and (to steal a phrase from New York) if you can make it there, you can make it anywhere.

Two other trails lie on the outskirts of town, Cam-Rock to the southeast and The Farm to the southwest. Both are excellent rides put together by

WORBA, with plenty of singletrack at both. The Farm, however, is only open to WORBA members and serves as one of many rewards of membership in the organization.

The other three trails covered here all fall within the state park system. Blue Mound, Governor Dodge, and Wyalusing are all open to some degree to mountain bikers and, in addition to riding, have camping facilities to boot. Governor Dodge has the most to offer to mountain bikers with two loops open, both with their own challenges and breathtaking views. The park is extensive, covering over 5,000 acres of grassland and forest.

Blue Mound is quite tame and serves as a family ride at the state's highest point of elevation. Wyalusing is also tame as far as the mountain bike trails go, but add in the road riding that can be done there through the Mississippi Valley and the story changes. As it is mapped in this book, the Wyalusing route is one of the toughest climbing courses found in the state and, in the setting of the river valley, is one of the most visually stunning and rewarding. Though the southwest corner of the state is somewhat less traveled, the riding found there is excellent and the state parks, particularly Governor Dodge and Wyalusing, are among the best.

6

Cam-Rock County Park

Cam-Rock County Park is a small parcel of land set in forest bordering the vast fields of farmland native to southwestern Wisconsin. The trails are new to the mix of WORBA-produced clusters, famous for utilizing the land granted to mountain bikers to the maximum. The three loops covered here were created in the fall of 1997 and are scheduled to open to the public in mid-1998. The park itself is located to the north of the small town of Rockdale, a quaint farming and mining community that passes by in the blink of an eye. The park has two entrances, one to the east of town, one to the northwest, the latter being used as the trailhead for this ride.

The three loops found here cover approximately 1.5 miles each with a grass connector path adding another 0.5 mile of riding between trails. The loops are solely ridden on singletrack over hard-packed earth, forest floor terrain, and at times broken cobblestone. The cobblestones and shelf-like stone formations found here are unique to this system and provide excitement for first-time riders. Channels or gullies running down the hills are utilized by routing S-curve cutback paths through them on downhills, forcing riders to think on each descent and plan their attack across each pass.

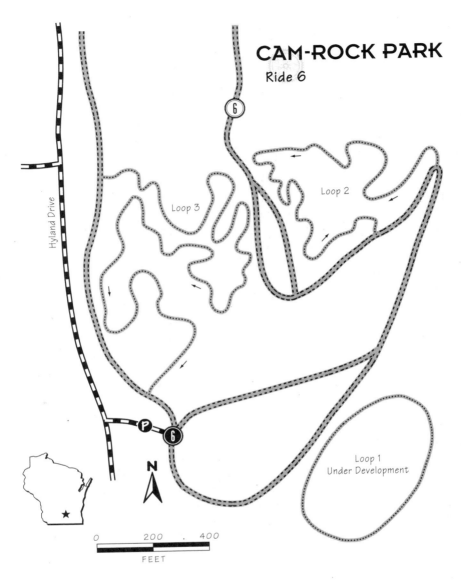

CAM-ROCK PARK
Ride 6

Hyland Drive

Loop 3

Loop 2

Loop 1
Under Development

N

0   200   400
FEET

The routes get better with each lap. Once you feel dialed in and have memorized some of the obstacles it is possible to make good time through the loops and get creative with technique. All three networks are set up on the same bluff, with trails cutting back and forth, climbing and descending along the same wall.

The entire network will take about an hour to complete for an intermediate rider with fresh legs. Multiple laps are a must and will add to the amount of time needed to ride the trails. This is another great example of the work WORBA is doing for the mountain biking community—obtaining, establishing, and maintaining trails throughout the state. And not simple trails, but technical trails, the type that challenge riders and make them want to skip out of work and other obligations so that they can ride. The routes here are of this variety.

General location: 20 miles southeast of Madison, on the northwest corner of the town of Rockdale.

Technical Difficulty: Level 3.

Aerobic Level: Moderate.

Tread: Singletrack, Grass Paths.

Length: Up to 5 miles.

Elevation Change: The entire bluff that the trails are ridden on is only 50 feet above the surrounding flats at the highest point. Several climbs are found on each route though most are taken on in short 10- to 20-foot spurts, with only a handful logging in at the 40-foot mark. The connector paths are relatively flat and serve as excellent areas for resting tired legs and lungs.

Camping: There are 300 sites to the south of the trails at Hickory Hills Campground on the shore of Rice Lake. The campground offers a lot in the way of creature comforts and doesn't pass for true backwoods survival. To find the sites follow County Highway B south out of Rockdale for 1 mile, then turn left onto Hillside Road and travel on this route for 4 miles. Hickory Hills is on the left (east) side of the road.

Season: Off-road trails are open May 1 to November 15.

Fees: A trail pass and vehicle admission sticker are required. Both are available as annual passes from the DNR.

Services: Water and restrooms are at the trailhead. Gas and groceries are available in Rockdale. For any other needs (including some of the best bicycle retail locations in the state), head to Madison.

Hazards: The singletrack trails have a good deal of obstacles and interesting crossings to negotiate. Stay back in the saddle and keep the majority of your weight on the back tire when diving down into gullies. The cobblestone sections are a bit tough and are not a great place to lay your body down. Keep the bike in an easy gear and creep over the top of the obstacles, using your body to push the bike up and over and out and around the stones.

Rescue: The trails are very close to the trailhead at all times and riders are never more than 0.75 mile away from the trailhead parking lot. In case of emergency, make your way back to the lot; the park is well used despite its small size.

Land status: Wisconsin DNR.

Maps: Maps are available in this book and at the trailhead. The trail area is shown on the USGS 7.5-minute quad for Rockdale.

Sources of more information: See Appendix A, in particular WORBA.

Finding the trail: Approaching Madison from the east on Interstate 94, take Wisconsin Highway 73 south from Deerfield. Follow WI 73 for 5 miles, cut across U.S. Highway 12/18 and continue on WI 73 for 3 more miles (set your trip odometer) to Koshkonong Road. Turn left (east) on Koshkonong Road and go 2 miles to Highland Drive. Turn right (south) and the trail parking lot is within half a mile on the left, over the crest of a hill.

WORBA rider Rita Nygren climbing through the leaves at Cam-Rock.

The trail departs from the southeast corner of the parking lot on a wide, grassy hiking path and cuts back on itself down a long, fast hill. Continue straight at the bottom of the descent, not veering to either of the options offered at the intersection there. The grassy path follows the shore of Rockdale Mill Pond for 0.25 mile and, at the bend in the trail, cuts off into the woods on singletrack to the right. The path, labeled loop 2, climbs to the top of the bluff and snakes back and forth across the midsection of the hill before returning to the hiking trail farther along the route.

Loop 3 is found another 0.25 mile along the hiking path around a gradual curve and up a small climb. The trail enters a field of waist-high grass to the right of the hiking path and quickly descends into the woods through a series of gullies and ravines. The path is well laid out, cutting back on itself several times on its way down through the stands of hardwoods. At the base of the first descent the trail cuts back up the bluff, crosses a series of rock shelves and cuts across the rim of a small plateau on cobblestones before descending back to the hiking trail connector path.

Loop 1 was still under development at press time and resides close by on a neighboring bluff, covering the same type of terrain as Loop 2.

7

The Quarry

The Quarry is, amazingly, the only sanctioned set of off-road bike trails within the Madison city limits. Madison is the classic college town with a massive campus and student body at the center and a unique blend of people occupying the city's main drag, State Street. The city has the highest per capita bike population in the United States, a fact that becomes obvious upon getting to town and watching the hordes of riders pouring down the street on bike paths. A local bike shop donated a good number of bikes to the city, spray painted red and sitting on street corners for anyone to ride. Probably none of them are ready for off-road riding but if that is your only option, it might be worth a shot to get yourself out on the singletrack.

The trails at The Quarry are quite simply the most technical in all of Wisconsin. The riding is insane and intense, reserved for only those well-trained in body English and bike control. The riding is not fast but instead is done at a much slower pace than usual, creeping and grinding over obstacles throughout the beehive network. Ridges, gullies, kettles, and natural

THE QUARRY

Ride 7

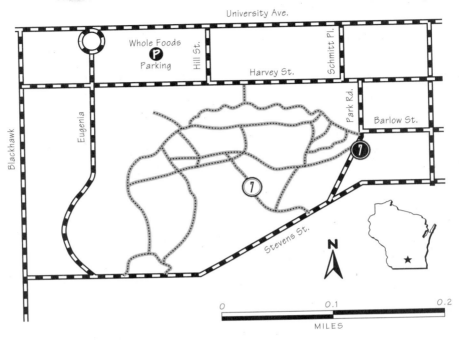

half-pipes are but a few of the types of terrain found in the cluster. All are ridden on extremely hard-packed and well-worn singletrack and all are strewn with glacial debris and root systems from the surrounding trees. For those not used to crashing or unplanned dismounts this is the place to learn. The "quick kick from the toe clips" and "handle-bar hurdle" are two techniques new to many riders that will be necessary for those wanting to avoid injury.

Excellent technique, balance, and leg power are needed to negotiate The Quarry. A lot of time is spent behind the seat with arms outstretched to keep weight over the back tire on hairy descents. A lot of time is also spent standing (something not normally recommended), hopping the bike over obstacles, cutting sharp corners through the trees and climbing dirt faces that at first do not look negotiable but with short bursts of power can be conquered. The Quarry is unlike any other legal trails in Wisconsin and contains terrain that normally is only accessible with a plane ticket out west.

The distance ridden in this cluster is tough to measure but comes in at approximately seven miles in all. It is not possible to ride this area without backtracking, which adds miles to the overall total. Time should also not be a consideration. Think of it this way. When you were five and out playing on a swingset or a big pile of tires bolted together on a playground, did you think of the time? Don't think of it here either. Just ride until you've had enough or your bike has given out beneath you, no sooner.

Mountain biker Scott Frey drops in to the "Champagne Glass" at the Quarry in Madison.

General location: Just west of the college campus within the city of Madison.

Technical Difficulty: Level 5.

Aerobic Level: Moderate to strenuous.

Tread: Singletrack.

Length: Up to 3 miles.

Elevation change: The hills are too numerous to count but none cover more than 30 to 35 feet of total elevation change. The entire network is located on a set of small mounds, most of which have extremely steep sides to climb.

Camping: There is no camping in the immediate vicinity, though most everyone has a friend of some sort in Madison that will allow camping in their living room.

Season: May to November.

Fees: None.

Services: The trailhead is located at Whole Foods, and therefore food and restrooms are readily available. The city has a great number of top-notch bike shops, including Budget (check out the used warehouse), Yellow Jersey, and Williamson Bike Works.

Hazards: Every hazard under the sun is found here and everything you encounter is a hazard. Thin ridges will send riders tumbling down steep faces. Roots, rocks, and ledges will provide challenges at every turn, and steep slopes will test riders' control both climbing and descending. Use good judgment and take on only challenges that match your abilities, but keep in mind, you don't learn until you conquer—and bashed-in shins are fun to show off at social gatherings.

Rescue: Ride these trails with a partner to be safe. In case of emergency, the trail is set in an urban area where people are easily found 24 hours a day. Get to the main road to summon help or head back to Whole Foods to use the pay phones there.

Land status: City of Madison.

Maps: This book only. The trail area is shown on the USGS 7.5-minute quad for Madison West.

Sources of more information: See Appendix A, in particular WORBA.

Finding the trail: Traveling west out of downtown Madison on University Avenue, watch for Whole Foods on the left, approximately 2 miles after leaving the University of Wisconsin campus. Park in the back of the lot and start riding on Harvey Road, which borders the back of the parking lot to the left. Take the first right, an unmarked park road just past Schmitt Place and begin looking for the trail entrances on the right hand side of the street. The first trail entrance comes up within 0.13 mile. The area will be better marked as WORBA does more development.

THE RIDE

There seems to be no rhyme or reason to the trail layout at The Quarry. Trails basically lead in all directions, following the lay of the land and kicking out onto the main road every now and again. Everything is fun, everything is ridable, no turn is incorrect, and getting lost is near to impossible. Markings will follow as WORBA becomes more involved.

8

The Farm

The Farm is an interesting new course designed by the Wisconsin Off Road Biking Association and managed under a new set of standards. The trails are on private land and are only open to WORBA members who have donated a set amount of time to trail development activities. The farmer who owns the land is a mountain biking enthusiast and active racer who was interested in setting up a set of training paths around the edges of his crops. After striking a partnership with WORBA, the trail crews got to work to open this unique section of singletrack. The area will be used to test new forms of erosion control and routing and will serve as a reward for membership in WORBA. The trails run over hard-packed soil throughout and climb back and forth over bluffs at the edge of the corn and bean fields. There are many tight squeezes that will scrape the ends of wide handlebars, and a number of log crossings can be found that add to the argument for equipping mountain bikes with rock rings to protect the front sprockets.

The trail covers three separate sections, two areas of singletrack riding set into the forest and a 0.75-mile section of singletrack connecting the two. The connector path runs along the edge of a corn field on the tree line dividing The Farm from neighboring properties. Completion of both sets should happen by mid-1998 and approved riders will be able to take advantage of it from that point forward. A nice aspect will be the limitless season for riding. Those interested in partaking well into winter can come out and ride singletrack after the first snowfall or in early spring when the trails are still frozen solid. The planned route will cover approximately 5 miles, with a 2-mile loop on either end of the 0.75-mile connector.

The surrounding area is beautiful, offering great views at the crests of each hill. The surrounding farmlands roll out to the horizon in all directions with patches of forest scattered throughout. The fields take on a bluish tint at midday and an amber tone from a distance as the sunlight reflects off the crops at sunset. Wisconsin farmland can be some of the most mesmerizing terrain to view from above.

Please be considerate of the crops while riding and stay on the trail at all times. Off-trail riding is not permitted and not at all necessary with trails as excellent as those offered here. To gain access, show yourself at a local WORBA chapter meeting or contact them through their website to join the group and become active in the local cycling scene.

General Location: Just west of Madison.

Technical Difficulty: Level 3 to 4.

Aerobic Level: Moderate to strenuous.

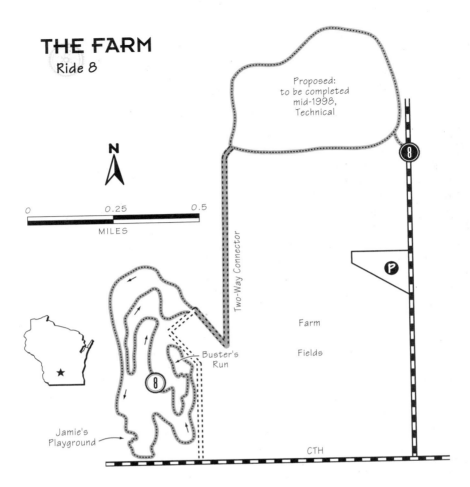

THE FARM
Ride 8

Proposed:
to be completed
mid-1998,
Technical

N

| 0 | 0.25 | 0.5 |

MILES

Two-Way Connector

Farm

Fields

Buster's Run

Jamie's Playground

CTH

Tread: Singletrack.

Length: Loops up to 7.75 miles.

Elevation Change: The connector path is very flat and runs up and over the gradual crest of a farmed hill. Both of the loops are built into the edge of steep bluffs with good climbs found on each. The most rigorous climbs cover 50 to 60 feet of elevation, though at times the climbing is spread out across the bluff and therefore is not at a very steep grade. The majority of the climbs come in quick spurts, with two larger climbs found on each loop.

Camping: There is no camping available in the immediate area, other than in the back of a self-provided VW bus.

Season: The trail is open to any rider ready to brave the harsh conditions. See the chapter on weather for winter riding tips.

Fees: Membership fees are due to WORBA and proper identification must be produced to get out on the course.

Services: Several grocery stores and gas stations are found at the intersection of Wisconsin Highway 12/14 and County Highway S. A pair of restaurant/bars are in the town of Pine Bluff, at the intersection of CH S and CH P.

Hazards: There are a great many log crossings with sprocket marks visible on all of them. A few of the corners are sandy and having the front wheel wash out in these spots is pretty common. There are a number of spots where it is necessary to pass between trees only 2 to 3 feet apart. Watch your hands when going through these at speed, to avoid crushing your knuckles. Look out for barbed wire on the connector path also, some of which has been buried for years and will take a year of riding to uncover.

Rescue: In case of injury make your way across the street to the farmhouse and ask that medical help be summoned. If no one is there, the roads are a bit desolate but passing traffic will happen along sooner or later. The best bet is to ride in pairs to assure safety.

Land status: Private land approved only for WORBA members.

Maps: Contained within this book only. The trail area is shown on the USGS 7.5-minute quad for Middleton.

Sources of more information: See Appendix A, WORBA.

Finding the trail: Contact WORBA, attend a local meeting, and find out more about how to get involved.

THE RIDE

The North Loop is the easiest to gain access to from the road and plans are in place for 2 miles of singletrack through the forest. In the woods the path is

A WORBA rider racing through cutbacks at the base of a climb at the Farm.

one-way only. On the southwest edge of the loop the path cuts back out into the sunlight and follows the fence line to the south over a singletrack connector path. The path is a bit bumpy from years of farming but will smooth out over time as riders get out and hammer it flat. The connector drifts along for 0.75 mile, at the end of the fence line cuts to the right along the edge of the cornfield, and within 0.13 mile ducks into the woods and onto the second loop.

This second loop runs in a counterclockwise pattern and immediately descends to the base of the hill. Several cutbacks and climbs entertain riders for the next 1.8 miles, taking them from the top to the bottom again midway through the ride before finishing at the connector path. With several passes on each loop and a couple of rides back and forth on the connector, an entire afternoon can be spent riding, and anyone who comes away without quivering legs should send in application for the next summer Olympics. The trails will become more refined and better marked as WORBA puts more time into them.

9

Blue Mound State Park

Blue Mound State Park is home to a set of three short but scenic mountain bike trails. The trails, found on the north side of the park, are an excellent place for beginners and families to venture into the woods and experience off-road riding in small doses. The John Minix Trail is listed in park literature as the easiest, logging in at 1 mile and providing a moderate challenge for intermediate riders. The loop takes about ten minutes to complete. The Willow Spring Trail is a bit longer, logging in at 2 miles, and is slightly more difficult with a rather long climb at the halfway point. This loop should take intermediate riders about twenty minutes. The Pleasure Valley Trail also covers 2 miles and, after passing through a forest of sugar maples, opens to a beautiful prairie leading down to a wooded valley. This loop takes about 25 minutes to complete, though stopping to take in views of the surrounding countryside is a must. The majority of the riding is over hard-packed dirt and gravel. The valley loop is on a mown path of grass.

The riding at Blue Mound is scenic but uneventful and may be uninteresting to advanced riders. Blue Mound is great for families looking to get out on the trail with young ones. (For more serious riders, there are better trails to the west at Governor Dodge and the extra drive time is well worth it. Technical riding can also be done around the Madison area without coming this far west.)

BLUE MOUND STATE PARK

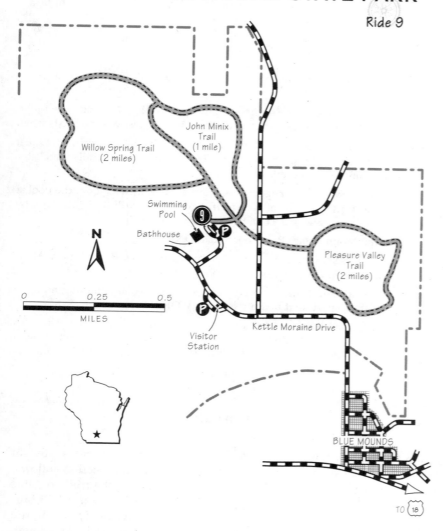

If you visit this park, the roads leading up to the observation towers and the swimming pool are good bets. The camping is very nice and a morning road ride through the area hills yields views of mist-covered farmland in all directions. The park can be very quiet during the work week and much more pleasant to explore than on weekends.

General location: 20 miles west of Madison on U.S. Highway 18.

Technical Difficulty: Level 1 to 2.

Aerobic Level: Easy.

Tread: Wide, smooth singletrack.

Length: 1- to 2-mile loops.

Elevation change: The trails are pitched on the side of a hill so some climbs are undertaken, none of which cover more than 30 to 40 feet in elevation.

Camping: There are 78 sites in the park. Showers and restrooms are available.

Season: May 1 to November 15.

Fees: A trail pass and vehicle admission sticker are required. Both are available as annual passes from the DNR.

Services: Water and restrooms are at the pool area. Gas and groceries can be found in the town of Blue Mounds to the south. Bike service is most easily found in Madison.

Hazards: Erosion control devices on downhills and climbs. Keep your front wheel light while tackling these. When traveling to the Pleasure Valley trails watch for traffic when crossing the park road.

Rescue: Help is available at the ranger station at the park entrance or at the pool at the trailhead. The trails get a lot of foot traffic and hikers will probably pass by sooner rather than later in the case of a bad wreck.

Land status: Blue Mound State Park, Wisconsin DNR.

Maps: The trail area is shown on the USGS 7.5-minute quad for Blue Mound. Maps are also available at the ranger station at the park entrance.

Sources of more information: See Appendix A, in particular Blue Mound State Park, the Wisconsin Department of Tourism, and WORBA.

Finding the trail: Head west out of Madison on U.S. Highway 18, then exit north on County Highway F. Jog left into the town of Blue Mounds. At the center of town turn right onto Mounds Park Road and follow this right into the park, which is northwest of town.

THE RIDE

The John Minix Trail begins with a paved path leading out of the parking lot to a double track path into the forest. A gravel downhill section follows, winding its way to the base of the forest. This portion of the trail contains erosion control devices in the form of 4-inch-wide wooden beams half buried in the gravel every 10 to 15 feet. These are best navigated with a little speed and a light jerk on the front handlebars as they approach. The downhill is about 5 feet wide and never cuts back too severely upon itself. At the bottom of the descent turn right and head out across the base of the forest through two small gullies. These are best taken with the front wheel in the air, dropping the back tire gently down into the base of the gully. Small creeks are scattered throughout the trail. These are most often covered with small wooden foot bridges that are easily crossed. The trail ends with a gradual climb through an open meadow, apparently where a railroad once passed through. A couple of exposed wooden ties explain the bumpy terrain along this section of the trail.

The author descending through the hardwoods and ferns on the John Minix Trail.
LAURA HUTCHINS PHOTO

The Willow Spring Trail shares the same opening descent as the Minix Trail. Instead of heading to the right at the bottom of the opening descent, head left and wind through the forest along hard-packed dirt and gravel. A couple of wooden bridges make small bog crossings a little less messy. Vibrant green ferns line the sides of the trail along the climb back towards the parking lot. The climb is made a bit more difficult by erosion blocks much like the ones encountered on the initial descent. Try to stay in the saddle and hop the front tire over each obstacle while keeping weight on the back tire to reduce slipping.

A connector trail leading off the Minix Trail heads east towards the Pleasure Valley Loop. The connector covers a half mile over dirt, gravel, and foot bridges under dense tree cover. Leaving the forest to cross into the valley means crossing the main road that skirts the edge of the park. Watch carefully for traffic, especially in summer when the crossing becomes quite overgrown and hard to see through. The path in the valley runs through waist-high meadow grass. It is a two-way path looping along the perimeter of the tree line with no coverage to escape the sun. Depending on which way the trail is traversed the ride either begins or ends with a dramatic view of the Blue Mounds to the east. The mounds appear bluish gray from a distance and give the park its identity.

10

Governor Dodge State Park

The trails at Governor Dodge State Park are consistently cleared of debris and overgrowth throughout the year by rangers and volunteers. This care helps to make the off-road trails found here some of the cleanest and most pleasant to ride in southwestern Wisconsin. There are 2 main loops open to bikers, both offering incredibly scenic views and challenging terrain. Both are ridable for intermediate riders, the Mill Creek Trail being the easier of the two.

The Mill Creek Trail is 3.3 miles long and departs from the south end of the Cox Hollow picnic area on the shore of Cox Hollow Lake. The entire loop takes about 35 minutes to complete. The path follows a one-way counterclockwise trail up into the sandstone bluffs surrounding the lake. The first mile is a black-top path with a fairly steep incline. At the top of the path the singletrack begins. The path rolls along the top of the bluff, darting into the forest and reemerging into sunlit meadows. Small climbs are scattered throughout followed by quick descents to reward tired legs.

A hilltop view of Twin Valley Lake, complete with a bench for resting tired legs.

The second ride in the park, the Meadow Valley Trail, is more difficult and covers 6.8 miles. This is a bit more advanced than the Mill Creek Trail and will take intermediate riders an hour and fifteen minutes to an hour and a half to complete. This loop starts off on the north side of the Cox Valley picnic area and climbs an incline out of the parking lot up into the forest. The trail weaves in and out of the woods as it circles the entire perimeter of the meadow that dominates the center of the park property. Magnificent views of Lost Canyon are the main attraction of the first half of the ride. At times, the trail rolls right out to the edge of the sandstone cliffs, peering down into the wooded canyon below. The second half of the ride is over wide dirt paths through the forest that borders the northern edge of the park.

The park covers 5,029 acres of land and is set in the midst of the driftless, unglaciated plain of southwestern Wisconsin. The area is interesting to imagine during the last ice age, when glaciers occupied the northern portion of the state and only this far corner remained untouched. The land teemed with plants and wildlife and, as the ice retreated, it was this area that re-seeded and populated the newly scoured land to the north. Sitting out on the central meadow it is easy to picture herds of deer crossing through the waist-high grass, feeding off the abundant foliage, and waiting for generations to return to their frozen home.

General location: 35 miles west of Madison on U.S. Highway 18.
Technical Difficulty: Level 2 to 3.

GOVERNOR DODGE STATE PARK

Ride 10

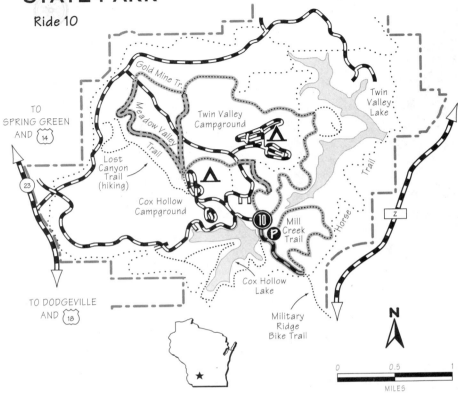

Aerobic Level: Moderate.

Tread: Pavement and dirt singletrack.

Length: 10.1 miles.

Elevation Change: Much of the riding is done atop bluffs, reached by large climbs on each of the two loops. The climbs cover approximately 80 to 100 feet in elevation. The rest of the climbs and descents cover 30 feet or less.

Camping: Riders can choose from 267 sites at the park. Showers and restrooms are available.

Season: Off-road trails are open May 1 to November 15.

Fees: A trail pass and vehicle admission sticker are required. Both are available as annual passes from the DNR.

Services: Restrooms and water are available at the trailhead parking lot as well as concessions. Dodgeville, to the south, is a good stop for gas or groceries.

Hazards: Watch the road crossing midway through the Meadow Valley ride. Both loops have their share of roots and rocks that are necessary to navigate, the Meadow Valley ride especially. I would suggest getting off of the bike when approaching the lookout cliffs over Lost Canyon about 2 miles in on the left. The descents on the Meadow

Valley ride are well marked but often washed out and eroded. Try to keep the front tire out of these ruts and hop them if necessary to keep from getting hooked in.

Rescue: Return to the trailhead to locate park rangers or to the park entrance ranger station. In the case of injury on the trail the main park road is the best bet for finding fellow park users. Pay phones are located outside the main park office and at the Cox hollow beach concession stand.

Land status: Wisconsin DNR, Governor Dodge State Park.

Maps: The trail area is shown on the USGS 7.5 minute quad for Pleasant Ridge. Maps are also available at the ranger station at the park entrance.

Sources of more information: See Appendix A, in particular the Dodgeville Chamber of Commerce, Wisconsin Department of Tourism and WORBA.

Finding the trail: Take U.S. Highway 18 west out of Madison 35 miles and head north on Wisconsin Highway 23 in Dodgeville. Take WI 23, 5 miles north to the park entrance on the right. After entering the park, take the road to the right just past the ranger station and follow it all the way to the Cox Hollow picnic area.

THE RIDE

The Mill Creek Loop departs the parking lot to the southeast and climbs 0.5 mile up the main bluff on pavement. At the top of the paved route the trail turns left and continues off-road on singletrack along the edge of a field of pines. To the right a connector path leads off to the state-sponsored Military Ridge bike/hike trail (not covered in this book).

The singletrack route continues across the top of the bluff, darting in and out of the forest and into a meadow of waist-high grass. The riding is pitched into the hill at times and short climbs are found throughout. Several excellent lookouts are found along the way looking down on Twin Valley Lake. The last 0.5 mile brings riders down off the bluff and back to the paved trail. Turn right at the end and cross back over the Cox Hollow Dam to the trailhead parking lot.

On the opposite side of the lot the Meadow Valley Loop departs to the north. The trail immediately climbs to the upper plain that makes up the central portion of the park. For 30 feet, the trail pitches at a very steep incline, making it tough to get good traction. The trail continues on before hitting the main loop, 0.25 miles in. The path covers single-, double-, and even tripletrack throughout the course of the ride. At the 0.5-mile mark the trail branches in several directions; stay to the left at this point, although the sign is easy to miss. Continuing straight at this intersection will take you into the Twin Valley Campground. Keeping left, the path heads across the central meadow and crosses back and forth from forest to meadow. Two miles in several short dirt spurs, approximately 10 feet long, lead to lookouts into Lost Canyon.

Back on the trail the path heads north again and crosses the main park road. After a section of meadow the trail dives back into the forest and stays there. The trails increase a little in technical nature and the next 3.5 miles

65

are some of the most challenging in the park. As the trail goes on, watch for several sandy areas that are very loose and tough to negotiate. The trail rubs up against the shore of Twin Valley Lake as it nears the end and finishes with a steep, steady climb back to the parking lot.

11

Wyalusing State Park

Any place where two rivers as large as the Mississippi and Wisconsin converge will be an area of diverse terrain and immense proportion. Wyalusing State Park is located at the confluence of these great bodies of water and offers 5 miles of challenging on- and off-road riding for mountain bikers (though most brochures say 6 miles, the route shown here ignores some areas open to mountain biking). The path covers the 2,596-acre park from end to end, beginning on the road with some serious descents and climbs, rolling through the forest on a set of singletrack trails, and returning to the road to backtrack over the climbs and descents that started things off. This route is meant for intermediate and advanced riders and will leave the lungs and legs of any class rider thoroughly wrung out and wasted. The entire course takes an hour and a half to complete at a good pace.

The off-road section included in the ride is marked as the hiking/ biking Military Ridge Trail. This forested section covers 1.6 miles of ground along a ridge looking out over the Mississippi. All day long and into the evening the Burlington Northern Railroad can be heard thundering along the banks of the river, adding an odd bit of nostalgia to the ride. This is a technical set of singletrack that is quite challenging and fun to ride, keeping riders awake with quick cutbacks and small obstacles in the form of roots and rocks. The turnaround at the end of the off-road trail is an open spot on an otherwise densely wooded bluff, which offers excellent views of activity on the Mississippi River below. Tugboats and barges dodge the river's many sandbars and offshoots on their way past the lookout.

The history of the park itself and its development is a familiar story in Wisconsin. In the mid-1930s, as the Great Depression descended upon the United States, the U.S. government formed the Civilian Conservation Corps (CCC). This outfit was responsible for constructing the buildings and paths presently found in many of our state parks. Even in such rugged terrain as Wyalusing or Devil's Lake these workers toiled to make these large-scale public wilderness areas enjoyable for people of all abilities. Many of the buildings and paths constructed by the CCC are still in use today, complimenting the surroundings while making them accessible.

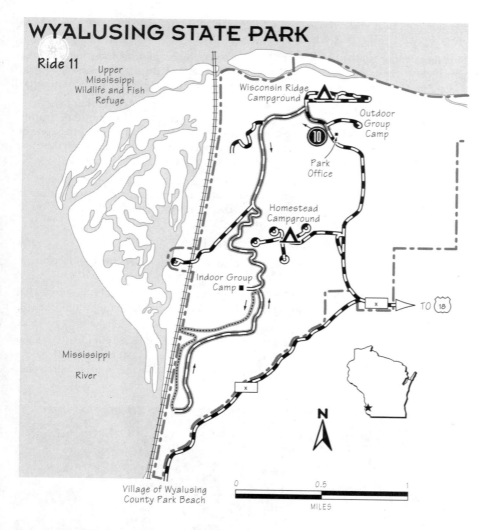

WYALUSING STATE PARK

Ride 11

Upper Mississippi Wildlife and Fish Refuge

Wisconsin Ridge Campground

Outdoor Group Camp

Park Office

10

Homestead Campground

Indoor Group Camp ■

Mississippi River

TO 18

Village of Wyalusing County Park Beach

N

0   0.5   1

MILES

General location: 5 miles east of Prairie du Chien off U.S. Highway 18.

Technical Difficulty: Level 1 to 3.

Aerobic Level: Strenuous.

Tread: Singletrack, Paved.

Length: 5 miles.

Elevation change: The Military Ridge Trail is all downhill, the climbing takes place on the road. Three climbs are included, covering 0.5 to 1.0 mile each. Grades up to 40 percent are encountered on 200-foot-plus climbs.

Camping: There are 132 campsites at the park. Showers and restrooms are available.

Season: Trails are open from May 1 through November 15. July and August can be uncomfortable due to temperatures in the 90s and high humidity.

Fees: A trail pass and vehicle admission sticker are required. Both are available as annual passes from the DNR.

Services: Water and restrooms are located at the main guard station found at the entrance to the park. Food is available in the town of Bagley south of the park. Prairie du Chien has a more extensive selection of stores, taverns, and restaurants.

Hazards: Most of the park roads posted at slow speeds, but tight corners and narrow forest passes can be tough to negotiate in the presence of automobile traffic. Some of the paved descents are very long and very steep. Keep speeds under control at all times and try to make eye contact with passing drivers to make certain they are paying attention before making any moves into traffic.

Rescue: Head back to the ranger station at the beginning of the park in case of injury or emergency. The majority of the riding is done on park roads, so other people visiting the park are around most all the time. Traffic on the main roads is not heavy but is constant throughout the day.

Land status: Wyalusing State Park, Wisconsin DNR.

Maps: The trail area is shown on the USGS 7.5-minute quad for Clayton, Iowa. Maps are also available at the ranger station at the park entrance.

Sources of more information: See Appendix A, in particular the Prairie du Chien Chamber of Commerce, Wyalusing State Park, Wisconsin Department of Tourism, and WORBA.

Finding the trail: When approaching Prairie du Chien on U.S. Highway 18 head southwest on County Highway C. After 2 miles turn right (west) on CH X. It is 0.75 mile to the park entrance. The park office is about 1 mile farther on the main road; its parking lot is the trailhead.

The author climbing the narrow forest floor terrain on the Mississippi Ridge Trail.
LAURA HUTCHINS PHOTO

Head north 0.13 mile past the baseball diamond on the right. The road breaks off to the left at this point. The path straight ahead takes riders to the top of a bluff looking down on the Wisconsin River. Turn left here and follow the main route, which descends rapidly for a little more than a quarter of a mile. The road forks here. Turn left, being very careful to bring the bike's speed down before entering the intersection. Another 0.5 mile of downhill riding follows, hugging the edge of the aptly named Long Valley. At the 0.5-mile mark make another left, following the sign to the Homestead picnic area. The next 0.5 mile seems more like 10. It's all uphill and winds a great deal back and forth through the sandstone cliffs. It's enough to make a rider feel like a Tour de France competitor in the Alps.

At the top of this climb stay to the right as you enter the Homestead picnic area. Continue to the right, going to the Indoor Group Camp, 0.13 mile farther on. The beginning of the Military Ridge off-road trail is on the left as you enter the group camp area. Hammer onto this trail and head downhill over one mile of singletrack through the forest, to the Mississippi River view clearing. This clearing is a good place to kick back for a few minutes, enjoy the countryside, and replenish thirsty, aching bodies.

Cathedral Tree Drive leads out of the east side of the clearing and climbs one mile at a moderate grade back to the Homestead picnic area. Check out the Spook Hill Indian burial mounds on the right side of the road during this climb, named so because of the howling winds that haunt this section of the forest on stormy nights. At the Homestead picnic area stay to the right and enter the road on the north end of the grounds. At this point the rest of the ride backtracks over familiar ground. Descend a half mile through the winding forest roads. At the base of the descent turn right and begin the painful 1 mile climb that finishes this ride. One right turn at the 0.6-mile mark disrupts the riders concentration on the masochistic activity at hand. Turn right at the top of the climb to find the parking lot.

Central Wisconsin

The trails covered in the area of central Wisconsin take up a large portion of this book, numbering fifteen in all. The area is a transition stage between the rolling southwest, the jagged southeast, and the wild and untamed north. The number of lakes and rivers begins to increase the farther north you travel in the state, and while water becomes more abundant, humans become less so, as Wisconsin's major population centers are in the south. Farmlands become more prevalent along the edges of highways and forests. To the west, a portion of the terminal moraine crosses the center of the state, making its way into the Mississippi River Valley and beyond to Minnesota. To the east, the Door County Peninsula juts into Lake Michigan, its lands filled with forests, farms, and small country towns edging the Green Bay shoreline.

The mountain biking opportunities in this central area cover the entire spectrum of riding styles and terrain varieties. The "Central Wisconsin" referred to in this book actually covers three diverse geographical segments; the Fox Valley and Door County Peninsula to the east, the Central Sands, and a land mass known as Upper Coulee Country to the west. The three form a swath of land across the state running from Lake Michigan to the Mississippi River and Minnesota border.

The Fox Valley fills in the area near the Lake Michigan shore at the base of Door County and surrounds inland Lake Winnebago. Historically, the Fox River provided the Indians and French with an efficient route between the Great Lakes and the Mississippi. This section of the state in its heyday of the 1800s was a booming industrial center, perfectly placed on the Great Lakes shipping routes. The Door County Peninsula, the thumb of mitten-shaped Wisconsin, contains three state parks with off-road trails, all of which are covered in the following section. The parks are lush, filled with vegetation and surrounded by water.

The Central Sands lie at the heart of the state around the cities of Stevens Point and Wausau. The area was at one time the floor of a glacial sea created by the melting glaciers, an area which drained through the southwest, forming several of the rivers including the Wisconsin that still flow today. When you are cleaning sand from your chain after a ride at Standing Rock or Hartman Creek you'll know where it came from. In addition to loose sand, towering sandstone bluffs, which were once islands in the glacial sea, crop up throughout the area. The rolling hills and marshes that are abundant here are also products of the glaciers and resulting waters that passed through here.

The western edge of this central section rubs up against the Mississippi River and is referred to as the Upper Coulee Country, an area of flat prairies boxed in by high bluffs. The formations were cut over time by various torrents of water, and the rich sediment this produced made the area prime farming territory. Much of this land is steep and rugged, climbing out of the plains to high plateaus and back down again. The Upper Coulee is centered around the cities of La Crosse and Eau Claire and contains rides with tougher climbing involved than the rest of the midsection.

When taken as a group, the trails available for riding are excellent throughout. From the cliffs overlooking Lake Winnebago at High Cliff State Park to the dense forest rim around Perrot Ridge at Perrot State Park, the riding is extremely diverse. Technical riders will drool over the Levis/Trow Mounds with its distant views serving as ample reward after the tough climbs there. The combination of camping and mountain biking at Newport will definitely change some riders' style, turning them from adrenaline mongers to peaceful naturalists, content to roll through the forest from their base camp to the spectacular sites in the surrounding area. Those who want singletrack can have their fill at the Nine Mile State Forest, while others can ride the cross-country ski trails around the amazing setting of Devil's Lake.

As you can see, the trails within the central portion of Wisconsin are hard to put a finger on. Whether the trails are 10 miles or 200 miles apart, each is unique. The area is a venerable mix and match of all the different types of terrain bikers like to ride. Though this guide should help riders choose the trails that best fit them, I urge you to explore them all. You may find yourself adding a new aspect of mountain biking to your normal routine.

12

Newport State Park

Newport State Park, at the northern tip of Door County, is one of the quieter sections of the peninsula. Most of the human traffic is confined to the western side of the Door County peninsula where the majority of the resorts, shops, and restaurants exist. The eastern side, where Newport is located, is a world unto its own, with forests and farmlands the chief attractions.

Newport is located directly south of the infamous maritime passageway known as Death's Door. This mile-wide stretch of water separates the mainland from Washington Island and its neighbor, Detroit Island. The dubious title was earned by the strait over the years as ships entered, using it as a shortcut into Green Bay, and got hung up on the rocks. Weather rips around the tip of the mainland, keeping the waters constantly rough and unpredictable. Sitting on top of the bluffs it's easy to imagine an old wooden schooner lying pitched on the rocks with a broken hull, and the crew scrambling to shore as it goes under. The nearby town of Gills Rock has a maritime museum housing artifacts of many of the wrecks from these waters.

NEWPORT STATE PARK

Ride 12

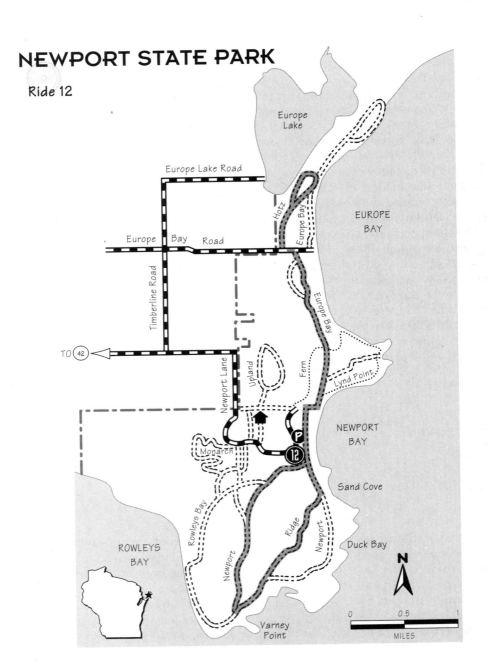

As for mountain biking at Newport, the trails are fast but uneventful. The trails explored here cover 8.75 miles and should take beginners an hour and fifteen minutes and advanced riders as little as half an hour. Other than avoiding a few roots that run across the trail, no technical maneuvers are necessary to master the course. There are no climbs either. The winning point on this trail is the tread, which is consistently hard and smooth. On some of the longer stretches it is easy to see far enough down the trail to really open it up without fear of running down an innocent pedestrian. All the trails are wide enough to handle two-way traffic.

An old, arched wood and stone gate is an interesting landmark to watch for at the head of the Hotz Trail. The entire area is set in a scenic hardwood forest that runs right to the edge of Lake Michigan.

A good way to ride this area is to camp at one of the park's secluded campsites and use it as a base from which to ride out and see the surrounding attractions.

After exhausting the trails in the park it is only a 4-mile road ride out County Highway NP and Wisconsin Highway 42 to the town of Gills Rock. From here it is possible to take the ferry across to Washington Island. While there are no trails offered on Washington Island the trip over is rather exciting and the island itself is fun to tour on bicycles. A second ferry off the northeast corner of the island leads out to Rock Island, a small state park that allows no motorized vehicles. It's all bikers, hikers, and wilderness on this small speck of land.

General location: 4 miles southeast of Gills Rock, or 40 miles northeast of Sturgeon Bay, which is the southernmost city on the peninsula.

Technical Difficulty: Level 1 to 2.

Aerobic Level: Easy.

Tread: Smooth, hard doubletrack.

Length: 8.75 miles.

Elevation change: Almost none. There are two climbs which amount to no more than 20 feet of elevation.

Camping: There are 16 sites located throughout the park, all of which must be hiked into and many of which are open to winter camping. The sites are located on the shores of Lake Michigan and Europe Lake and are each beautiful in their own regard. Fire pits are found at each site; restrooms and water are available in the park.

Season: April 15 to November 15. The trails are open only to cross-country skiers in the winter months.

Fees: A trail pass and vehicle admission sticker are required. Both are available as annual passes from the DNR.

Services: Water is available at lot 3 nearest the beach and also at the farthest point north on the Hotz Trail overlooking Europe Lake. Bathrooms are located at lot 3 and at the picnic area east of lot 2. Food and lodging are abundant starting at Gills Rock and most other small towns along the western coast. The nearest bike shop is in Fish Creek, 15 miles south on Wisconsin Highway 42.

An old stone farm gate leads onto the Hotz Trail at Newport State Park.

Hazards: Watch for hikers on the trail. There are many campers packing in gear and beach-goers making their way down from the parking lot to the beach. Small rocks and roots litter the trail but pose no threat. There is one road crossing approaching the Hotz Trail that has some fast traffic. Watch for the ash-gray sand that covers some portions of the trail; it holds up well when you're traveling straight over it, but cornering can make your front tire wash out.

Rescue: Help is available from the park office or from campers scattered along the trailside.

Land status: Wisconsin DNR, Newport State Park.

Maps: The trail area is shown on the USGS 7.5-minute quad for Spider Island. Maps are also available at the ranger station at the entrance to the park.

Sources of more information: See Appendix A, in particular Newport State Park, the Door County Chamber of Commerce, Wisconsin Department of Tourism, and WORBA.

Finding the trail: From the town of Ellison Bay, take Wisconsin Highway 42 east for 3 miles to CH NP. Turn right (south) and follow CH NP for 3 miles to the park office. The trail departs not from the main station but from the second parking lot.

THE RIDE

From lot 2, the trail heads east toward Lake Michigan. There are two entrances from this point and it doesn't matter which is taken—they both lead for all practical purposes to the same spot. The main trail comes up within

500 feet: take it to the right (south). Within 0.25 mile the main series of loops comes: keep to the right and stay on the Newport Trail. The other two loops in this section, Rowley's Bay and Ridge, do not allow biking.

The Newport Trail heads out in a counterclockwise circuit toward the waters looking out at Spider Island. Many of the campsites are along this shore, all under cover of forest but within feet of the water. The trail loops around for three miles before rejoining the connecting path. Continue north on this path that leads along the shore of Newport Bay.

Within 0.75 mile, lot 3 comes up and the trail breaks out of the forest and into the clearing at the main beach. Watch for pedestrians here and the only sand of the entire ride. Follow the trail to the right and out to the beach. Just before entering the deep sand the trail breaks to the left and heads into the woods again on the Europe Bay Trail. This rolls along for one and a half miles before reaching Europe Bay Road. The Europe Bay Trail on the other side is closed to bikes. Instead, head to the left and pick up the Hotz Trail marked by an old, arched stone gate. The trail forks within 0.5 mile. Stick to the right and follow it as it loops around and climbs twenty feet to an overlook on Europe Lake. If your water supply is low, this is the place to fill up at the green hand pump in the clearing.

The rest of the trail backtracks from this point. Continue on the Hotz Trail back to where it originally forked and continue south to Europe Bay Road. Carefully make the crossing and head south on the Europe Bay Trail all the way to the beach and back to lot 2.

If Gills Rock and Washington Island are of interest, exit the park on the main road, CH NP. Take this back out to WI 42, which leads into Gills Rock in just two miles. At the farthest point north a small dock serves as the port for the ferry leading across to Washington Island. This makes a nice day trip while staying at Newport. For more information on the ferry, including current rates, call 414-847-2546.

13

Peninsula State Park

Peninsula State Park was developed in 1909 from a protruding section of Door County that was, until that time, heavily logged and farmed. The area is a geological wonder made up of sandstone and limestone which accumulated millions of years ago at the bottom of a prehistoric sea. The area, along with the rest of Door County, is part of the Niagara Escarpment, the massive shelf of rock that extends from Lake Winnebago to Niagara Falls, New York. The terrain the mountain bike trails cover has more recently been scoured and compressed by glaciation, the same glaciers that carved out the surrounding waters of Green Bay.

Peninsula State Park offers 8 miles of off-road trails and a 9-mile gravel bike path. The off-road trail covers a mix of double and singletrack over hard-packed soil. The trail is rather uneven and obstacles are numerous making it a challenging and exciting ride. More technical riding is found on the trails that cross back and forth across the main loop. An intermediate rider can easily traverse the entire network within an hour and a half, counting the time spent backtracking over familiar trails to get to each crossing path.

After completing the off-road loop, riders may enjoy taking the relaxing and scenic ride up the Sunset Trail bike path. Adventure Island, Chambers Island and to the North Horseshoe Island are all visible from the mainland. An old lighthouse on the northwest corner of the property adds character and history to the park. On the eastern shore a 75-foot observation tower takes travelers 200 feet over the water of Green Bay. Careful explorers wandering the woods may still be able to locate the foundations of buildings from the original farms and logging camps of the area. Sighting a red-tailed hawk perched along the trail is not at all uncommon.

General location: Right in the center of Fish Creek, which is 20 miles northeast of Sturgeon Bay.

Technical Difficulty: Level 2 to 3.

Aerobic Level: Moderate.

Tread: Singletrack and doubletrack.

Length: 8 miles.

Elevation change: While there are quite a few flat stretches, small rolling hills make up the majority of the terrain. Small climbs are commonplace, none over 30 feet in elevation.

Season: May 1 through November 1. The season here is a little shorter than most state trails because of erosion control. The area often floods and trail closings are not uncommon. Call for trail conditions before making the drive.

PENINSULA STATE PARK

Ride 13

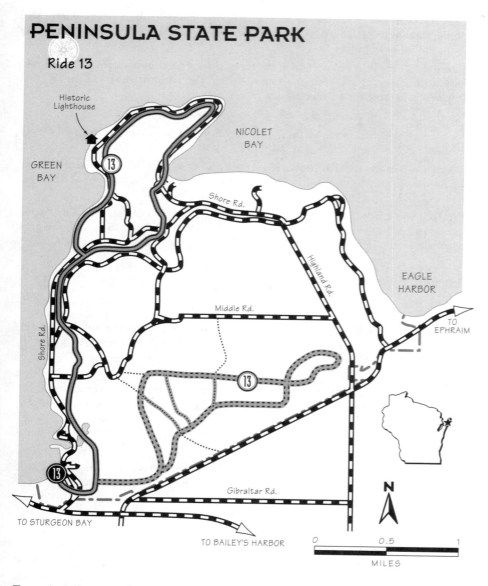

Fees: A trail pass and vehicle admission sticker are required. Both are available as annual passes from the DNR.

Services: All services, from gasoline to food to lodging, are available in Sturgeon Bay.

Hazards: Watch for roots and rocks on the quick downhills: they have the ability to pull the front tire wherever they want if given the chance. The best bet is to hit them with a little speed, with the rider's weight back in the saddle to keep the front end light. Most trail literature in the park states that the trails are minimally maintained and therefore obstacles crop up with every rainfall or group of riders that pass through.

Erosion control blocks must be dealt with on the opening climb and therefore also on the final descent. There is one road crossing on the path connecting the parking lot to the off-road trails.

Rescue: The trails in this section of the forest do not get a lot of traffic but are boxed in by rather heavily traveled roads on all sides. The park office should be the first stop when looking for assistance.

Land status: Wisconsin State Park, Peninsula State Park.

Maps: The trail area is shown on the USGS 7.5-minute quad for Ephraim. Maps are available at the ranger station at the entrance and through the DNR.

Sources of more information: See Appendix A, in particular the Door County Chamber of Commerce, Peninsula State Park, Wisconsin Department of Tourism, and WORBA.

Finding the trail: Take Wisconsin Highway 42 north out of Sturgeon Bay. When you reach Fish Creek, WI 42 heads to the right. Follow it for 0.25 mile to the park entrance on the left. Parking for bikers is on the left just past the ranger station.

THE RIDE

Departing from the south end of the bicycle trail parking lot follow the gravel path for 0.5 mile. This is the Sunset Bike Trail which runs the length of the park. At the 0.5-mile mark is a sign directing riders to the off-road bike trails. Take this right turn which leads onto a wide dirt path climbing up into the forest. Erosion control devices on this part of the trail make it a bit tricky, but remain seated and things will go just fine. The climb is about a quarter of a mile and leads to the top of the bluff where the trails are located.

The main loop begins at the top of the climb. Stay to the left and follow the easy markings out and around in a clockwise direction. On the far side of the loop is an intersection with a second loop. The two loops together actually form a figure eight, with three shorter paths intersecting it. Try out the short paths, each filled with drumlins and minor eskers for more technical riding.

Riders may also enjoy exploring the surrounding area on the Sunset Trail, from which this off-road trail branches. The trail runs the full length of the park, one step further from the shoreline than Shore Road which follows the same route. The trail is very easy and asks little of a rider's endurance. Be careful of hikers while riding, there is a great deal more foot traffic on this route than on the off-road sections.

A narrow strip of singletrack bisecting a meadow at Peninsula State Park.

14

Potawatomi State Park

Potawatomi State Park is located in a peculiar geographical position at the inlet of Sturgeon Bay that cuts off Door County from the mainland of Wisconsin. An observation tower at the northern end of the park yields spectacular views of Sawyer Harbor and the sandstone bluffs leading from the forest down to the waters of Sturgeon Bay. The forest is made up of a hardwood mix of birch, hemlock and maple. The vegetation on the forest floor is always at a minimal height and never grows over the trail.

The park itself is named for the Potawatomi Indians who once inhabited the surrounding area. The tribe held all of Door County, including the main villages on the islands at the tip of the peninsula, Rock Island being the main trade center. The name *Potawatomi* means "keepers of the fire."

The park's trails are rather plain, but that's not to say they are completely uninteresting. Big-ring, high-speed riding is easily manageable on the main route. Whereas many trails in this book are filled with debris, climbing, and cutbacks, this route is smooth, flat, and lends itself to swooping corners. The result is fast terrain with no surprises that lets riders take advantage of momentum and high-speed handling. Beginners can make the circuit easily in an hour at a moderate pace, advanced riders can swing 20- to 25-minute laps at racing pace.

If lodging in Sturgeon Bay, a quick connecting path that leads through the woods from Duluth Avenue on the northwest side of town is a quick way to and from the park. The town serves as the gateway to Door County and still has the historic appeal of the shipbuilding town it once was. Don't be surprised to wait while crossing the bridge into town as the taller sailing ships and shipping freighters make their way through the drawbridge.

General location: 3 miles northwest of Sturgeon Bay off Wisconsin Highway 42/57.

Technical Difficulty: Level 1.

Aerobic level: Easy to moderate.

Tread: Wide singletrack.

Length: 5.75 miles.

Elevation change: The trail is flat throughout, other than a climb at the trailhead to get to the top of the bluff. The climb covers no more than 30 feet of elevation.

Camping: The park has 123 sites, divided into two sections, one of which is open year round for winter camping. Fire pits are found at all sites and restrooms and water are within walking distance.

Season: Open April 15 to November 15. The trails are open only to skiers after the first snowfall. The trails may be closed after heavy rainstorms, so calling ahead is a good idea. The trail is mostly on higher ground but can still become saturated.

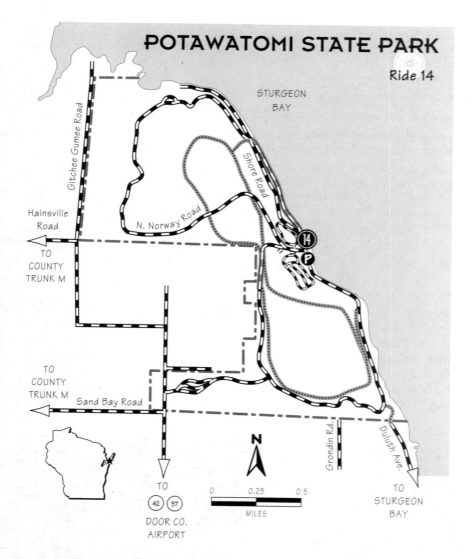

POTAWATOMI STATE PARK

Ride 14

STURGEON BAY

Gitchee Gumee Road

Shore Road

Hainsville Road

N. Norway Road

TO COUNTY TRUNK M

14
P

TO COUNTY TRUNK M

Sand Bay Road

Grondin Rd.

Duluth Ave.

N

TO
42 57
DOOR CO. AIRPORT

0   0.25   0.5
MILES

TO STURGEON BAY

Fees: A trail pass and vehicle admission sticker are required. Both are available as annual passes from the DNR.

Services: Water and restrooms are located at the trailhead. Food, lodging, and even bicycle repair can be found in Sturgeon Bay.

Hazards: Hiking is allowed on the trails so it is necessary to watch for hikers. There are no blind corners to speak of, however, so it is rather easy to see others in the distance. There are quite a few road crossings that can be dangerous if time is not taken to look down the road for traffic, much of which is moving rather quickly. Debris may litter the trails after storms but for the most part is not to be found. Some rough limestone rocks make the first climb a bit difficult. Lean back a bit to keep the weight on the back for traction and hop the front wheel over obstacles while selecting the path of least resistance.

Rescue: Help is available at the park office or in the town of Sturgeon Bay. The trails are fairly unpopulated in all seasons. The best bet is to get back to the main road in case an emergency. Remember, it is only a mile and a half back to Sturgeon Bay using the connector path.

Land status: Wisconsin DNR, Potawatomi State Park.

Maps: The trail area is shown on the USGS 7.5-minute quad for Sturgeon Bay West.

Sources of more information: See Appendix A, in particular the Door County Chamber of Commerce, Wisconsin Department of Tourism, and WORBA.

Finding the trail: Go 1.5 miles west of Sturgeon Bay on Wisconsin Highway 42/57 and turn right (north) on Park Road. Follow the signs for 2.5 miles to the park entrance on the right. After entering the park follow the main road for 0.5 mile to the first intersection. Turn right and follow the road through the forest to picnic area #2. Ride down to the water to find the trailhead.

THE RIDE

Leaving from the Hemlock Trailhead, head north along the paved trail along the shore of Sturgeon Bay. Just after passing a gate at the end of the paved path, the main road comes in. The Hemlock Trail continues on the opposite side of the road. The trail splits at this point. The Hemlock Trail veers to the right and is closed to bicycles while another trail, marked with a green bike silhouette sign, leads to the left and is the correct route to take. A quick climb to the top of the bluff takes riders to the beginning of the loop. I

The fast singletrack of Potawatomi State Park winding through a stand of birch trees.

choose to ride in a counterclockwise direction, as the corners are worn in this direction, although two-way riding is allowed.

Follow the bike sign straight ahead to join the main loop. The only tricky intersection comes up shortly after this. Watch for a bike sign to the right a little way down the correct path. The tendency is to go straight which leads out to the paved road and the connecting path to Duluth Avenue. Stay right here and keep moving.

At the 2-mile mark a sign points to mountain biking in either direction, take the trail to the left and head across the park road and back onto the trail. The other option serves as a cutoff for tired riders wanting to head in early and leave out the remaining two miles of riding.

At the end of each loop, riders can elect to spin another loop or return to the lot. Head to the right to take another lap; turn left to find the paved Hemlock Trail and parking lot.

15

Point Beach State Forest

Point Beach State Forest offers 3.1 miles of mountain bike riding on the Red Pine loop of its trail system. The forest, covering 2,900 acres, is located on the shores of Lake Michigan just south of the Door County Peninsula. The main feature of this narrow strip of land is the 6 miles of sandy beach that runs the length of the eastern side of the park. After a morning ride the temptation to spend the afternoon lounging on the beach is hard to resist.

Point Beach is a historic location in maritime history. The Rawley Point lighthouse, at the southern end of the grounds, is one of the largest lighthouses on the Great Lakes, visible from 20 miles away. It is still in operation, coming to life a half hour before sunset and running through the night until a half hour past dawn. The treacherous waters of the bay that borders the point claimed twenty-six boats before the existing steel light tower was erected in 1894.

The Red Pine Trail takes approximately thirty-five minutes to complete and covers an odd mix of tread—singletrack, doubletrack, and wide-cut paths. Most of the loop is through pine and birch forest, over grass, wood chips, and hardpack. Because of the area's unique geological history, much of the trail is covered in sand or is composed of a soil/sand mixture. Throughout time this area has been occasionally submerged, most recently by Lake Michigan, more distantly by a prehistoric ocean that covered the entire state. This accounts for the sandstone poking its way up through the sand-based soils.

POINT BEACH STATE FOREST

Ride 15

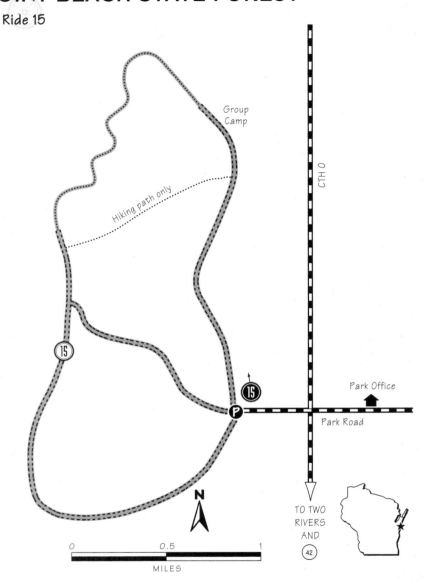

General location: 4 miles north of Two Rivers along the Lake Michigan coast.

Technical Difficulty: Level 2 to 3.

Aerobic Level: Moderate.

Tread: Singletrack and doubletrack.

Length: 3.1 miles.

Elevation change: All hills on this loop are very minor, with none gaining more than 20 feet of elevation. The majority of the trail is flat with small hills encountered in groups.

Camping: There are 127 sites within the park. Restrooms and water are available and firewood can be purchased near the park entrance.

Season: The park is open year round; however, the trails do close to mountain bikers as soon as enough snow gathers for cross-country skiers to begin using the trails.

Services: Water, toilets, and pay phones are available throughout the park.

Fees: A trail pass and vehicle admission sticker are required. Both are available as annual passes from the DNR.

Hazards: Sand is the only problem plaguing this trail. It is easy to lose the front end of the bike on this terrain. The best tip is to keep the front end light by distributing body weight out over the back end. This keeps the front tire from digging in and helps to keep the back tire weighted down for traction.

Rescue: Park rangers are found throughout the park, in the camping areas and main entrance booth, and are your best source of aid in case of emergency. The phone number for the Ranger Station Office is 794-7480.

Land status: Wisconsin DNR, Point Beach State Forest.

Maps: The trail area is shown on the USGS 7.5-minute quad for Two Rivers. Maps as well as camping information are available from the ranger station at the entrance to the park.

Sources of more information: See Appendix A, in particular the Point Beach State Forest, Wisconsin Department of Tourism, and WORBA.

Finding the trail: When approaching Manitowoc on Interstate 43, exit north onto Wisconsin Highway 42. Follow WI 42 along the lake for 9 miles into Two Rivers. At

The author crunching through leaves at the Point Beach State Forest.
LAURA HUTCHINS PHOTO

85

the center of town take County Highway O north out of town. Take CH O for 6 miles to the park entrance on the right. After purchasing a trail pass return to the main entrance and head directly across the street to the Red Pine entrance on the west side of CH O.

The ride

The Red Pine Trail starts out from a parking lot on the southeast corner of the loop and runs in a counterclockwise circuit. The trail starts out over a wide-cut grass path with a sandy bit of singletrack running down the middle, heading over small, rolling hills with wide, arcing bends. A half-mile-long sandy section appears on a small downhill leading into the group camp off to the left. Choose a good line to navigate around it, and the sand will not present much of a challenge.

After passing the group camp a short, grassy section leads into a wide trail area covered in roots and littered with pine needles from the surrounding trees. A couple of deep sand pits will stop riders in their tracks if finesse is not used to push the bike through. At the 1.25-mile mark the trail switches to a welcome mix of singletrack and hard-packed soil that winds through the forest for the next half mile. Many tight switchbacks must be navigated through this primarily unobstructed section. At the two-mile mark the trail switches back to doubletrack over a grass and sand base. This section heads south and bends down and around a corner introducing a bit of gravel to the mix leading back to the parking lot.

An unmarked path bisects the Red Pine Loop, starting off from the parking lot and leading out to the northwest. This section rolls more than the main loop, taking riders up small climbs and descents over a mix of singletrack and wide-cut paths. The total mileage for this abbreviated loop is 1.2 miles.

16

High Cliff State Park

High Cliff State Park overlooks Lake Winnebago on its northeast shoreline. High above the water, a massive memorial statue of Red Bird, chief of the Winnebagos, stands guard over the lake. The mountain bike path that runs the length of the cliffs takes its name from this historic figure.

The park itself is named for the towering limestone cliffs that border this corner of the lake. The cliffs are part of an enormous ledge known as the Niagara Escarpment that runs northeast from this site and makes up the land mass of Door County, Wisconsin, and Niagara Falls, New York. This is one of the most beautiful locations in Wisconsin regardless of what season mountain bikers choose to visit.

The main trail, the Red Bird Trail, runs the length of the main cliff wall and covers 3 miles—1.5 miles out and 1.5 miles back—over a mix of 5-foot-wide dirt and limestone paths. The entire circuit takes a half hour to cover, but riders will no doubt want to stop and sightsee along the way. Many small side trails lead off the ledges and down into rock formations surrounding the lake. These are not ridable but are definitely hikable and can easily fill an afternoon with exploration. Be careful not to ride too close to the edge of these ledges. To the east of the trail a set of Indian effigy burial mounds constructed more than 1,500 years ago are scattered throughout the woods. The Indians of this area often came to the shores of the larger waters to lay their dead to rest.

The bridle trail that runs the length of the park to the east is also open to mountain bikes. This is an 8.5-mile trail basically divided into two small loops and connected by a long two-way traffic connector. A small connector also runs off the Red Bird Trail to the bridle trail, taking riders out across a breathtaking meadow along the edge of a rustic stone fence bordering local farmland. A stone grain silo sits on the edge of this property, evidence that the park land was also once farmed.

Only 100 yards north of the statue of Red Bird and the mountain bike trail entrance is a 40-foot observation tower, offering excellent views for miles in all directions—forest, limestone quarries, and the waters of Lake Winnebago to the west.

General location: Three miles south of Sherwood on Wisconsin Highway 55, 20 miles southeast of the city of Appleton.

Technical Difficulty: Level 2.

Aerobic Level: Easy.

Tread: Doubletrack, Gravel Path.

Length: 3 miles.

HIGH CLIFF STATE PARK

Ride 16

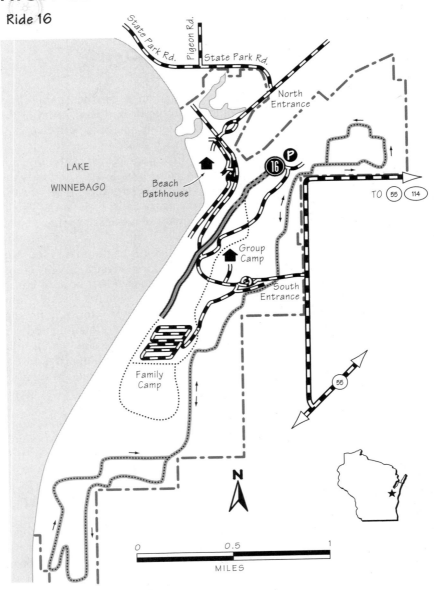

Elevation change: The trail is relatively flat, with two 25- to 30-foot climbs found on either end of the quarry. If the intent of the ride is to get out and do some climbing, ride back down to the main lot and come back up on the road, a killer climb that takes you from the lakeshore to the top of the bluff over the course of a mile.

Camping: There are 112 sites within the park. Water and restrooms are available.

Fees: A trail pass and vehicle admission sticker are required. Both are available as annual passes from the DNR.

Season: Open year round.

Services: Water and restrooms are located in the parking lot at the beginning of the Red Bird Trail.

Hazards: Be careful when approaching the edges of the bluffs and cliffs. Loose gravel, wet surface, and leaves can all lead to dangerous conditions. Also, watch for the drop-off midway across the limestone quarry on the Red Bird Trail. Because of the light color of the rocks, this drop-off is hard to measure from a distance and, if the rider is surprised by the drop, it could lead to a nasty face plant. The ledge is 2 to 4 feet high in most places.

Rescue: The park is well used and other park visitors are usually not far off. Rangers also do a good job of patrolling the park. In case of emergency, make your way out to the park road or back down to the lower ranger station at the north park entrance.

Land status: Wisconsin DNR, High Cliff State Park.

Maps: The trail area is shown on the USGS 7.5-minute quad for Sherwood. Maps are also available at the ranger stations at either entrance to the park.

Sources of more information: See Appendix A, in particular High Cliff State Park, Wisconsin Department of Tourism, and WORBA.

Finding the trail: Approaching Menasha from the east on U.S. Highway 10, exit south onto State Park Road, one mile after passing County Highway 55. Follow State Park Road south for 3.5 miles to the park entrance. Once past the ranger station, turn left and follow the park road to the top of the bluff. At the first intersection on top of the bluff, turn left and follow the road to the Red Bird parking lot where the Red Bird statue is plainly visible.

THE RIDE

The mountain bike trail at High Cliff starts out from a picnic area already high up the wall of the bluff. The statue of Red Bird unmistakably marks the trailhead. The trail heads off to the southeast across a path of wood chips under cover of the forest. The trail winds a bit here but no major obstacles or climbs are found. After a quick descent out of this section on a gravel hill the trail leads out into an old limestone quarry. The flat limestone field can be a bit deceiving—halfway across the quarry a 3- to 4-foot ledge runs for about 100 yards. Keeping to the far right on a narrow gravel path proves to be the easiest way past this nasty obstacle.

On the other side of the quarry is the main road, which riders will have to cross on a blind corner. On the opposite side of the road the trail continues over gravel and limestone with two short but steep climbs that take you back to the top of the bluff. To the right are startlingly beautiful views of the lake below. The path ducks back into the forest at this point and winds its way along for another half mile with no major climbs or descents to challenge the rider.

Chief Red Bird watches over the waters of Lake Winnebago and the entrance to the off-road trails.

At the 1.5-mile mark the Family Campgrounds are visible on the left just past the Indian effigy mounds. A walking trail has been established between the mounds, some of which are over 1,500 years old.

The Family Campgrounds are the end of the line for mountain bikers. Hikers are allowed to continue on the trail, while bikers are asked to turn around and trace their route back to the Red Bird statue. The horse trail is also open to mountain bikers, although, like most bridle trails, it is rather chewed up by the horses' hooves. This trail runs along the easternmost side of the park, away from the views of Lake Winnebago.

Hartman Creek State Park

Hartman Creek State Park is an excellent location for a weekend of family camping and mountain bike riding. The trails found throughout the park are extensive, covering the full width of the park's property and skirting the edges of two of its lakes. All in all, just over 8 miles of trails are open to mountain bikers, all of which can easily be tackled by beginners not ready to explore the more technical rides in the book or families who want to bike together in this beautiful forest setting. And when the riding is finished, what better way to wash off the dust than to wade into Hartman Lake at the beautiful sandy beach which serves as this ride's trailhead?

The trails found at Hartman Creek at first may look disappointing, from a seasoned mountain biker's perspective, since the first mile is over black-top. But soon after reaching the shore of Allen Lake, the terrain turns to hard-packed doubletrack and takes off through the pines along the shore-line. The path is wide throughout, allowing riders to ride two abreast or at least to keep away from dense vegetation at the edges of the path at the peak of summer. The far western edges of the trails get a bit exciting with rolling hills and one excellent descent that will thrill just about any rider. Watch for the two hiking paths that bisect the Glacial Trail mountain bike path. Both of these are off limits to bikers and are marked accordingly. A fine will be doled out to any bikers found on these trails.

Overall, Hartman Creek is a perfect park for spending a weekend in the wilderness with your family. The trails run right out of the campground on both ends, one set leading to Hartman Lake, the other to Allen Lake and beyond. The riding offers beginners a taste of the glaciated terrain that in other areas of Wisconsin is much more difficult. Here, the glaciers sheared the top of the land, flattening it into a series of small, rolling hills by scrap-ing across it, receding, and then pushing forward time after time. The rich soil left behind is a perfect bed for thick, heavy woods. The entire area is packed with trees—large expanses of pines in some areas and mixed hard-woods in others—all of which are beautiful in the late summer and fall months. Riders just starting out will love this trip for its beauty and easy introduction to riding; advanced riders may find trails more to their liking in other corners of the state.

General location: 8 miles west of Waupaca off Wisconsin Highway 54.

Technical Difficulty: Level 1 to 2.

Aerobic Level: Easy.

Tread: Paved path and wide, hard-packed doubletrack.

Length: 8 miles.

HARTMAN CREEK

Ride 17

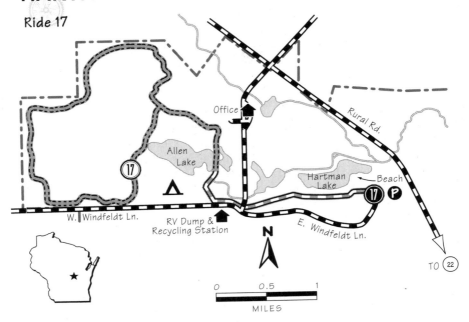

Elevation change: The trails are very moderate in this area with only minor 20- to 30-foot climbs found on the far west side of the Glacial Trail. For the most part the trail is very flat.

Camping: The park offers 101 sites in the family camp area, each with fire pits. Toilets, showers and drinking water are also available. Five group sites are found to the southwest of the family camp area, and each can handle up to 50 occupants.

Season: The trails are open from April to November. The park is consistently good through this season. Spring brings cooler temperatures for comfortable riding. Summer is great for morning rides and afternoon swims. Fall is the most picturesque, with the trees displaying a vivid panorama of colors, cool temperatures, and perfect nights for sitting at the edge of a campfire.

Fees: A trail pass and vehicle admission sticker are required. Both are available as annual passes from the DNR.

Services: Water and toilets are found at the family camp area. Toilets are also found at the trailhead. The city of Waupaca to the east is the closest point of civilization and a good place to stop for gas or groceries.

Hazards: Watch for other trail users. Because of the easy nature of the trails, they are popular with hikers as well as bikers. Wide trails make passing easy, but announce your presence well in advance to avoid collisions.

Rescue: The trails are well used and seldom get away from the park's population centers. The camping areas are good places to look for assistance any time of year. The park office at the entrance to the park is also a good place to stop in case of injury or emergency.

Singletrack winds through the tall pines at Hartman Creek State Park.

Land status: Wisconsin DNR, Hartman Creek State Park.

Maps: The trail area is shown on the USGS 7.5-minute quad for Blaine and King. Maps are available at the ranger station at the entrance to the park.

Sources of more information: See Appendix A, in particular the Waupaca Chamber of Commerce, Hartman Creek State Park, Wisconsin Department of Tourism, and WORBA.

Finding the trail: From Waupaca follow Wisconsin Highway 54 west for 8 miles to Hartman Creek Road. Turn left (south) and follow it for 4 miles directly into the park.

THE RIDE

The trail starts out from the Hartman Lake Beach parking lot on the far east end of East Windfeldt Lane. The bike path is paved at the start and heads off to the west around the southern shore of Hartman Lake. The trail is very gentle at this point, traveling over subtle hills on fresh blacktop. After 0.75 mile the trail enters the family campground. Stay to the right on the campground road and within twenty feet the paved trail continues on to the north.

Allen Lake is immediately visible and the path follows its eastern shore. After passing the fishing pier the trail turns to hardpack on wide paths, some single lane and some double. The terrain stays like this until passing this point later in the ride. The trail continues on for another 0.5 mile before coming to the beginning of the Glacial Trail Loop which heads off to the right in a counterclockwise direction. Be sure to follow the bike icon signs: there are several entrances to the hiking paths that bisect this loop, all of which are forbidden to bikers. The path on this loop increases a little in difficulty with some minor climbs and quick descents. The path makes a complete circle, passing the west edge of Allen Lake near the end of the loop and returning to the connector trail to finish.

Backtrack over the same terrain that you followed to get to the Glacier Trail to return to the parking lot. Upon your arrival at the Hartman Lake lot, take advantage of the beach so conveniently placed at the trailhead. If more riding is in the picture, the Windfeldt Trail to the south is also open to bikers though it is even more basic than the Glacial Trail. To find it, go to the intersection of East Windfeldt Lane and Hartman Creek Road and travel to the east about 100 yards. The trail departs south from there, connecting to the main loop within the first quarter of a mile.

18

Standing Rock Trails

The Standing Rock Trails near Stevens Point are named for the glacial erratics that dot the surrounding forest and cover some areas of the trail. Erratics, or "hitchhikers," are rocks that caught a ride south in the ice of glaciers, which scooped them up in one area and deposited them in another. In some areas of the state the rocks ended up perched precariously atop bluffs or other erratics. At Standing Rocks the rocks are doing just that, standing. Many are the size of a Volkswagen; others, like the ones encountered on the trail, are much smaller and just add some challenge to the terrain.

The mountain bike trails cover 10 miles along the western shore of Bear Lake and in the surrounding forests. The deer population is high in this area of the state and several may be spotted during each ride. Some of the better-traveled portions of the trail are on single- and doubletrack, but the majority of the riding is on the forest floor—uneven grass, rocks, and worn patches of soil. Some of the hilly sections, especially climbs, are filled in with red gravel and riders are asked to stay on this to prevent further erosion of these high-use areas. The red gravel is actually great for traction and helps make each pedal stroke count. The entire system can be conquered in an hour and a half at a good pace. The loops, however, form a great number of variations that could easily fill an afternoon.

Most importantly, this trail offers bikers a chance to "show what they're made of"—but not in terms of technical prowess. There is a warning sign at the base of the ski hill stating that mountain bikers must stay off the ski slopes and that future use of the facility by bikers depends on their cooperation. It is in areas like this that bikers need to show their true colors and prove to the management that they not only obey the trail rules but help maintain them. If you see litter on the trail, stop and pack it out. Obey signs, respect erosion control areas, and be careful of other trail users, especially those who are a little slower. By doing this, the trails will not only stay open, but word will get out that mountain bikers are eco-friendly, and that these trails will help boost small town economies.

General location: 16 miles southeast of Stevens Point, 6 miles southwest of Amherst.

Technical Difficulty: Level 2 to 3.

Aerobic Level: Moderate.

Tread: Singletrack and doubletrack.

Length: 10 miles.

Elevation change: Though the terrain is seldom flat for more than a few feet there are no huge climbs to tackle. Two climbs, each around 75 feet, must be taken on, but the majority of the climbing comes in short spurts.

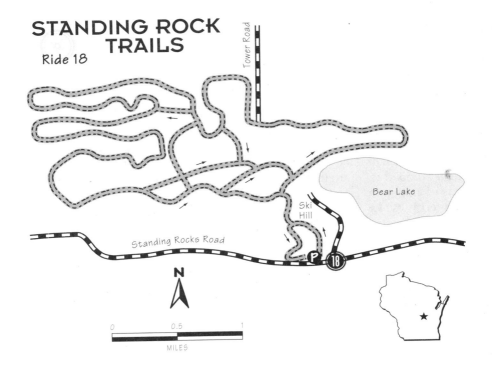

STANDING ROCK TRAILS
Ride 18

Tower Road

Bear Lake

Ski Hill

Standing Rocks Road

N

0   0.5   1

MILES

Camping: No camping is available in the immediate vicinity.

Season: May to October. Fall riding is enjoyable because of the temperatures, but any time is nice in this area. The forest will protect riders from summer sun, and trailside vegetation is not thick enough to hold heat the way meadow grass can in the summer. After rains, call the area Chamber of Commerce to see if the trails are closed for erosion reasons.

Fees: A self-pay donation station is set up at the trailhead.

Services: There is no water at the trailhead. Food, water and gas can all be found in Amherst. Everything else, including bicycles, can be found in Stevens Point.

Hazards: Watch on corners which at times are loose with sand. Tree falls are common, though easily avoidable, on such a wide track. As always, take the time to move branches to the side of the trail for future riders, unless they provide a cool obstacle for others to bunny hop.

Rescue: The trails are out in the woods and farmlands and are not known for heavy traffic. Ride in pairs, and in case of emergency use the pay phone outside the ski lodge.

Land status: Portage County Park System.

Maps: The trail area is shown on the USGS 7.5-minute quad for Amherst.

Sources of more information: See Appendix A, in particular the Wisconsin Department of Tourism and WORBA.

Finding the trail: When entering Amherst on U.S. Highway 10 from the southeast, turn left (west) on County Highway B and travel south 4.5 miles. Turn left (south) onto CH K and go 1 mile. Turn right onto Standing Rocks Road. Follow this for 1 mile and turn right into the park entrance. The parking lot is immediately on the left.

THE RIDE

The trail departs the parking lot to the north under a thick forest cover and rolls through the hills with a couple of minor climbs. After 0.5 mile the trail exits the forest and travels across the top of the ski slope, offering a grand view of Bear Lake and the forest below. Stay tight to the tree line on the left and do not give in to the temptation to bomb down the ski slope, no matter how fun and dangerous it looks.

The trail quickly reenters the forest and immediately comes to an intersection. Stay to the right and head down the hill toward the Red Pine Run. Continue on this trail, passing the cutoff to the left at the 0.25-mile mark. The Red Pine Run stays among the aspens and follows along the northwest corner of Bear Lake. At the 1-mile mark the trail doubles back and heads west for two miles past the gated entrance to Tower Road. The trail then heads due north along the road and within 0.75 mile the cutoff trails begin to appear. Three of them are found within a half a mile, all taking riders across the center of the loop.

Continuing on the main trail the Red Pine Run turns into the Loggers Loop section, where the trail starts to double across itself, back and forth through the forest on its way south to the Ice Age Trail. This is where the majority of the cutoff trails end up. The Ice Age Trail leads back to the initial intersection at the top of the ski hill. Follow the same path that led from the lot to this point, across the backside of the ski hill summit.

Tall pines line the side of the wide paths leading through the Standing Rock Forest.

19

Nine Mile State Forest

The Nine Mile State Forest Trails are very fun, very technical, and much less strenuous than many of the trails listed in this book. Imagine taking the best technical singletrack and knocking out all the climbs, leaving just the switchbacks, hazards, and washboard areas to navigate. Then weave the entire network into a complex maze that cuts back in on itself time and again offering an entire afternoon of riding. These features are what make this cluster a perfect introduction to singletrack riding for the amateur or a reduced-strain playground for the more advanced rider. The trails are divided into three categories: Green, the easiest trails, closest to the chalet; Blue, intermediate riding; and Red, the expert loops labeled the Alps and Little Alps because of their climbing.

The maps for the area are unusual, marking each tiny loop with its own letter designation, thus showing loops B through Y (minus H for some reason). Although at first this appears to be a tough system to master, it quickly becomes easy to pinpoint a location in the field. The trails are marked with letters and maps at many intersections and, with a printed map in hand, it is easy to stay on a course within the maze.

The entire trail system covers 18.6 miles of ground, though the total distance means little with the amount of backtracking done in a system of this sort. The majority of the trail system is on singletrack over hard-packed earth. There are also several gravel and clay roads that run throughout the system; these serve both as connectors between the singletrack routes and as a mainline back to the chalet. Riders of all levels can spend an entire afternoon riding this cluster, doubling back over the same trails at times, finding unexplored routes at others. The only rule is to follow the direction arrows painted on trees to avoid nasty head-on collisions and off-trail riding.

This trail set is very conducive to groups of four or five riders or more, all heading out in different directions and meeting up at various intersections throughout the day. By doing so everyone can ride at their own pace, out of each other's way but still in a group setting as riders zig and zag through nearby trails.

General location: 3 miles southeast of Wausau.

Technical Difficulty: Level 4.

Aerobic Level: Moderate.

Tread: Singletrack.

Length: up to 18.6 miles.

Elevation change: Nearly the entire trail system is run over flat land with climbs of only 10 to 20 feet over very moderate grades. The only trail with any climbing is the

NINE MILE

Ride 3

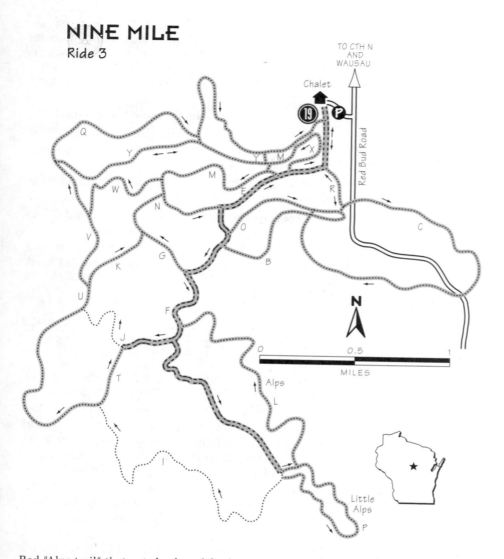

Red "Alps trail" that cuts back and forth across the same bluff with several steeper climbs of 90 to 100 feet.

Camping: There are 30 campsites at Rib Mountain State Park south of the trails. To find the park, exit U.S. Highway 51, going south on County Highway N. After a quarter of a mile, turn right (north) onto Park Road and follow it all the way to the center of the park. Rib Mountain is thought to be over a billion years old.

Season: May through November. When snow is on the trail it is the skiers' domain. This trail system is primarily a ski area, and is open to bikers only in the off-season.

Fees: A self-pay station for trail passes is found at the trailhead. Parking is free.

Services: All necessities are available in Wausau to the northeast. Toilets are found in the trailhead parking lot.

Hazards: Watch for the typical hazards found on singletrack. Roots and rocks are the main obstacles. Sudden dips in the trail come up frequently. The best bet for making it through these is to allow the bike to pivot away from you; only when the rider's body weight follows the bike down into these depressions is there a possibility of an endo. Let the bike stick to the trail while the rider's body floats above in a static position.

Rescue: On most days other riders will be present on the trails to lend a hand. The first stop in case of emergency should be the chalet at the trailhead, although it is often closed in the summer season.

Land status: Nine Mile County Forest.

Maps: The trail area is shown on the USGS 7.5-minute quad for Wausau West. Maps are available at the trailhead in the parking lot.

Sources of more information: See Appendix A, in particular the Wausau Chamber of Commerce, Wisconsin Department of Tourism, and WORBA.

Finding the trail: Approaching Wausau from the south on U.S. Highway 51, take the County Highway N exit. Travel west on CH N for 3.5 miles to Red Bud Road. Turn left (south) and drive 1.5 miles; the road will turn from paved to gravel. The parking lot is on the right just after reaching the forest.

THE RIDE

All of the trails start out at the chalet on the northeast end of the property, adjacent to the more-than-adequate parking lot. The trails start out on doubletrack dirt, leading out across an open field to the Main Street Trail that serves as the main artery through the system. By turning to the right and following the main trail, singletrack loops become visible to the right and left almost immediately. The trails closest to the chalet are Green and, while easier than the rest, are still very technical and challenging.

Approximately 0.75 mile out on Main Street and after a short jog to the left, the "D" marker appears. This is in the vicinity of the intermediate Blue section. More climbing is found here, especially in the southernmost corner on the Bushwhacker Trail.

Off the Bushwhacker Trail to the southeast, the Alps and Little Alps trails take off in a northerly direction. The one-way trails cut back and forth across the same small bluff, climbing and descending 90 to 100 feet at a time. The trails are only 2.75 miles in length but provide a heavy workout in a short distance. They are the only Red expert trails in the entire system.

The area that these trails covers is rather small, with the longest loop under three miles and the majority not covering more than a fraction of a mile each. The best idea is just to explore the grounds on an individual basis. It is rather difficult to get lost in this cluster. By trying to keep a good sense of direction, carrying a map, and checking the posting now and again, it is easy to navigate these trails and have a great time in the process.

Technical singletrack snakes its way through the tall pines in Nine Mile State Forest.

20

Devil's Lake State Park

Mountain biking at Devil's Lake State Park takes place high on the East Bluff of this ancient glacial canyon. The park is famous for its glacial remains including stunning examples of erratics in the Balanced Rock and Devil's Doorway formations. Hikers and climbers are the main populace of the park, and they definitely have the upper hand. The hiking trail system and climbing sites were developed by the CCC and hug the lake on both sides, providing spectacular views at every turn. You may wish to visit the park with the intention of hiking and camping, but bring a mountain bike to spend an afternoon spinning loops in this unique corner of the terminal moraine.

The Ice Age Loop is the only trail open to mountain bikers and covers 4 miles over hard-packed singletrack, grass and gravel paths. A 1-mile connector starting off in the main parking lot takes riders up the back lip of the bluff to the upper trailhead parking lot. The loop takes about 35 minutes for an intermediate rider to complete and will challenge the climbing stamina and handling skills of all riders.

Devil's Lake is one of the most profoundly odd and beautiful locations in all of Wisconsin. The cliff walls and fields of tumbled boulders, many of which are larger than a compact car, illustrate the massive restructuring this state underwent during the ice age. The lake itself is carved so deep that in some areas the depth was unknown until advanced methods were available to gauge the depth.

From the top of the bluffs it becomes obvious that park visitors were not the first to be amazed by the glacial structure. The Indians that explored and traversed this area of Wisconsin built lasting memorials into the ground itself to express their appreciation. From the East Bluff an effigy mound is visible in the shape of a large bird. Any time of year, during any type of weather, the park offers striking views of untamed and unique nature all around.

General location: 3 miles south of Baraboo.

Technical Difficulty: Level 3.

Aerobic Level: Moderate.

Tread: Singletrack, Gravel.

Length: 6 miles.

Elevation change: Most of the trail rolls without a great deal of climbing. The climb out of the parking lot to the main loop covers 0.6 miles of ground and 250 feet of elevation. Another smaller climb is encountered midway along the Ice Age Loop.

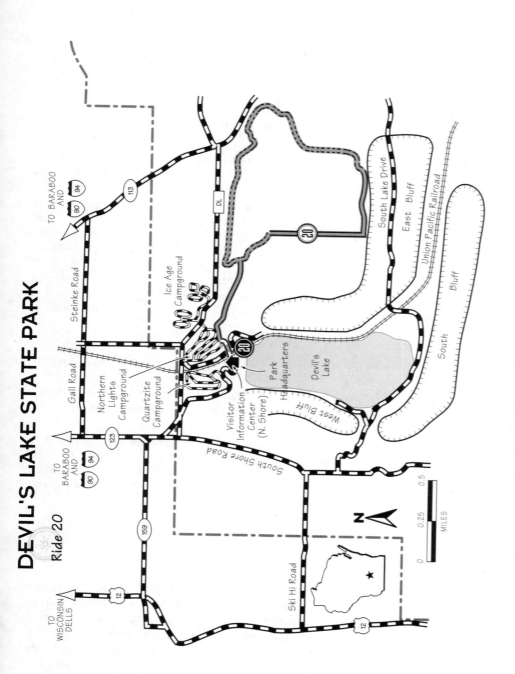

DEVIL'S LAKE STATE PARK
Ride 20

TO BARABOO
AND
90 94

113

DL

20

South Lake Drive

East Bluff

Union Pacific Railroad

South Bluff

Steinke Road

Ice Age
Campground

Gall Road

Northern
Lights
Campground

Quartzite
Campground

20

Park
Headquarters

Devil's
Lake

West Bluff

123

Visitor
Information
Center
(N. Shore)

TO
BARABOO
AND
90 94

South Shore Road

159

12

TO
WISCONSIN
DELLS

Ski Hi Road

12

N

0   0.25   0.5
MILES

Camping: The Ice Age Campground has a great many sites available, all with fire pits and within walking distance of water and restrooms.

Season: March 15 to November 15. Mid-summer can be rather stifling, and proper hydration is a must. Don't be surprised to see snow in March, April and November. The swimming beach at the trailhead is open all summer from Memorial Day weekend through Labor Day.

Fees: A trail pass and vehicle admission sticker are required. Both are available as annual passes from the DNR.

Services: Food is available at the beach house on the north end of the lake. Water and toilets can also be found here. Nearby Baraboo (7 miles to the north) is a good source for groceries and bicycle repair and parts.

Hazards: Watch for loose gravel on the descent leading back to the parking lot from the Ice Age Loop. Try keeping your weight in the saddle when climbing on this stuff, and when descending crouch over your ride with bent knees and elbows to gently absorb the bumps and "float" through corners. Watch for the occasional hiker on blind corners.

Rescue: Park Rangers can be found throughout the park although the less-traveled Ice Age Loop is not heavily monitored. If injured, slowly navigate the path back to the main grounds and either head toward the main office or ask for the assistance of campers found nearer the beginning of the trail.

Land status: Wisconsin DNR, Devil's Lake State Park.

Maps: The trail area is shown on the USGS 7.5-minute quad for Baraboo. Maps are also available at the ranger station in the main parking lot.

Sources of more information: See Appendix A, in particular the Baraboo Chamber of Commerce, Devil's Lake State Park, Wisconsin Department of Tourism, and WORBA.

Finding the trail: Take Interstate 94 to U.S. Highway 33 (Exit 92). Follow US 33 west for 10 miles to Baraboo. Turn left (east) onto Wisconsin Highway 129. Then turn right on WI 123 and follow it to County Road DL. This leads directly to the park entrance. Follow the road down to the parking lot for the main ranger station and beach house; this will serve as the trailhead for this ride.

THE RIDE

The connecting path to the Ice Age Loop starts out from the northeast corner of the main parking lot. Follow signs to the Northern Lights Campground out of the lot and across the Union Pacific Railroad Tracks. The next mile is all uphill starting on hardpack, passing through a grassy meadow and finishing with 0.5 mile over gravel to the top of the bluff. The trail cuts its way across the backside of the bluff under forest cover for the next 0.5 mile. At the 1.5-mile mark the tread turns to wide-cut grass and descends into an enormous meadow sprawling out to the tree lines a half mile on either side. A short climb follows, taking the rider back into the forest and past the entrance to the Steinke loop. Continue straight, as this is closed to mountain bikers. Rounding the far edge of the loop a series of climbs take the rider to the very edge of the East Bluff's south face. It is necessary to dismount and find a path to the edge for unobstructed views of the surrounding terrain.

After a view of the surrounding area the path cuts along through the woods and leads out to a gravel path heading north. This section really rolls, making it easy to carry speed from the downhills into the uphills. After following this gravel route for 0.8 mile, follow the mountain bike signs to the left, across a field and back into the woods. Another 0.33 mile returns the rider to the starting point of the loop. What will it be? Another lap to the right or back down to the trailhead for a swim to the left? Check how much fuel is still in your tank and make the decision.

Mountain biker Jonathan Bykowski combatting the trail and the heat at Devil's Lake.

Mirror Lake State Park

Mirror Lake is a beautiful park located at the center of the state just outside the true terminal moraine. The park has a mountain bike course consisting of three loops connected at their edges, forming a wide circuit nearly 9 miles in length. The riding is fast and climbing is not as common as in other areas of the moraine. The singletrack portions of trail lend themselves to big-ring cruising, and the wide paths offer quick, swooping cornering and all-out straightaways. The trails cover hard singletrack mixed with sand and wide grass paths, most with a well-worn groove down the center. The middle Fern Dell Loop is prepared for skate style cross-country skiing in winter and therefore is wider and grassier than the Turtleville and Hastings loops to either side. The entire network takes about an hour for an intermediate rider to complete at a moderate pace. Most riders will also want to take an extra pass on their favorite of the three loops.

The riding can be tough at times, especially in the transition areas between the loops where high grass meadows have been mown to form trails. The riding here is particularly bumpy and it is hard to keep any semblance of momentum. On the bulk of the three loops, however, momentum is the rider's friend and is easily sustained through proper shifting and hard cranking. The path is surrounded nearly constantly by trees to both sides of the trail, a mixture of pine and oak throughout. The trails are quiet and the chance of seeing whitetail deer sprinting out ahead of you is very good.

Beware: the trails described in this chapter lie dangerously close to the tourist wasteland known as the Wisconsin Dells. This once-beautiful area has become cluttered with billboards and covered over by water parks and go-cart tracks during the past several decades. The land it covers is truly remarkable, with intricate stone channels once thought by the Indians who inhabited this area to have been created by an enormous mythical snake that had forced its body through the earth. Unfortunately, it is now only an exploitation of the state's natural beauty. Riders are better off at Mirror Lake or Devil's Lake in the true wilderness, enjoying the land for what it is, meditating on its old age and intrinsic splendor high atop a cliff or in a meadow of whispering grass.

General location: 3 miles south of the small town of Lake Delton.

Technical Difficulty: Level 2.

Aerobic Level: Easy to moderate.

Tread: Wide singletrack.

Length: 9 miles.

MIRROR LAKE
Ride 21 STATE PARK

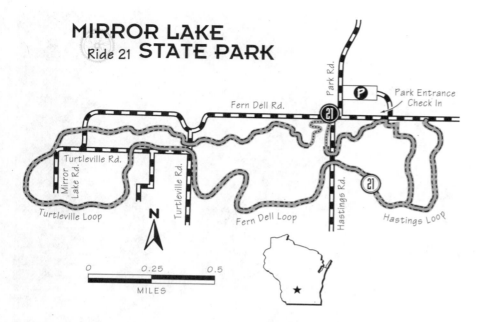

Elevation change: While there are quite a few flat stretches, small rolling hills make up the majority of the terrain. The Hastings loop definitely has the larger climbs, with a few moderate hills on the others.

Camping: The park offers 27 sites. Restrooms and water are available and fire pits are found in each unit.

Season: May 1 through November 1. The season here is kept a little shorter than most state trails because of erosion control. The area often floods and trail closings are not uncommon. Call for trail conditions before making the drive.

Fees: A trail pass and vehicle admission sticker are required. Both are available as annual passes from the DNR.

Services: Water is available at the campground just around the corner from the park office, to the northeast. Gas, groceries, and lodging are available in Lake Delton. Bicycle repair is available in Baraboo, approximately ten miles south on U.S. Highway 12.

Hazards: Watch for hikers on all three loops, although these trails are specifically for mountain bikes and hiking trails closed to bikers can be found in the north end of the park. The trails are all well maintained and marked. Occasionally tree falls are encountered after storms, but for the most part the trails are very clear. Sand can be challenging on all three loops. The best way to battle the sand is to keep body weight over the rear tire as if you are riding a unicycle.

Rescue: The trails in this section of the forest do not get a lot of traffic but are boxed in by heavily traveled roads on all sides. The park office should be the first stop when looking for assistance.

Land status: Wisconsin State Park, Mirror Lake.

Maps: The trail area is shown on the USGS 7.5-minute quad for Wisconsin Dells South. Maps are available at the ranger station at the park entrance and through the DNR.

Singletrack leading onto the main loops at Mirror Lake.

Sources of more information: See Appendix A, in particular Mirror Lake State Park, the Wisconsin Department of Tourism, and WORBA.

Finding the trail: At Lake Delton, exit Interstate 90/94 east onto U.S. Highway 12. Go south 0.5 mile on US 12 and turn right (west) on Fern Dell Road. The park entrance is 1.5 miles down the road on the right.

THE RIDE

The park office at the Fern Dell Road entrance serves as the trailhead for all three loops. The trails start to the south of Fern Dell Road, kitty corner to the park exit. Follow the main park road out of the park and south, cross Fern Dell Road and enter the single track Beaver Pond Loop. This short winding section leads out to the middle Fern Dell Loop, a two-way trail. To the left the trail meets up with Hastings Road within 0.5 mile. On the other side of Hastings Road, the Hastings Loop picks up, rotating in a one-way counterclockwise direction. The Pioneer Loop, an additional short section of trail found at the far east edge of Hastings Loop, offers an additional mile of riding.

Riders deciding to turn right from the Beaver Pond loop onto the wide Fern Dell path will come to the Turtleville Loop in 1.5 miles, west of the dirt Turtleville Road. This 2.75-mile loop is a two-way path, though a great deal of it is singletrack. Because of this it is important to watch and listen for oncoming riders, especially on the downhill sections.

The park stresses that there is no riding north of Fern Dell Road. So everything to the south is fair game and after completing the off-road sections, touring the park roads to cool down is a great way to finish the day.

Smrekar Trail Cluster—Black River State Forest

Black River State Forest riding can be divided into two sections. The first, covered in this chapter, contains the Pigeon Creek connecting trail that joins the state forest campground to the Smrekar Trail Cluster. The riding in this area is exciting, rugged, and wild. When combining this section of trails with the Wildcat trails to the northwest (covered in the following chapter), an entire weekend can easily be spent spinning loops in this diverse section of central Wisconsin. The trails are all ridden under the cover of the oak, pine, and aspen forest that makes up the Black River State Forest. Keep a watchful eye open for the wild turkeys that have been released into the area since the mid-1980s.

The area's most outstanding geographical features are the tower-like mounds rising up along the horizon. These are remnants of the ancient glacial sea that covered the entire southwestern portion of the state about the time the glaciers receded. The mounds are made up of sandstone deposited on the floor of the sea and later blasted into shape by thousands of years of rain and winds. It is easy to envision the surrounding countryside as the floor of a lake, with thick vegetation and massive reefs reaching up to the surface of the water.

The Pigeon Creek Trail is just under 5 miles long with no climbs to speak of. The entire path is wide-cut grass running alongside the Pigeon Creek Flowage and surrounding marsh. Nearly the entire length of the trail is swampy and soft. Expect this part of the trail to be submerged after heavy rains and during the spring thaw. After a hard day on the Smrekar Cluster, this flat route to the campground is a welcome stretch.

The Smrekar Cluster covers 14 miles of wide-cut grass paths with a smattering of singletrack in a few sections. An endless combination of routes is possible by mixing loops together. The area is well mapped and, with this guide and a compass, getting lost should not be a problem. Excellent views of the surrounding area are visible from the tops of ridges on this route. The North and Central loops are marked as difficult, with many climbs and descents to negotiate. The Ridge Loop is the most difficult, with massive climbing and descending, but it is also the route with the best views of the area, so the extra effort is definitely rewarded. An easy 1.2-mile loop is also part of this cluster, to the south of the trailhead parking lot.

A couple of interesting diversions are worth mentioning here. A mile west of the main Smrekar Cluster is the site of a mid-1800s farm. The stairway down into the cellar of the farmhouse is still in existence and sits in the

SMREKAR TRAIL CLUSTER— BLACK RIVER STATE FOREST
Ride 22

middle of a clearing in the trees. The hand-dug well that sat to the side of the home looks as if it still might work. A cemetery that served the small logging community near the turn of the century is just west of the Central Loop and just east of Smrekar Road.

The entire cluster along with the time spent on the connecting trail will take a minimum of four hours for intermediate riders keeping up a good pace. But with so much to see, riders may want to camp at Pigeon Creek and take a day to do this section and a day to do Wildcat.

General location: 2.5 miles northeast of Millston off Interstate 94.

Technical Difficulty: Level 2 to 3.

Aerobic Level: Moderate to strenuous.

Tread: Wide-cut grass paths and singletrack.

Length: Loops up to 21 miles.

Elevation change: While there are no climbs whatsoever on the Pigeon Creek Trail, the Smrekar Cluster has a countless number of climbs, many in the 100-foot range. The Ridge Trail in particular is a bear with two main climbs of 200+ feet, both taking every bit of energy a rider can muster.

Camping: Pigeon Creek Campground, the trailhead for this ride, offers 38 sites. Fire pits are found at each unit and water and restrooms are available within the campground.

Season: May 1 to November 1. The season is a little shorter than in many state-managed areas because of erosion control. The Pigeon Creek Trail in particular can be a mess during the spring thaw.

Fees: A trail pass and vehicle admission sticker are required. Both are available as annual passes from the DNR.

Services: Water is available at the Pigeon Creek Campground as well as the Smrekar Trailhead. Bathrooms are located at the Pigeon Creek Campground. Food and gas are available in the village of Millston—if you blink you might miss it. The town shuts down early, with only the bars lighting the way. The larger town of Black River Falls lies 12 miles to the north and provides all the necessary items for survival in the wilderness, including bicycle repair.

Hazards: The trails are wide and well kept but, because of the vast expanse here, tree falls are not cleared promptly, so watch for them. Depth perception on the downhills can be a bit hard to judge, with many bumps hiding in the grass. Sand washouts at the bases of the hills can also cause trouble. By leaning back and keeping weight off the front end of the bike, the front tire is allowed to cut through the sand instead of sinking in. Sinking in leads to face plants, which everyone should strive to avoid.

Rescue: The trails are not heavily populated and are rather desolate. It is a good idea to ride with a partner to avoid dangerous situations. The surrounding roads are mainly gravel logging paths which are not well traveled. If worse comes to worse head for North Settlement Road, north of the cluster. Help is often available at the

Climbing into the hills amongst the hardwoods on the Wildcat Trail.

trailhead or the Pigeon Creek Campground. The town of Millston can also be a source of emergency aid.

Land status: Wisconsin State Forest, Black River State Forest.

Maps: The trail area is shown on the USGS 7.5-minute quad for Warrens West.

Sources of more information: See Appendix A, in particular the Black River State Forest, Wisconsin Department of Tourism, and WORBA.

Finding the trail: From Interstate 94, take the Millston exit onto County Highway O. Travel east 0.1 mile and turn left on North Settlement Road. Go 2 miles down, and the entrance to the Pigeon Creek camping area is on the right.

THE RIDE

The beginning of the Pigeon Creek connector is on the south end of the picnic area parking lot. The trail runs out and around the Pigeon Creek Flowage before entering the forest. The trail in this area is rather uneventful. Watch for the stately blue herons that occasionally erupt from the swamps alongside the trails in a flurry of majestic flapping wings.

At the 4-mile mark the trail leads out onto the gravel Smrekar Road. Follow this for 0.5 mile directly into the parking lot for the trailhead. The South Loop, to the right, covers 1.2 miles inside the trees. This is an easy loop and one to bypass for more advanced riders.

A large wooden sign hangs to the left of the parking lot with a map of the entire cluster. The main Smrekar Trail itself takes off to the left of the sign, starting on the Central Loop. By riding out in a counterclockwise direction the extremely difficult Ridge Trail comes up within the first 0.5 mile. The connecting trail to the abandoned farm mentioned earlier also takes off along this route. The Ridge Loop gets into the climbing right away, leading up through an interesting ravine in the bluff. Park benches are welcome at viewing spots at the top of each climb.

The North Loop doesn't pick up until quite a bit further along the trail. The Ridge Trail meets with it after two miles of climbing and descending, the Central Trail after 1.5 miles over slightly less technical terrain. The connector to the Wildcat Cluster lies in the middle of the North Loop and at the pinnacle of the Central Loop. Signs point the way from all the converging loops.

Wildcat Trail Cluster—Black River State Forest

The Wildcat Cluster is the second portion of the Black River State Forest trails, connected at the southeast corner with the Smrekar Cluster from the previous chapter. The Wildcat Trail loops are very difficult and are meant for more advanced riders. Three separate loops offer 10 miles of trails. The Norway Pine and Red Oak loops are laid out side by side like the chambers of a massive heart. The Norway Pine Trail measures 2.7 miles and is the most difficult, rising out of the parking lot immediately with two quick, difficult climbs taking riders out to the edge of a ridge looking out across the forest. The Red Oak Trail covers an equal distance but with subtler climbs. Both are one-way trails ridden over a mix of grass, sand, and hardpack. Both share the same return path that runs a full mile down the center of the loops. The descent that ends the ride is sure to get the adrenaline flowing.

The Wildcat Loop covers 4 miles and is found at the intersection of the Red Oak and Norway Pine loops. This is a very difficult loop with several hard climbs, rough descents and, of course, glorious views of the countryside. In contrast to the Smrekar Cluster, which takes riders along the edges of ridges, the Wildcat Cluster is a mound in itself, visible from miles around and covered in snaking, fat-tire paths.

The entire cluster takes an hour and a half to cover at a good pace. As mentioned in the previous chapter, this Cluster makes a perfect second day of riding after day one on the Smrekar Trails and a night camping at Pigeon Creek.

General location: 5 miles northeast of Millston, off Interstate 94.

Technical Difficulty: Level 3.

Aerobic Level: Strenuous.

Tread: Grass doubletrack and singletrack.

Length: 10 miles.

Elevation change: All of the trails are filled with climbs, many in the 100- foot range. The Norway Pine and Wildcat Loops in particular are difficult climbing routes.

Camping: There are 38 sites at the Pigeon Creek Campground, used as the trailhead for the Smrekar Trails (see preceding chapter for directions). All sites have fire pits, and restrooms and water are available within the campground.

Season: May 1 to November 1. The season is a little shorter than in many state-managed areas because of erosion control.

Fees: A trail pass and vehicle admission sticker are required. Both are available as annual passes from the DNR.

WILDCAT TRAIL CLUSTER—
BLACK RIVER STATE FOREST
Ride 23

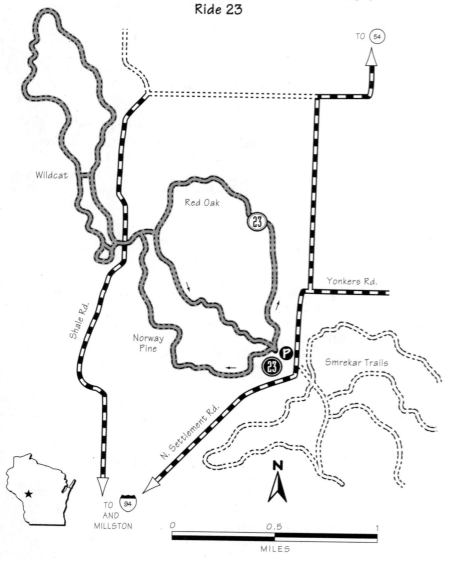

TO (54)

Wildcat

Red Oak

(23)

Yonkers Rd.

Shale Rd.

Norway
Pine

(23) P

Smrekar Trails

N. Settlement Rd.

TO (94)
AND
MILLSTON

N

0   0.5   1

MILES

Services: Water is available at the Wildcat Trailhead. A shelter and toilet are found at the head of the return trail between the Red Oak and Nordic Pine trails. Food and gas are available in the small village of Millston. The larger town of Black River Falls, 12 miles to the north, provides all other necessary items including bicycle repair.

Hazards: The trails are wide and well kept but, because of the vast expanse here, tree falls are not cleared promptly, so keep a watchful eye for them. The downhills in this section are dotted with rocks and roots and demand the total attention of the rider. Sand is present on climbs and descents. Stay seated while climbing to keep the back tire anchored in the sand for traction. The pedaling is harder this way but far more productive than standing and slipping in loose sand. Watch for hikers at all times: they outnumber bikers by quite a bit at this trailhead.

Rescue: The trails are not heavily populated and are rather desolate. Ride with a partner to avoid dangerous situations. North Settlement Road is the best bet for flagging down a passing car. The road is located just south of the parking lot. Help is often available at the trailhead station. Millston can also be a source of emergency aid.

Land status: Wisconsin State Forest, Black River State Forest.

Maps: The trail area is shown on the USGS 7.5-minute quad for Warrens West.

Sources of additional information: See Appendix A, in particular the Black River State Forest, Wisconsin Department of Tourism, and WORBA.

Finding the trail: Exit Interstate 94 at Millston onto County Highway O. Travel east 0.1 mile and turn left on North Settlement Road. The trailhead is on the left in 4.25 miles (1 mile past the dirt Smrekar Road).

THE RIDE

The Norway Pine and Red Oak loops are closest to the parking lot. The Red Oak Trail takes off to the right in a counterclockwise direction. It rolls out through heavily forested hills until it meets up with the Norway and Wildcat Loops. Turn left to head back in to the trailhead. After a series of small climbs and descents a fast downhill takes riders quickly back into the lot over a mix of sand and hardpack littered with small debris. This is very fun stuff.

The Norway Pine Loop starts off to the left and heads in a counterclockwise direction. The climbing starts right away with two major climbs in the first half mile. The views to the west are magnificent and show a large section of the Black River Forest. It is easy to pick out the sections currently being logged and others that have been reforested and are still young in comparison to the surrounding old forest.

At the farthest point of both the Red Oak and Norway Pine loops is the connector to the Wildcat Loop. Riders should use caution, as this connector crosses Shale Road, then picks up the Wildcat Loop on the other side. The Wildcat Loop takes off to the left in a clockwise direction and gets into the climbing right away. Be prepared to stop at the tops of climbs to recover, especially in hot weather.

24

Perrot State Park

Perrot State Park has an interesting history, both in terms of how it formed naturally and of the people who have called it home. The formations found here had their beginnings under water. The sandstone bluffs throughout the park were formed when this area was the floor of an ancient sea, piling sand and mud on top of itself until under its own weight the mixture was crushed into stone, forming the bluffs we ride on today. After the sea receded, glaciers moved through, shearing the tops off the bluffs and, amazingly, rerouting the Mississippi from one side of the park to the other.

The park's human history goes back over 7,000 years, starting with the Archaic Indians that passed through here on their way to various hunting grounds. Many other tribes have utilized this area as well, building effigy mounds that are still visible today. In the late 1600s, the French fur trade brought Indians and French together here, one group collecting the furs, the other reaping the rewards. During his travels, French explorer Nicholas Perrot spent the winter in the area in 1685 and, 45 years later, the French established a permanent fort here.

The trail system lies in the center of the park surrounding the 500-foot-high Perrot Ridge. The trail entirely encircles the ridge and offers grand views of the Mississippi below, with boats bustling on its waterways and Burlington Northern trains moving along its shore. The off-road trail covers a wide path of grass and at times hard-packed soil. Because of the nature of the terrain, climbing is common, in some cases over rather extended routes. In comparison with other parks, Perrot puts mountain bikers right at the heart of the park's true splendor, instead of pushed off to a remote edge. The scenery is beautiful throughout, with the trail cutting through thick forests and occasionally breaking out into meadows of waist-high grass. The Mississippi is visible near the end of the ride as the trail sweeps around the southern edge of Perrot Ridge.

All in all, the riding is excellent for those not as interested in technical terrain as in exploring the park's beauty. Benches are set up at a couple of the more scenic meadows, allowing for a few minutes of stretching and relaxation during the ride. The entire loop will take an hour to an hour and a half for intermediate riders. Make certain to apply bug spray, as the surrounding waters are ample breeding grounds for mosquitoes.

General location: 23 miles north of Lacrosse, 1 mile west of Trempealeau.

Technical Difficulty: Level 3.

Aerobic Level: Strenuous.

Tread: Singletrack and wide-path grass.

PERROT STATE PARK
Ride 24

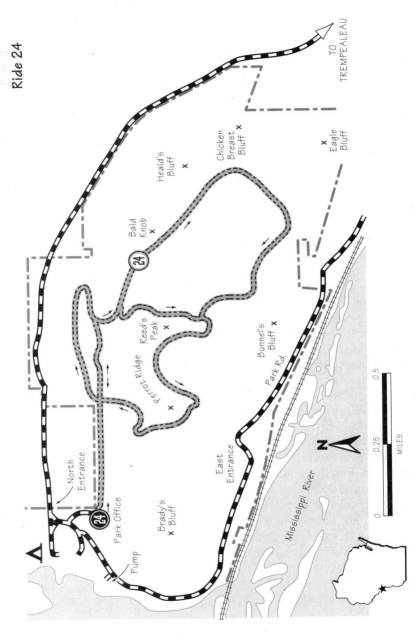

Views of the Mississippi are commonplace at Perrot State Park.

Length: 6.5 miles.

Elevation change: Nothing in this section of Wisconsin is flat. At best the hills are rolling; at worst they are monstrously steep and long. The trailhead, on the low ground, is 250 feet below the highest ridge bikers pass over. Most of the climbs cover heights of approximately 60 feet, with two logging in around 175 and 200 feet.

Camping: The park has 96 sites, all with fire pits. Many are located along the river. Showers and restrooms are available.

Season: Trails are open from April 15 to November 15. However, erosion is a concern, and often after heavy rains or in the early part of the season when snow runoff is still affecting topsoil, the trails will be closed. It is a good idea to call ahead and check on the conditions of the trail.

Fees: A trail pass and vehicle admission sticker are required. Both are available as annual passes from the DNR.

Services: Water and soda are available at the nature center directly to the west of the trailhead. Nearly all services, from groceries to lodging, are available in both Trempealeau and Lacrosse.

Hazards: Watch high speeds on the steeper descents, as the trail can be fairly chewed up and difficult to maneuver on. It is easy to find the front tire of the bike stuck in a deep washout. Erosion control devices have been put in to help this problem somewhat, but these are obstacles in themselves as they become more and more exposed. The last descent actually feels like going down a set of short stairs. Try popping your front wheel off of them to catch enough air to clear the obstacle entirely. Watch for hikers on all blind corners and make a verbal announcement when passing anyone.

Rescue: The park is rather busy and rangers are easily found. The park office serves as the trailhead. Even on the farthest point of the trail other hikers and bikers are normally close by to lend a hand. If no one is around, use the map to locate a nearby road and wait for a passerby to come along.

Land status: Wisconsin DNR, Perrot State Park.

Maps: The trail area is shown on the USGS 7.5-minute quad for Trempealeau. Maps are available at the ranger station, located at the park entrance, and at the park office at the trailhead.

Sources of more information: See Appendix A, in particular Perrot State Park, the Wisconsin Department of Tourism, and WORBA.

Finding the trail: Take Interstate 90 to Wisconsin Highway 35 north of Lacrosse. Take WI 35 northwest 15 miles to Trempealeau. Turn left on Main Street, then right on First Street (unmarked), which leads right into the park within the next 4 miles. Follow it to the far end of the park to the sign for the park office and service area. Turn right on this road and follow it to the office and trailhead.

THE RIDE

The trail leads away from the paved road into the forest in a westerly direction starting out on a doubletrack path. A hiking trail closed to bikers comes up on the right within the first 0.5 mile; continue going straight. At the 1 mile mark the trail splits. Continuing straight leads riders onto a short 1-mile loop that serves as an excellent warm-up before tackling the main trail. The main loop leads to the right and starts out with the biggest climb of the day. The "tow-rope" climb (as in, you wish there was a tow rope to drag your tired body up the hill) is fairly steep, and on top of that, it's long. This climb covers about 250 feet in elevation, with more climbing to come.

At the top of the climb the trail forks. The main loop continues to the left; a cutoff route goes to the right, severing nearly three miles of riding from the main loop and sticking to the east edge of Perrot Ridge. The main loop, to the left, travels clockwise and passes by Heald's Bluff and Eagle Bluff along its route. The riding along this edge is all up and down, with an excellent extended descent marked by the Ski Jump downhill, which kicks things off with a quick, steep drop on a curve followed by a long section of fast-paced riding. Several climbs in the 50-foot range are found on this portion of the trail, along with another climb of 200+ feet that is at a more gradual grade. This loop connects with the cutoff at the southeastern tip of Perrot Ridge and follows its south face around to the main connector back to the trailhead. This section features several meadows along with an interesting descent over staggered erosion blocks. Watch the signs along Perrot Ridge denoting the mountain bike trail with bicycle icons. The Brady's Bluff hiking trail also follows this route.

Perry Creek Trail

The Perry Creek Trail is one of the most pleasant rides in Wisconsin. What starts out looking like a fairly uneventful afternoon of riding quickly turns into a beautiful look at nature in a quiet corner of the Black River State Forest. As the trail winds through the forest, first along the base of Castle Mound, then later high above Perry Creek, the immersion in nature pulls riders farther and farther along. The path seldom pitches, and only in two places near the turnaround is there any climbing involved.

The trail first passes beneath high tension lines in a clear cut field, but the route quickly becomes more scenic. Midway along, the path begins to hug the edge of Perry Creek, its crimson tint resulting from the red clay beneath its clear water. The trail seldom strays from the creek and, as the journey goes on, the scenery gets more stunning and unique. At times the bluffs rise 40 feet above the waters as they flow quickly toward the Black River. At the far end of the trail an old railroad bridge, used for decades, still hangs over the creek.

The ride is best suited for beginners, families, or riders not wanting technical challenge but instead scenic views from the saddle. The path is two-way and is not ridden in a loop but instead in an out-and-back manner. The entire trail will take under an hour at a quick pace but is best ridden more slowly, with plenty of breaks to walk down to the water's edge or sit atop the bluffs in the quiet woods. The majority of the path is wide, short-mown grass with occasional sections along dirt ATV trails.

The state forest campground that serves as the trailhead for this ride enables visitors to spend an entire weekend exploring the area. The campground is very nice, set back in the woods at the base of Castle Mound. While mountain bikes are not allowed on the trails to the top of Castle Mound, foot travel is encouraged. The views from the trail are excellent, and an impressive erratic at the far east side of the mound makes the climb particularly worthwhile.

General location: 1 mile southwest of Black River Falls.

Technical Difficulty: Level 2.

Aerobic Level: Easy.

Tread: Wide-path grass and doubletrack.

Length: 9 miles out and back.

Elevation change: The trail is perfectly flat except for two moderate but steady climbs near the turnaround point. Each of the climbs covers around 50 feet of elevation.

PERRY CREEK TRAIL

Ride 25

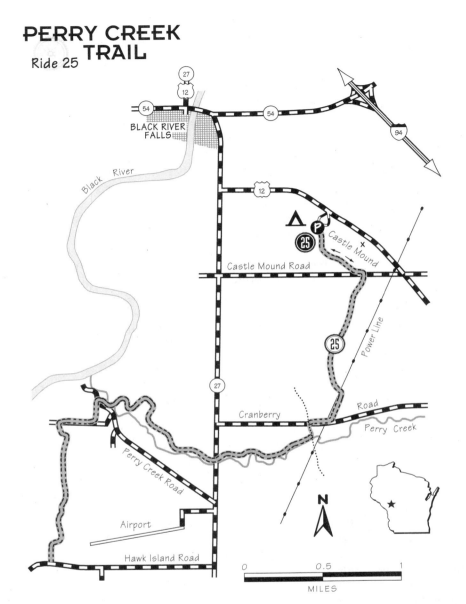

Camping: Several campsites are located within the park at the base of Castle Mound. Restrooms are available and fire pits are located in each unit.

Season: The trails are open April to November. Spring is a nice time to see the creek at its fullest and fastest. Fall brings spectacular changing colors.

Fees: A trail pass and vehicle admission sticker are required. Both are available as annual passes from the DNR.

Services: Everything can be found in Black River Falls, from water and gas to groceries and lodging.

Hazards: There are road crossings at three separate places (six in all on this out-and-back route). Wisconsin Highway 27 is particularly busy and care must be taken when crossing.

Rescue: In case of emergency make your way out to one of the roads or back to the ranger station at the park entrance. The trails are well used by other campers, mainly those on foot.

Land status: Wisconsin DNR, Black River State Forest.

Maps: The trail area is shown on the USGS 7.5-minute quad for Black River Falls.

Sources of more information: See Appendix A, in particular the Black River Falls Chamber of Commerce, Wisconsin Department of Tourism, and WORBA.

Finding the trail: From Black River Falls travel north on Interstate 94 and take the Wisconsin Highway 54 exit. Head west on WI 54 and after 1 mile turn left (south) onto WI 27. Follow WI 27 for a 0.5 mile and turn left (east) onto U.S. Highway 12. Travel on US 12 for 0.5 mile to the park entrance on the right, then follow the park road to the picnic area parking lot.

THE RIDE

The trail departs the parking lot to the south on a wide grass path and follows the base of Castle Mound for half a mile. The mound itself is not really visible because of the trees, but hiking paths along this route will take individuals to the top on foot. Do not ride these trails, which are located to

Rock ledges edge Perry Creek and provide excellent rest spots for bikers.

the left of the bike path. At the 0.75 mile mark the bike path crosses Castle Mound Road. After another mile through forest, the trail breaks out into a clearing and heads across a field underneath a set of high tension power lines that stretch in both directions as far as the eye can see. The trail shortly breaks to the right away from the power lines and back into the forest, and within a quarter mile begins to follow an ATV trail, crossing Cranberry Road and heading back into the forest. (Cranberry Road is named after the cranberry bogs it leads to just east of the trail.)

Across the road, Perry Creek is visible immediately on the left. In 0.75 mile the path crosses WI 27. The speed limit on this 2-lane highway is 55 mph, so use caution. The path continues for another mile, down two descents along the creek and to a sharp bend in the waters. It then cuts across the water and heads up the bluff to the left, where it ends at the road. This is the turnaround point. Follow the trail back along the same route to return to the parking lot.

26

Levis/Trow Mounds

The trails in this section of Wisconsin, just north of the Black River State Forest, are among the most exciting and rewarding in all the state. This cluster is one of the most overlooked in all the land and offers climbing of a sort not normally found outside of mountainous regions. Every ingredient necessary for great mountain biking is found here—stunning, unobstructed views, incredible singletrack, and beautiful medium-paced cross-country trails to transport riders around the grounds.

Two towering mounds dominate the diverse terrain. Levis Mound to the south is covered with ribbons of narrow hard-pack trails cutting back and forth on their way to the peak. Trow Mound to the north juts out of the forest and has two trails leading to the top. The riding is exhilarating and time passes quickly on this circuit. It is hard to think of anything but the trail while climbing and descending along the mounds, not even how stressed your legs and lungs are feeling.

Once at the top of the mounds the treetops are at your feet, and the views stretch out for miles over the surrounding forest. From Levis Mound, Trow Mound stands up tall among the neighboring farmlands, as does Levis when at the crest of Trow. The trails are seldom crowded, and meditation on a high peak is sublime.

The main trails that lead riders around the base of the mounds and to all the singletrack starting points are comprised of wide, cross-country ski paths

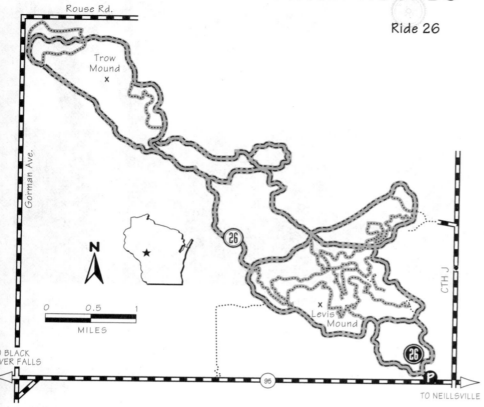

over sand, dirt, and some grass. The trails are extensive and completely encircle both mounds. These trails are, for the most part, rated as easy to moderate, with little climbing and no technical terrain. One section to the northwest, however, dubbed the Moundbounder, receives the park's most difficult rating, and though the 1.5-mile length of trail is not very technical, the repeated climbing and descending is intense.

The singletrack is most heavily concentrated on the south end of the property around Levis Mound. Names like "switchback" and "the corkscrew" atttest to the nature of the terrain. Climbing and descending on these routes takes concentration, skill, and nerve. Sardine Hill and Fox Hole Hill on Trow Mound offer the same excitement.

All in all, the riding is excellent and the trails are exceptionally well laid out and marked. Intermediate riders can cover the system in three hours, though an afternoon can easily be spent backtracking on favorite routes to reach the tops of the mounds from different angles.

General location: 16 miles northwest of Black River Falls, 5 miles west of Merrillan.

Beautiful views of the surrounding forest and mounds are visible from every precipice.

Technical Difficulty: Level 3 to 4.

Aerobic Level: Moderate to strenuous.

Tread: Singletrack and doubletrack.

Length: Up to 12 miles.

Elevation change: The singletrack climbing to the tops of the mounds makes up some 200 + feet of elevation, though in quick bursts instead of drawn out sections. The climbing is actually so fun and intense, taking place on narrow ledges, that it is easy to ignore the physical strain.

Camping: There are 26 sites at the East Forks campground south of the Black River. Follow CTH K south from the Levis/Trow area, through the town of Hatfield around the southern tip of lake Arbutus to West Clay School Road. Turn left (east) and follow this route for two miles to Campground Road. Turn left (north) and drive the remaining 0.5 mile to the sites. Water and toilets are available.

Season: Winter is off limits, even to hikers, in order to maintain the meticulously groomed ski trails. Any of the other three seasons, however, are fair game. Fall is particularly breathtaking from the vistas as the colors change, spring provides clear trails, and summer as always is a bit hot, but the shade of the forest and the breezes on the peaks make it bearable.

Fees: A self-pay station is set up at the trailhead. Parking is free.

Services: Toilets are located at the trailhead parking lot. Gas and groceries can be found in the town of Merrillan, five miles west. Black River Falls is a bit farther but offers a greater selection of restaurants and the like.

Hazards: Watch for sand, both on the singletrack and the main trails, as well as tree falls. It is easy to wash out the front tire in sandy sections and tumble off the edge. The ledges that lead to the top of the mound are narrow, loose, and at times filled with obstacles such as roots and rocks. Stick tight to the wall and use body English and athletic skill to make it through. It's all ridable.

Rescue: The trails are well ridden though riding with a partner is always a good idea. Rangers do not patrol the inner trails enough for you to assume they will be around to help. Get out to the road and flag down help in an emergency or get in the car and go to Merrillan for assistance.

Land Status: Wisconsin DNR.

Maps: The trail area is shown on the USGS 7.5-minute quad for Merrillan. Maps are available at the trailhead.

Sources of more information: See Appendix A, in particular the Clark County Forest, Wisconsin Department of Tourism, and WORBA.

Finding the trail: When approaching Black River Falls from the south on Interstate 94, exit Wisconsin Highway 12/27 north. Follow WI 12/27 for 11 miles to Merrillan. Turn right (east) onto WI 95, and go 6 miles to the trailhead on the left (north).

THE RIDE

Leaving from the north end of the parking lot the trail takes off on a wide forest-floor-type path on a warm-up loop. The loop heads out to an intersection, letting riders go right to return to the lot or left to continue on. By heading left the first set of singletrack will depart quickly on the right side of the trail. This is the Switchback Trail which carves back and forth across Levis Mound. Halfway up Switchback, the path forks. To the right the trail leads back down to the East Levis Loop; to the left it continues to the top. On top of the bluff several different trails take riders to the scenic vistas, or to the three downhill trails on the far side-Corkscrew, Northface, and Piledriver.

To the north of this section another loop encircles a shorter portion of the mound. The 0.5-mile Porky Point Trail leads to the top of this formation. East of these two loops, the wide-track trails lead out and across the flat land to Trow Mound. The only difficult wide-track riding in this cluster is found here in the form of the Moundbounder, a 1.5-mile trail edging the east face of Trow Mound. There are also three singletrack trails here, Sardine Hill on the southeast face, and Buck and Fox Hole Hills on the north face. All three provide excellent routes to the top.

Northeast Wisconsin

The northeastern portion of Wisconsin is the land of pines. The Nicolet National Forest covers an area from the small town of Mountain north into the Upper Peninsula, where it melds with the Ottawa National Forest and continues on into Canada. The true expanse of the trees is hard to fathom and even from well above the top branches, in the Mountain fire tower, it is not possible to see the edge of the forest in any direction except on a very clear day when Lake Michigan is visible to the east. The seemingly endless miles of timber are what brought the logging industry to northern Wisconsin in the 1800s and started the hearty tradition of the north woods logging camps.

The small town of Hurley on the Upper Peninsula border was one of the most notoriously rough and tumble locations in all the world at the turn of the century. Historically, the town topped the list of dangerous places, reportedly ranked just above Hayward to the west and Hell to the south. In Hurley's wild days, hordes of lumberjacks would return from the woods to drink heavily, in spite of prohibition, and visit the town's prostitutes. The town, and those surrounding it, have mellowed with time and, while taverns are still commonplace, brothels are not, and visitors can enjoy a relatively quiet walk down the once-boisterous streets.

In addition to the Nicolet National Forest, this area includes the Northern Highland American Legion State Forest, covering approximately 222,000 acres, and a small portion of the Chequamegon National Forest edging Vilas County. The terrain was pock-marked throughout by the receding glaciers, and the depressions left behind soon filled with water, creating hundreds of interconnected lakes. Rivers flow from lake to lake, pounding over rocks and waterfalls. The setting makes for tough wilderness riding, not for those without a tolerance for the elements and an outdoor lifestyle. The off-road riding in this section of the state is mainly on grass paths. Razorback Ridge and the Anvil Trails along with Washburn are the most technical of the group, ridden on wide paths over tough terrain. Escanaba and the Lumberjack Trail lend themselves to exploration, with their desolate grass paths leading through the plush undergrowth of the forest. Topping the list of expansive trails are the Pines and Mines Units of Iron County. Though only a small portion are covered in this book, the logging roads lead on for hundreds of miles, allowing riders to spend weeks traversing the north woods, fishing and camping along the way. Iron County is named for the vein of ore that runs through the ground in this part of the world. It was iron that brought miners to the area to mix their own brand of toughness with that of the lumberjacks.

In comparison to the northwest corner of the state, the northeast is a bit more accessible for tourists. The lakes and towns are populated with boaters and vacationers every weekend during milder weather. Boulder Junction, Eagle River, and Minocqua are some of the most popular destinations in the upper part of the state. The excellent riding combined with the small-town atmosphere makes for a great escape. Consider camping at one of the many campsites located throughout the state and national forests. Sites away from lakes provide the most serene camping, without the often disruptive noises of vacationing families.

Anvil Trails

The Anvil Trails are one of the most popular mountain biking destinations in the Nicolet National Forest. The cluster itself is just east of the main vacationland of the North Country—the triangle of Eagle River, Minocqua, and Boulder Junction. This is another section of true northern Wisconsin riding—desolate, rugged, and enclosed by pines on all sides; and in this case enclosed by water, in the form of Ninemile Creek and Upper Ninemile Lake along the eastern and southern edges.

Most of the riding is very basic save for one trail, Devil's Run. The paths cover a wide variety of surfaces, from wide doubletrack paths on the West and North trails, to narrow cross-country ski paths on the Ninemile and Lake trails, to rough and challenging singletrack on Devil's Run. Intermediate riders should have no trouble exploring the full set of trails within two hours.

It is uncertain where the name "Anvil" comes from, but a possibility is that it stems from the hammering that riders take on the Devil's Run. The climbing is tough and the descents are not only filled with debris but also are pitched at rather steep angles, making it tough to keep everything together and under control on the way down. Because of this, good shifting skills come in handy. Halfway up a climb is no time to be making a huge jump across the cassette. Knowing what gearing will propel the bike up the face of the ridge is of key importance and will keep your feet in the clips.

To totally immerse yourself in nature, try camping across the street on the shore of Anvil Lake and riding over to bike. The sites are beautiful and there is really nothing to compare with waking up to campfire coffee, heading out from the site in the saddle and, when the trails are complete, returning to the campsite for an afternoon beside the lake and a night beside the campfire. Through the night, owls in the surrounding forest call out across

ANVIL TRAILS

Ride 27

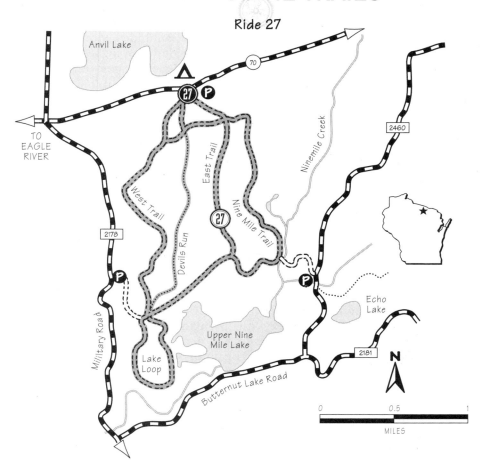

the silence while whitetail deer bed down in nearby meadows. The stars in this part of the north woods are spectacular and fill the sky from horizon to horizon. Counting satellites and falling stars while tuning derailleurs is a wonderful way to spend an evening here.

General Location: 9.5 miles east of Eagle River.

Technical Difficulty: Level 3 to 4.

Aerobic Level: Moderate to strenuous.

Tread: Doubletrack and singletrack.

Length: 16 miles.

Elevation change: The terrain in this area is rather flat to the edges of the property and rather hilly down the center. The beginner and intermediate loops are ridden over rolling hills while the expert trail encounters 5 tough climbs. Most of the climbing covers 20 to 40 feet of elevation while the Devil's Run Trail has several in the 75- to 100-foot range.

Camping: The Anvil Lake National Forest campground is right across the street on the Southwest corner of Anvil Lake. Only 18 units are available, all with picnic tables and fire pits. Drinking water and swimming are the main attractions.

Season: April to November. The optimum time for riding is fall when the trees have changed and the temperatures are a bit cooler. Bring bug spray for the late spring and summer months.

Fees: A trail pass available from a trailhead self-pay station is required.

Services: There is a water pump at the trailhead parking lot on Wisconsin Highway 70 as well as a restroom. A shelter is found at the major trail intersection north of the Lake Loop. Groceries, gas and bicycle maintenance necessities are all available in Eagle River, 9.5 miles west.

Hazards: The beginner and intermediate loops have some roots running across the trail, most being avoidable because of the width of the trail. On the Devil's Run Trail the path is more narrow and roots and rocks are more abundant. No erosion control devices are in place on the climbs and descents making them rather loose and prone to rivulets that need to be avoided to maintain control on the steep descents. This is a good trail to learn the skills necessary to pick a good line through the hazards.

Rescue: The nearest source of aid is found in the town of Eagle River. I would suggest riding with a partner in an area this far off the beaten path. In the case of an injury, find a way out to Wisconsin Highway 70 to the north or Military Road to the west. This is not a heavily ridden trail in some parts of the season nor a heavily trafficked area outside of Highway 70.

Land status: Nicolet National Forest, Anvil Trails.

Maps: The trail area is shown on the USGS 7.5-minute quad for Anvil Lake. Maps are also available at the trailhead or from the Nicolet National Forest office.

Sources of more information: See Appendix A, in particular the Vilas County Chamber of Commerce, Wisconsin Department of Tourism, and WORBA.

Finding the trail: From Eagle River at the junction of U.S. Highway 45/47 and WI 70, head east out of town on WI 70. Travel 8.5 miles and watch for the Anvil Lake Trail sign on the right (south) side of the street.

THE RIDE

The trails depart the parking lot to the south on a wide path with singletrack worn down the center. The basic layout of the trail network has two paths leading away from the trailhead and two returning. The outer West Trail and Nine Mile Trail both are one-way leading away from the lot. To get to the Nine Mile Trail, follow the West Trail away from the parking lot for 0.5 mile and take the cutoff path running to the east all the way across the network to the Nine Mile Trail. Both of the outer trails follow forest floor terrain mixed with worn single and doubletrack patches to the same meeting place at the far south end of the loop. It is at this intersection that all the trails combine with a wooden shelter as a landmark.

The 1.75 mile Lake Loop departs from the south and covers ground along the edge of Upper Nine Mile Lake on more forest floor terrain. Upon returning to the shelter there are two options for returning to the trailhead. The two center paths, the Devil's Run to the left and East Trail to the right both return to the lot. The Devil's Run is for advanced technical riders with legs like tree trunks. A good deal of climbing is involved and the downhills practically demand V-brakes to keep the speed under control. The East Trail, on the other hand, is a pussycat in comparison and will roll riders back to the lot safe and sound without a great deal of effort and no technical skills necessary.

28

Washburn Trails

The Washburn Trails are a great location to head for when the crowds are getting thick at some of the more well-known northeastern Wisconsin trails. These are less well known and yet offer some excellent singletrack riding on a rather simply designed course. The trails are always under development and expansion; they consist mostly of rough dirt paths blazed by local riders across the network of established trails. The main trails are ridden on wide grass paths with single- and doubletrack running over them. This portion of the network covers approximately 7 miles and, though it is the easiest of the terrain found here, has its share of fast descents and climbs. Picking a good line around the erosion on the climbs is necessary.

The singletrack, shown on the map included here but not marked at the trail itself, is ridden over hard-packed earth, strewn with small rocks, root systems, and the occasional stump. The trails are rather rough and offer a challenge to riders of all abilities. Total concentration is necessary to keep the bike upright through the dips, dives, and narrow passages between trees.

The idea at Washburn is to ride the main ski trails and duck into the woods whenever a path is visible. The paths lead back out to another portion of the main circuit within half a mile at most. By doing this the entire area can be explored and, as it is all good singletrack, riders won't mind backtracking over a good section.

For intermediate riders, the main ski trails can easily be conquered in half an hour to forty minutes. Throw in the singletrack and the ride can take the better part of an afternoon depending on how much of it is covered. The entire system is set in a dense hardwood forest over a series of rolling hills. Like most of the surrounding area, the hills were formed by glaciers and are pock-marked throughout with kettles and kames.

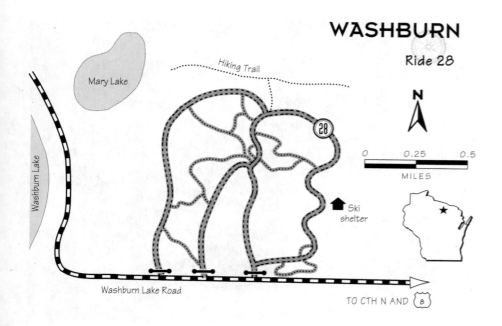

One note that should alleviate some confusion: The signs at the front gates designate hiking only, but the trails have been approved by the local chamber of commerce and all the signs within the gates clearly show bike icons.

General location: 6 miles west of Rhinelander off U.S. Highway 8.

Technical Difficulty: Level 3.

Aerobic Level: Moderate.

Tread: Singletrack and grass doubletrack.

Length: 7 miles.

Elevation change: The entire set of trails is on one large hill with climbs on the front side leading up to the singletrack. The climbing is seldom more than 40 feet with most coming in short spurts of 10 to 20 feet of elevation.

Camping: The Terrace View Campground is 10 miles southwest of the trails, just south of the intersection of U.S. Highway 8 and US 51. The campground is set on the shore of Muskellunge Lake (named for the massive, razor-toothed fish that live in these waters) and has 42 sites to choose from. Fishing, swimming, fire pits, toilets, and water are all available.

Season: Specific dates are not available but the trail is shared with cross- country skiers and becomes their trail from the first snowfall until the spring thaw. In summer the trails are not maintained and the singletrack can become very overgrown. Autumn is probably the best time of year to ride, especially as the trees turn and humidity and temperatures both fall.

Fees: None.

The author rapidly descends the singletrack at the Washburn Trails.
JONATHAN BYKOWSKI PHOTO

Services: There is a small shelter on the east side of the cluster. Other than that, there are no services at the trailhead to aid riders. The closest town is Woodboro, which is a good stop for gas and snacks. To the east, Rhinelander has everything including gas, water, restaurants, and bicycle maintenance.

Hazards: The singletrack trails are very roughly developed and small stumps are fairly common. It is also quite easy to hook a handlebar or bar-end around small trees that tightly line the singletrack. Sway side to side around these. The hills on the ski trails can change drastically due to erosion. Watch for small channels caused by rainwater running down these sections, waiting to suck in front wheels and dump riders from their bikes.

Rescue: Ride in pairs to be safe. The trails are not well used and traffic along Washburn Lake Road is rather sporadic. Head to Rhinelander in case of emergency.

Land status: County Forest.

Maps: The trail area is shown on the USGS 7.5-minute quad for Rhinelander. This book is the only source of maps.

Sources of more information: See Appendix A, in particular the Rhinelander Chamber of Commerce, Wisconsin Department of Tourism, and WORBA.

Finding the trail: From Rhinelander go west on U.S. Highway 8 about 6 miles to County Highway N. Turn right (north) and follow CH N for 0.75 mile to Washburn Lake Road. Turn left (west) and follow Washburn Lake Road for 1.5 miles. Watch for 3 gates spaced about 0.25 mile apart on the right. Each of these serves as a trailhead.

From the trailhead at the third gate, the trail heads north following a grassy path up a small hill into the forest. The ski trail continues from the top of this hill around to the right, passing the entrance to four singletrack paths along the way. The trail curves sharply at the far end of the cluster and heads east, then splits within 100 yards, each fork heading south back to the other two gates. The trail to the right splits again halfway back to gate 2. The trail to the left goes through a series of moderate climbs and fast descents with singletrack leading off on both sides. The singletrack leads out to the ski trails on the far east and west sides of the network.

The trail to the left of the main split covers the easternmost side of the trail cluster and offers only two singletrack opportunities. It has the largest climbs and descents, including a rather fast descent on a curving pass dubbed by locals as "Herringbone Hill." Halfway down the path a shelter has been constructed on the east side of the trail, mainly for skiers but in case of a bad storm it can help bikers, too.

There are trails to the north of this unit but their status at press time was too uncertain for them to be included in this book. It is advised to call ahead for the status of the trails in this northern set.

29

Razorback Ridge

Razorback Ridge is the true definition of rugged northern Wisconsin riding. The trails in this area lead through a thick forest of pine, maple, and birch trees, occasionally peeking out into a valley of meadow grass. For the most part, the trails in this cluster are made up of wide-cut grass paths with single- or doubletrack running down the center. The trails are rather bumpy and keep the rider bouncing around in the saddle nearly constantly. The area offers 30 miles of trails through the woods, and countless side routes branch off, offering a more challenging variety of singletrack.

Maintenance on the trails is nonexistent. No erosion control devices are found here and the trails are basically left as is, giving riders who prefer *au naturel* to structured courses a chance to ride on real, untamed terrain. By midsummer what starts out as an already wild area explodes into an overgrown, densely vegetated region. While the main routes are wide enough to easily pilot in any season, the singletrack sections become more and more

RAZORBACK RIDGE

Ride 29

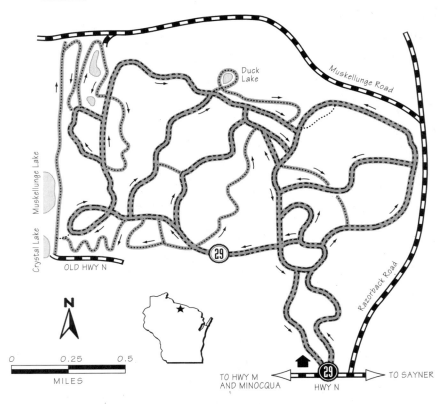

difficult as spring turns to summer. Fall and early winter bring a light dusting of snow, and the trails are wide open and free of clutter.

The trail markings are the only real drawback to the riding in this area. The maps seldom face the same direction you are, which makes it tough to determine what the "you are here" markings on each map actually mean. The singletrack off the northwestern edge of the main circuit is definitely worth exploring, but most paths are marked with paper plates on posts (really!) with names like "Face Plant" or even more simply, "Experts Only." In the summertime these technical routes are nearly impossible to ride because of the dense overgrowth of trailside vegetation. In the spring and fall, however, the riding is as challenging as it gets with exhausting, high-concentration climbs—doled out in short spurts—and insane switchbacks, many of which lead directly into more climbing. Here the mind is equally important as the body, with attentive handling and excellent timing necessary to clear some of the more intricate sections. Singletrack riding such as this also demands expert shifting, the gift of knowing what gear will be needed 20 to 30 feet before the terrain actually changes.

The entire trail complex will take 2 to 2.5 hours to complete at a good pace. An entire afternoon can easily be spent riding different combinations of loops. The nearby small towns of Sayner and St. Germaine add a little north woods realism to the scene, with restaurants like the Muskie Queen creating the ambience and log cabins serving as everything from banks to hardware stores.

General location: 2 miles west of Sayner.

Technical Difficulty: Level 3 to 5.

Aerobic Level: Moderate.

Tread: Grass doubletrack and singletrack.

Length: Up to 30 miles.

Elevation change: The terrain is typical of the north woods, being primarily shaved off by glaciation. There are no terribly extended climbs but many in the 30- to 40-foot range. The singletrack has the same elevation changes in terms of feet, but at much more severe grades.

Camping: In spring through fall, camping is found on the shore of Big St. Germaine Lake at Lynn Ann's Campground, west of St. Germaine. Follow Wisconsin Highway 155 south to the town of St. Germaine. Head west on WI 70 for 2.5 miles to the campground on the right.

Season: April to November. Springtime is very sloppy and comes late in this part of the world. Fall is ideal with mild temperatures and clear trails. Summer is the main season but can be very hot and humid with overgrown trails. Winter is interesting here; you get to experience the northwoods in its harshest season—until the trails are buried and become the domain of cross-country skiers.

Fees: Donations are requested at the trailhead.

Services: McCay's general store, at the trailhead, has gas, food, and beverages for needy bikers. Water and restrooms are also available at the camp, directly behind the store.

Hazards: Poor trail markings can be as dangerous as tree stumps. Razorback is not well marked, and a good sense of direction comes in handy. Carry a map to avoid frustration. The singletrack trails are loads of fun but also rough and technical. In a few years, when enough riders have gone through to fully establish the trails, they are sure to get better, but for now think of it as being a part of trailblazing history. The famed Suicide Hill is steep and bumpy, but the name is extreme and the hill is definitely ridable.

Rescue: Ride in groups or pairs for safety. The trails are not well ridden except on weekends, so help along the trail is sporadic. The best bet in case of emergency is to travel back to McCay's general store.

Land status: Northern Highland American Legion State Forest.

Maps: The trail area is shown on the USGS 7.5-minute quad for Sayner. McCay's also has a handful of maps behind the counter.

Sources of more information: See Appendix A, in particular the Vilas County Chamber of Commerce, Wisconsin Department of Tourism, and WORBA.

Finding the trail: From St. Germaine go north on Wisconsin Highway 155 for 7 miles to Sayner. Follow WI 155 through Sayner and turn left (west) onto County Highway N. Follow CH N for 2 miles to McCay's general store, at the corner of Razorback Road (unmarked). Turn right, then park along the left side of the road.

The ride

For everyone's safety, all the trails in the system are one way and are marked as such. The trails depart the parking lot on single- and doubletrack to the north. Within the first 1.5 miles the first 2 loops approach—the short Ridge trails and the shorter Old Timer's Loop. Both of these are warm-up loops that stay close to the parking lot. From either edge of these 2 sections of trail the path diverges: to the left is the Long Rider, to the right is Hair Raiser.

The Long Rider is the longest of all the loops and carries riders out to the far west corner of the cluster to the area where most of the singletrack is found. Trails departing to the right are wide grass paths much like the Long Rider. Roller Coaster and Mary's Frolic are two such trails that both end up at the heart of the system, Big Valley, where all the trails converge.

Left of the Long Rider Trail is more technical riding in the form of the singletrack Bear Claw, Corkscrew, Face Plant, and Rat'l Snake. Several others will be marked when you arrive, all at various stages of development. This portion of the trail draws in technical riders and keeps them captivated

Rider Jonathan Bykowski descending the infamous Suicide Hill at Razorback Ridge.

for hours. The riding is excellent and the uncharted feel adds to the sensation of trailblazing and adventure. After returning to the main Long Rider Trail the path eventually leads into Big Valley, just as all the others do.

Getting back to the first two beginner loops, the Hair Raiser Trail, which departs to the right, takes riders out to the smaller eastern side of the cluster. The only singletrack in this area is the Deadman's Curve path, kitty-corner to the entrance of Suicide Hill on the far side of Hair Raiser. Doug's Folly leads to the base of Suicide Hill in Big Valley after crossing Hair Raiser.

Since all the main trails lead back to Big Valley, this trail system is very easy to navigate. The singletrack, on the other hand, is ever-changing and developing and the signs marking these trails can literally blow away in a high wind. Plan on doing some exploration to locate the truly choice rides.

30

Lumberjack Trails

The Lumberjack Trails, on the outskirts of the small tourist town of Boulder Junction, form a scenic cluster of wild, natural paths, good for exploring the north woods in any weather. The adjoining town is small and, despite the weekend crowds, is very appealing with its rugged appearance and "old main street' buildings. The town is one of the farthest north in the Northern Highland American Legion State Forest, deep in the heart of the "land of lakes" only twenty miles from the Upper Peninsula border. The riding in this part of the state is not as much sought after for technical thrills, but instead for the pedaling at a slower, exploratory pace. The idea here is to move through the forest gracefully in an effort to quietly appreciate the surrounding area. The edges of the trail are thick with pines and stands of various hardwoods, and lakes and streams hide in many of the valleys the trails pass by.

The Lumberjack Trail system consists of two smallish loops at the northern trailhead, and a long connector trail that leads to a southern trailhead near the Boulder Junction Chamber of Commerce. These three main trail sections cover ten miles of terrain over grass and soil on wide paths. The trails are not well ridden yet and have not worn smooth. The Boulder area bike enthusiasts who maintain the trails have included this network as part of the Boulder Area Trail System (BATS), and signs throughout the trail system are decorated with their bat logo. The entire network takes about an hour and a half to complete for an intermediate rider at a moderate pace. Side trails taking riders to the edge of the water will take a bit of extra time to explore.

LUMBERJACK TRAILS

Ride 30

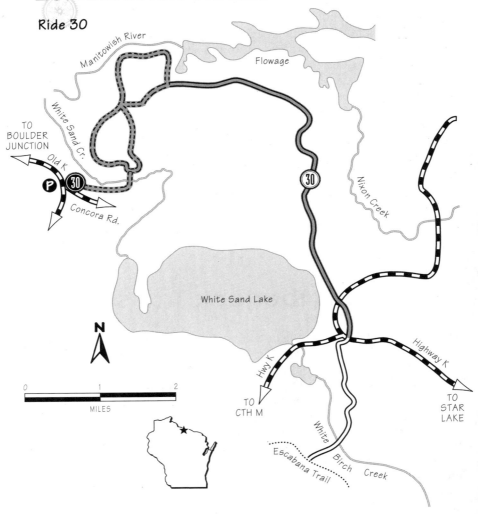

The trails pass some large bodies of water along the way, including White Sand Lake, Fishtrap Flowage, and the Manitowish River. The system runs through mostly old-growth forest, although a large portion was recently logged and reforested. A connector from the southern trailhead to the Escanaba trail—2.5 miles to the south—is covered in the following chapter. This connector is actually a snowmobile trail cutting through forest and marshlands much like the other trails in the system.

All told, the Lumberjack Trails are excellent for isolated, detached riding. I tend to like them when a little added adversity is factored in, perhaps a light rain or cold wind to make the ride unique. There is nothing quite like a slow paced ride in the north woods on the cusp of winter when most other

A wooden bridge crosses the White Sand River on the way to the main loops.

bikers have packed it in and the trails are empty and all but abandoned. It is easy to go back in time this way and grant some empathy to the explorers who first had to make their way through this part of the world on horseback and foot.

General location: 2 miles east of Boulder Junction.

Technical Difficulty: Level 2 to 3.

Aerobic Level: Moderate.

Tread: Gravel, grass, and doubletrack.

Length: 10 miles.

Elevation change: The trails are very moderate with only a small number of climbs. The climbing covers 30 feet at the most and takes place almost entirely on the two loops. The connector trail from the second trailhead to the Escanaba Trail is flat.

Camping: The North Trout Lake Campground just south of the trails offers 48 units, all with fire pits. Toilets are also available. To find the campground follow County Highway M from Boulder Junction south past CH K. The entrance is 1 mile past this intersection on the right.

Season: The trails are open to skiers in the winter, so snow riding is not allowed. Summer and fall are the best seasons, after the spring thaw has dried until it snows in late October or early November. The bugs can be vicious in summertime and bug spray is advised. On a hot summer day there is nothing more annoying than a huge pack of horse flies and various other biting bugs trailing behind you as you try to make your way through the forest.

Fees: None.

Services: Gas and groceries can be found in Boulder Junction. It is a good idea to fill up on water in town, as none is offered at the trailhead.

Hazards: Erosion is common on the descents and climbs—riders should use caution. It is easy to miss a nasty rut under the cover of grass. Tree falls are common on all trails but are easily avoidable. Try to be considerate and drag them to the side for future bikers.

Rescue: Ride in pairs on these trails as they are not well ridden and are far from any major paved routes. In case of emergency, make your way back to town.

Land status: Northern Highland American Legion State Forest.

Maps: The trail area is shown on the USGS 7.5-minute quad for Boulder Junction and White Sand Lake. Maps are easily obtained by stopping at the Boulder Junction Chamber of Commerce on the way into town on County Highway M.

Sources of more information: See Appendix A, in particular the Boulder Junction Chamber of Commerce, Wisconsin Department of Tourism, and WORBA.

Finding the trail: From the south, follow County Highway M into Boulder Junction and turn right in the center of town onto Old County Highway K. Follow this for 1 mile and turn left (north) onto Concora Road. The trailhead is almost immediately on the left.

The trails depart to the north from the Lumberjack parking lot on a wide grass path. The moderately rolling terrain found at the onset never changes throughout the two main loops. A short connector starts things off hitting the main trails in 0.5 mile. Along the way the connector crosses a small wooden bridge over White Sand Creek. On the far side of the bridge the first of the two loops is found. Stay to the right as you enter this first loop and follow the trail over sand and grass for 1 mile until it meets with a path on the right. This short, 40-foot path tethers the two loops of this northern section together, connecting the far north end of loop 1 to the south end of loop 2. Stay to the right as you enter loop 2. After 0.5 mile on loop 2 another trail departs to the right. This is the long, out-and-back trail that leads to the south trailhead. The connector follows a grass and gravel path for 6 miles to the Boulder Chamber of Commerce. A 2.5-mile trail at the south side of the Chamber parking lot connects the Escanaba trails to the south.

Back on loop 2, a short unmarked path is found in another 500 yards that takes riders out to the Manitowish River where it flows out from the surrounding flowage over the Fishtrap Dam. A picnic bench here makes this a nice resting spot. Back on the main loop the trails continues for another 1.5 miles, completing the full circle and returning to loop 1, carrying on through the rolling hills to the short connector back to the parking lot.

Escanaba Trails

The Escanaba Trails are yet another set of north woods mountain bike trails near the small town of Boulder Junction high up in the Northern Highland American Legion State Forest. The trails are connected at the north end of the cluster to the Lumberjack Trails covered in the preceding chapter. The Escanaba Trails, however, differ from the Lumberjack Trails in the sense that they cover much more technical ground. There are two main loops, one surrounding Pallette Lake, the other surrounding the system's namesake, Escanaba Lake. The much smaller Mystery and Spruce lakes lie to the east of the network in the swampy section of the area. The technical aspect of the trails comes in the form of bumpy sections reminiscent of the "whoop-de-do" portions of BMX tracks in the 1970s.

The scenery to either side of the trail consists of thick, hardwood forests and marshlands with tall reeds and cattails. Wooden bridges span many of

ESCANABA TRAILS

Ride 31

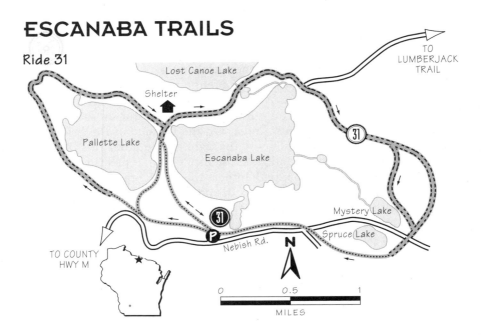

the sections that would be too wet to cross otherwise. Because of the large amount of water in the area, it makes sense that the base of the soil is comprised of sand. Even on the hard-packed sections sand is obviously present and a good cleaning of the bike's drivetrain will be necessary upon return to the parking lot. In some cases the soil-to-sand ratio is weighted heavily in favor of the sand and the tread is apt to break apart, making for loose corners and slippery climbs.

Fishing is permitted in both of the larger lakes, with a great deal of shore-line accessible along the bike trails. For a good long day of riding, try the Escanaba Loops, ride north to the Lumberjack Trail, return to Escanaba and spend the rest of the day on the shore of Pallette Lake casting for small-mouth bass. The entire set only takes an hour to complete for an intermediate rider with fresh legs, but if Lumberjack is added the ride can stretch to several hours and provide a rigorous workout. The beauty of Escanaba is the quiet that can be found there nearly any day of the week. The trails are located far enough within the forest that no noise from traffic or the town of Boulder Junction can penetrate. Usually there is just the sound of leaves rustling, birds chirping, and bike tires humming.

General location: 4 miles south of Boulder Junction.

Technical Difficulty: Level 3.

Aerobic Level: Moderate.

Tread: Doubletrack and singletrack.

Length: 8 miles.

The wide forest floor path that edges the shore of Escanaba Lake cuts through stands of pines.

Elevation change: The trails are rolling, more bumpy than hilly. A few climbs must be tackled but none over 40 feet in elevation.

Camping: The South Trout Lake Campground offers 24 units for tired riders. To find the camp area follow County Highway M south 3 miles from the Nebish Road intersection. The campground is on the right.

Season: When trails are free of snów they are open to mountain bikers, basically April to early November. Marshlands mean bugs and sloppy trail sections in spring. The best riding is in summer and fall, ideally late fall after the first frost when the ground is hard and bugs are scarce.

Fees: None.

Services: Food, lodging and gas can all be found in Boulder Junction to the north. The trailhead parking lot is just that—a parking lot with no services.

Hazards: The trails are not very well traveled and so tree falls, potholes, and erosion tracks can be expected. Be aware on the trail and look ahead of the bike, not at the front tire.

Rescue: In case of emergency, head back into town or at least to County Highway M. Nebish Road, which borders the trails on the south side, is not very well traveled, especially during the week. Ride in pairs on these trails because of their remoteness.

Land status: Northern Highland American Legion State Forest, Wisconsin DNR.

Maps: The trail area is shown on the USGS 7.5-minute quad for Boulder Junction. Maps are easily obtained by traveling north to the Boulder Junction Chamber of Commerce located on CH M just before the entrance to the town.

Sources of more information: See Appendix A, in particular the Boulder Junction Chamber of Commerce, Wisconsin Department of Tourism, and WORBA.

Finding the trail: When traveling north toward Boulder Junction on CH M, turn right (east) onto Nebish Road 4 miles before entering town. Follow this gravel road for 3.5 miles to the sign pointing to the trailhead parking lot. (It seems like more than 3.5 miles because of the slower speeds on gravel so set your trip odometer to measure the distance.) Turn left and follow the road a few hundred feet to the paved lot on the left. The trail departs from here.

THE RIDE

The trails depart to the north on singletrack and, once they have entered the forest, they seldom peek out from underneath its cover. The trails immediately turns west and carry riders in the direction of Pallette Lake. The main trail is one way in this westerly direction, but there are a pair of 2-way trails that break off from it during the first half-mile and cover the thin strip of land separating the lakes. These trails are very bumpy and hilly but provide a good, quick route to the far side of the loop, or can be used as a direct route to the Lumberjack Trail connector. The main one-way trail comes to the edge of Pallette Lake within the first mile and follows its shore, hugging the edge of the forest; this is one of the more scenic sections in the system. On the far north side of the lake the trail meets back up with the two-way trails that bisect the cluster and with the second loop that circles Escanaba Lake. There is a shelter at this intersection, which comes in handy during surprise bouts of inclement weather.

The trail departs from the shelter to the east, again traveling one way in a clockwise direction. The trail passes between Lost Canoe Lake and Escanaba Lake over a series of small wooden bridges and paths in this rather marshy section. Within 1.5 miles the connector to the Lumberjack Trail comes up on the left. The trail is well marked.

After another mile the main trail forks. The path to the left stays on higher ground through the forest, while the path to the right ducks down to the shore of Mystery Lake. The trails join again in just 0.5 mile. The path then cuts across Nebish Road, continuing on the other side for a mile, then crossing the road again before returning to the parking lot, over more of the same bumpy terrain that started the ride.

32

Pines and Mines Trails

This chapter is written more as an overview of a trail system than as a turn by turn guide, and in the end focuses on only a small portion of this enormous network. The Pines and Mines Trails in Wisconsin's far northern country cover more than 300 miles of ground stretching from Iron County into Upper Michigan along the eastern shore of Lake Superior. The idea to keep in mind while riding this system is exploration. The only way to ride here is to spend time here, and more than just an afternoon. Consider setting up a base camp from which to ride out and view the surrounding forests and towns or to travel to the area lakes and streams to spend a portion of the day fishing. Bikes equipped with racks for carrying gear are necessary. For some truly adventurous types, it is possible to put enough gear on the bike frame to become completely mobile and move from campground to campground.

The riding here is of a completely different style than most people are acquainted with, suited to those more used to road riding than to technical mountain bike trails. Ninety percent of the trails are ridden on logging roads over gravel, clay, and dirt, while the remainder is on old railroad beds and doubletrack. The distances are great and 40- to 50-mile rides are common to get from site to site. The riding must be undertaken with a spirit of adventure in mind. It is best to throw out the ideas of technical riding and technical equipment. A steady pedal stroke in a comfortable gear coupled with durable equipment and clothing will make the journey more enjoyable. Ample camping is available throughout the entire network.

For the purpose of this book, only the trails on the Wisconsin side of the border will be covered and more specifically a tough climbing section near Montreal. The Iron County network of trails extends from Manitowish in the south all the way to Hurley and the Bad River Indian Reservation in the north, covering nearly 150 miles in all. The entire county has been heavily mined and forested, hence the bounty of logging roads still available to ride on. The towns are small and considered tourist areas, though none could be described as anything but rustic. The streets are narrow and the buildings are old, making the area interesting to travel through at a leisurely pace. Eight waterfalls can be found on the network, from Lake of the Falls Dam in Mercer to Superior Falls near Saxon Harbor. The land in this northern country is both rugged and beautiful, with massive expanses of pines and water at every turn.

Across the border and into the Upper Peninsula of Michigan, two additional sets of trails are found. The Ehlco Mountain Bike Complex just north of Bergland, Michigan, offers 27 miles of trails, the majority on gravel roads with some double- and singletrack thrown in on the northeast side for fun. The Big Iron River splits and runs through the center of the system, adding some wild scenery. To the south the Pomeroy/Henry Lake Complex surrounds the northern town of Marenisco. The system expands to the east and west, covering over 100 miles of fire roads and singletrack. The area is desolate and shares land with a remote state prison. The roads skirt many lakes throughout the area and pass through some of the densest pine and hardwood forests in the country.

General location: Iron County, Wisconsin. Trailheads are found in many of the towns including Mercer, Montreal, Hurley, and Saxon. The trail described below and mapped out within this chapter departs from Montreal, just west of Hurley.

Technical Difficulty: Level 3.

Aerobic Level: Moderate to strenuous.

Tread: Doubletrack and paved path.

Length: 23 miles covered here, 300+ in entire network.

Elevation change: Logging roads are notoriously flat though in an area such as this climbing is inevitable at times, in most cases on a steady grade instead of a steep pitch. Trail 6 feels mountainous for flatlanders, with two climbs of 200+ feet.

Camping: There are camping areas in several locations throughout the Iron County system. Weber Lake County Park is north of Upson on the shore of Weber Lake, the farthest west point on the loop.

Season: The prime riding time is fall when the trees have changed and the weather is ripe for campfires and flannel shirts. This cooler weather is ideal for long days in the saddle and nights under the stars. Spring comes late this far north and snow is not unusual in April and even into early May. Winter is quite rugged, but because the trails are mainly run on logging roads and old rail beds, there are no restrictions on winter use. Snow piles high and sticks around from November to April, but frozen, plowed roads can present some of the most challenging rides around. When thawed and damp, however, they turn into miles and miles of sticky mud.

PINES & MINES

Ride 32

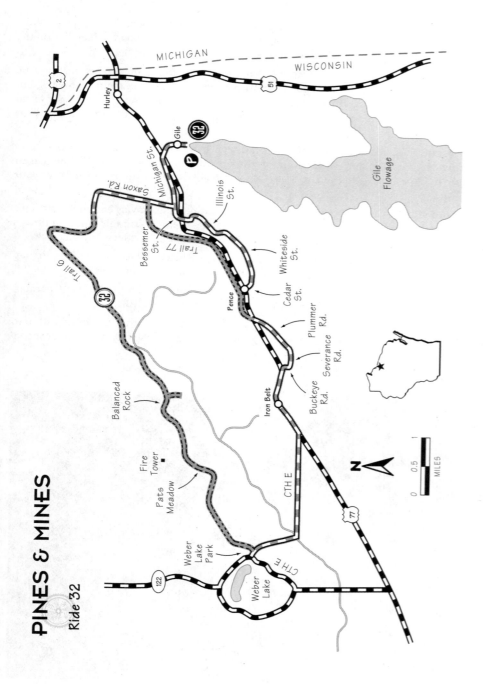

Fees: None.

Services: Montreal is quite small but is the obvious first stop for food and gasoline. East of here, Hurley is larger and has more options, and Ironwood, which lies on the Upper Peninsula, is even bigger and is the source of all other necessities.

Hazards: There are a wide variety of hazards to be found on the network, traffic being the foremost. Cars frequent the fire roads less than the main highways, but reckless driving is common even on these less regulated routes. Take care at all times, ride defensively, and consider strapping an amber light to the back of your bike.

Rescue: The roads in the forest are not well traveled and group travel is recommended. Use the map to get an injured rider out to a major road or to the nearest town. On a trip of this sort it is also a good idea to carry a full medical kit in your gear.

Land status: County logging roads and trails throughout. Pay attention to any signs indicating no trespassing or no bikes and abide by them. Using this guide and maps available at area chamber of commerce offices should help riders stay on track.

Maps: Stop in the Mercer Chamber of Commerce listed below for a complete map of the area. The selection of literature found there is quite complete.

Sources of more information: See Appendix A, in particular the Mercer Chamber of Commerce, Wisconsin Department of Tourism, and WORBA.

Finding the trail: When approaching Hurley from the south, turn left (west) onto Wisconsin Highway 77. Upon entering Montreal, park at the city hall, which serves as the trailhead.

Long, desolate dirt roads leading to the horizon are found throughout the Pines and Mines System.

THE RIDE

The best bet for planning an extended trip through the Pines and Mines Trail system is to stop in the town of Mercer at the Chamber of Commerce to stock up on maps and information on current trail conditions. The workers at this station are excellent help for on-the-spot planning. For the purposes of this book, only a small section is mapped and detailed below. The trail departs from the Montreal City Hall and departs west on Michigan Street.

After a mile on Michigan, turn left on Bessemer Street, follow it south across Wisconsin Highway 77, then turn right onto Illinois Street. After a short distance, turn left onto Whiteside and follow it for just under a mile before turning right onto Cedar Street. Follow Cedar back across WI 77 to where it meets with Trail 77. Turn left on Trail 77 and follow it southwest, parallel to WI 77. After a mile, turn left onto Plummer Road and follow it for a mile until you come to another set of cross streets. Plummer turns into Severance Road as you roll into this section.

Shortly after Plummer becomes Severance Road, turn right onto Buckeye Road. Head north briefly before turning left onto County Highway E. Of course, all this while you have been leaving a path of breadcrumbs to assure your safe return. This last turn thankfully marks the end of the cross street sections and County Highway E leads all the way out of Iron Belt to Weber Lake Park. The park is an excellent spot to stretch and drink before continuing on with the second half of the ride.

After the break, continue on the trail and head east along Trail 6. Several scenic vistas come up just off the sides of the trail within the first 2 miles. The riding here covers forest floor terrain and includes some rather tough climbs. After approximately 9 miles the off-road section hits Saxon Road, marking the end of Trail 6. Turn right onto Saxon and follow it south to Michigan Street. Turn left on Michigan to return to the Montreal City Hall. For another scenic view, continue past the trailhead and south into Gile [approximately 1 mile] to view Gile Falls pouring into the Gile Flowage. The vista offers another excellent place to stretch and relax.

Chequamegon Area Mountain Bike Association Trails

The Chequamegon Area Mountain Bike Association (CAMBA) trails in the far northwest corner of the state offer the premier Wisconsin off-road experience. The trails surround small towns and villages whose names have forever become tied to the sport of mountain biking. Drummond, Delta, Hayward, Seeley, and of course Cable are all familiar names in the biker's vocabulary. As Moab is to Utah and Big Bear is to California, Cable is to Wisconsin. It is the destination to which all serious mountain bikers in the state at one time or another find themselves drawn. All told, the CAMBA system covers over 300 miles of trails on a 1,600-square-mile section of land that CAMBA has taken upon themselves to manage and maintain.

As the name suggests, the setting is that of the Chequamegon National Forest, a venerable sea of pine and hardwood forest. The world is spread out here, with towns widely spaced across the land, interconnected by dirt logging roads. These logging roads form a large part of the CAMBA network, though terrain diversity is the big draw and everything is found here from sweet singletrack to paved, scenic roads. Though the word "paved" is used here, this is an off-road sector of the state and only a few sections of riding are on asphalt; the rest is all directly on dirt. The CAMBA area has it all and serves riders from beginner to expert. The rides are lined up in six distinct clusters from north to south, with those in the north being the most expansive and desolate and trails in the south presenting more technical terrain. All trails are well marked, with signs throughout letting riders not only know that they are still on the right path but also pinpointing their exact location by means of a numerical system.

The Seeley and Hayward clusters are the first that travelers approaching from the south encounter, and both are filled with riding of all sorts. Big climbing, technical singletrack, and scenic cruising are but a few of the riding types to choose from. Even on days when you are burnt from earlier hammering, there is always something accessible to ride, if you just have to be out in the woods moving.

Just to the north, the Cable and Namakagon trails take off, covering heavily glaciated and rugged terrain. The trails begin to open up more and more and the extent of the marking efforts begins to show. A sunny summer afternoon in Cable is hard to beat for a die-hard Wisconsinite biker. A short drive north to Drummond, the Delta and Drummond clusters pick up. These are the wild ones, covering an enormous amount of ground and demanding a great deal of endurance from riders. This is a good part of the world in which to take it easy and learn to cruise. There is no sense in burning your legs in the first five miles when twenty more are coming your way.

While inside the CAMBA system, ride the trails with a watchful eye. This is a big wilderness, with wildly overgrown forests housing animals of all sorts from bears to chipmunks. Bald eagles and red-tailed hawks soar over lakes, and in the fields wild berries are ripe for picking in the warmer months. The area is a perfect setting for relaxed cruising and, for those with a competitive nature, racing in the form of the Chequamegon Fat Tire Festival and Firehouse 50. Be warned, however: the Fat Tire Festival fills up quickly each year and it isn't a bad idea to send in your registration a year in advance to hold your place.

The Chequamegon area is the legendary center of Wisconsin mountain biking, so make certain to take advantage of its existence.

33

Hayward Cluster

The Hayward Cluster is the farthest south of all the CAMBA trails and for those just arriving the first possible stop on the road leading to Cable. Hayward is a legendary place in Wisconsin lore, known for decades as one of the toughest logging towns in all the north. The endless span of trees brought brawny men to the area for work, ready to take on the hardship of the north woods. I would guess many of their descendants are still here, still rough and ready but now pedaling mountain bikes through the forest with thick thighs and calves passed on from generations gone by. These days, the roughness of the town has been toned down a little though it is easy to see its roots after a few days on the trails in the elements.

There is only one trailhead at this cluster and one connecting trail leading to the rest of the network. Six trails are laid out running from Hayward northeast and into the Seeley cluster. The first path encountered out of the parking lot at the Mosquito Brook Trailhead is the Whitetail Trail, covering 4.5 miles of single- and doubletrack paths with a small section on the road. A small portion of this covers the famed Birkebeiner Trail, the site of North America's most important cross-country ski race. The Birkie Trail is also ridable as a mountain bike course, though good judgment must be used by riders when evaluating trail conditions. It is important not to ride on the trail in wet conditions, in order to maintain its groomed appearance. The trail covers a total of 26 miles in the summer and, after departing the Whitetail Trail, rolls through surrounding hills to the northeast, making stops at the County Highway OO trailhead and finishing at the Telemark Resort. The riding is on wide grass paths with singletrack worn in at places.

CAMBA–HAYWARD CLUSTER
Ride 33

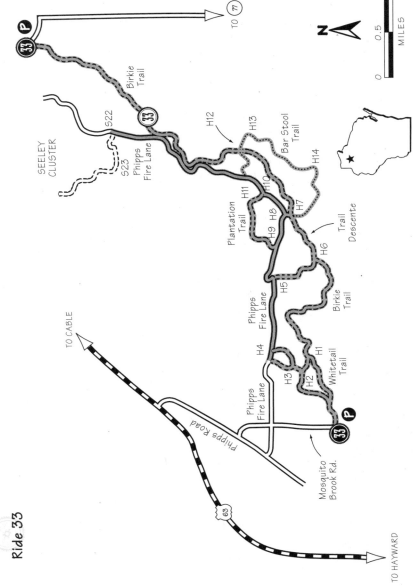

SEELEY CLUSTER

S22

S23

Phipps Fire Lane

Birkie Trail

H12

H13

Bar Stool Trail

H14

Plantation Trail

H11

H10

H9 H8

H7

H6

Trail Descente

H5

Phipps Fire Lane

Birkie Trail

H4

H3 H2 H1

Whitetail Trail

Phipps Fire Lane

Mosquito Brook Rd.

Phipps Road

TO CABLE

TO HAYWARD

N

MILES

The Phipps Firelane, in existence since the early part of the century, connects to the northern pinnacle of the Whitetail Trail. This dirt road covers nearly 8 miles when measured from the trailhead to the point where it connects to the Seeley Cluster. The riding is fast and furious on earth packed hard by truck tires. This is a quick route to get into some of the trails further back in the cluster.

There are three loops set back in the forest that round out the Hayward area biking experience. All three are accessible by either the Birkebeiner Trail or Phipps Firelane, depending on how quickly you want to get there. The Trail Descente is the first loop you will come across, logging in at 8.6 miles including the ride out from the trailhead. The trail covers singletrack and doubletrack over a patch of terrain set into the hills. The Plantation Trail is next and is one of the few in the cluster not to brush up against the Birkie Trail. The trail covers dirt road for the most part with some double- and singletrack on the southern portion. The trail gets its name from the Red Pine plantation it runs through—a serene yet surreal expanse of land with rows and rows of trees spreading out as far as the eye can see.

The last of the loops and the one farthest out from the trailhead is the Bar Stool Trail, which covers just under 12 miles in all. The entire run is made on dirt roads, some on the Phipps Firelane, some on snowmobile trail roads. This is one of the densest sections of forest you will encounter in this area and, for a road ride, one of the more exciting as you sail through the forest listening to the whir of your bike going by the trees.

All in all the trail is great for venturing into deep woods in any season of the year. It also serves as a terrific spot for picking up the Birkebeiner Trail and riding it in its entirety, something every Wisconsin biker should do. For those anxious to get away from their steering wheel and behind their handlebars, this is a great introduction to what lies ahead.

General Location: 2.5 miles north of Hayward.

Technical Difficulty: Level 3.

Aerobic Level: Moderate.

Tread: Singletrack, doubletrack, and fire roads.

Length: Up to 51 miles.

Elevation Change: The hills in the area are numerous but gentle in comparison to the eskers farther north. Climbs in the 20- to 40-foot range are commonplace.

Camping: See Cable Cluster. Also try the KOA campground off U.S. Highway 63 in Hayward.

Season: May to November. The best time of year to ride is in the spring and fall when the temperatures are cooler and the bugs are dormant. In a place as dominated by trees as this, the fall is of course dazzling. Once snow has fallen the trail becomes the domain of cross-country skiers, and marring their paths with tread marks is not allowed.

Fees: The Mosquito Brook/Birkie Trail parking costs $5 per day or $30 for an annual pass. Stop in at the Cable Area Chamber of Commerce to see how you can become a member of the Chequamegon Area Mountain Bike Association and help support the trails.

Services: Toilets are at the trailhead. Everything else from food to bike repair can be found as you pass through the city of Hayward or north at Seeley.

Hazards: Watch for trucks on the fire roads, as speed limits are often ignored on these desolate roadways. Tree falls as always are found on networks as vast as CAMBA and it is appreciated by future riders if you move debris to the sides whenever possible (unless it creates a really cool obstacle to navigate around or over).

Rescue: Ride in groups whenever in an area this large, for safety reasons. Use the Phipps Firelane to get injured riders back to the parking lot. Hayward to the south is the closest town and the first stop in an emergency.

Land status: Sawyer County Forest.

Maps: Available at trailheads, or through CAMBA. The CAMBA package includes an area map and five cluster maps. See Appendix A.

Finding the trail: From Hayward follow US 63 north and turn right (east) onto Phipps Road after 3 miles. Follow Phipps Road for 1.75 miles to Phipps Firelane and turn right (east). Follow the fire lane just briefly until you reach Mosquito Brook Road. Turn right and go south 0.75 mile to the trailhead parking lot.

THE RIDE

The entire network is well marked with a numerical system, an H denoting that you are on the Hayward Cluster followed by a number stating where you are on the map. Leaving the parking lot on the Whitetail Trail the path quickly comes to a split. Stay to the right and follow the one-way path to the H1 marker. At this point the Birkebeiner Trail diverts and heads northeast where it picks up the Trail Descente at marker H6 within 1.5 miles. Staying on the Whitetail Trail, stay to the right at marker H3 and follow the one-way trail to H4 where the path meets Phipps Firelane. At this point, tired riders can head back to the trailhead and the more durable mountain bikers can continue on to the main loops.

Phipps Firelane heads due east through the river valley on a fast dirt road. At marker H5 the path meets with the Trail Descente Loop and breaks to the right on a one-way path. Within half a mile the trail picks up the Birkebeiner Trail briefly and follows it northeast to marker H7. The Birkebeiner Trail continues on to the east from this point and leads all the way to the CH OO trailhead and beyond. To the left (north), the trail continues for 500 feet or so to another intersection that picks up Phipps Firelane again. To the left is the start of the Plantation Trail, to the right is the beginning of the Bar Stool Trail. After completing either of these, ride back to the Mosquito Brook Trailhead to the south or on to the Seeley Cluster to the north using Phipps Firelane.

34

Seeley Cluster

The Seeley Cluster is the second stop on the road north into the CAMBA network. The trails here are tethered to the Hayward Cluster to the south and the Cable Cluster to the north by the Birkie Trail and Phipps Firelane. Those more zealous in their endeavors can bike all three connected networks without need of auto transportation in between. An entire day can easily be spent riding through the ridges and valleys surrounding the glacier-carved lakes of this north woods area. Taking a breather by one of the many lakes can be detrimental to the afternoon's ride however, as it is easy to be drawn into the silence and scenery of the surrounding land and the pleasant slumber that often follows.

Two trailheads serve the Seeley Cluster: Silverthorn Park off U.S. Highway 63, and the County Highway OO trailhead, which serves as a back-door entrance to the system. There are five trails in all, ranging from hard-packed doubletrack to paved roads. It can easily be said that there is riding to suit anyone's tastes in this section of the CAMBA network.

The trails are divided in two ways, those that border on the Cable Cluster, and those that border on the Hayward Cluster. The first trail leaving the Silverthorn lot is the Northern Lights Trail 5.2 miles, named for the road it parallels and of course for the Aurora Borealis that lights up the skies at night. The Northern Lights Trail is ridden almost entirely on paved roads leading back to the main off-road routes. The path carves through several low-lying cranberry bogs in the Namekagon River Valley. This is an easy ride, good for beginners or for those who have worn themselves out after days of hard riding and need to give their bodies a break.

To the east the next trail in the system is the Winding Pine Trail, which delves into some off-road riding on doubletrack and gravel roads. The trail covers 8.5 miles from the Silverthorn lot, crossing over the Birkie trail at a couple of points on its way out to the Lake Helane Trail farther east. The Lake Helane Trail covers nearly 15 miles when measured from the trailhead and offers some technical riding over a portion of the Chequamegon 40 race course. The majority of the ride is off-road on doubletrack with a small section of gravel road. The climbing is moderate with several longer climbs on minor grades. Descending can be a bit hairy at times, with both solid and loose rocks to contend with on the way down. The loop brushes up against the east side of Lake Helane, with a couple of inviting grassy rest stops along the way.

To the north, the Fire Tower Trail completes the northern section of the Seeley Cluster. The trail surrounds a bluff that was once home to the Seeley Fire Tower but is now just a bare hilltop. A spur heading to the center of the

CAMBA–SEELEY CLUSTER

Ride 34

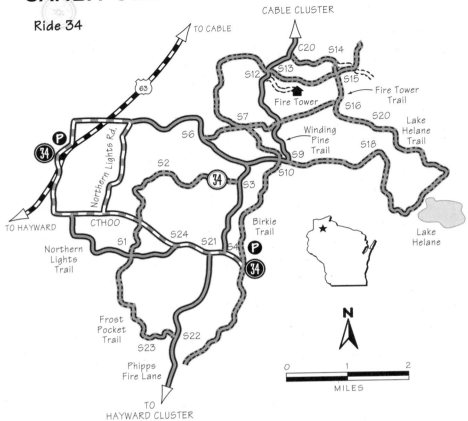

loop offers the toughest climb in the entire CAMBA network. The doubletrack path leads to the top of the bluff and a side detour leading off the opposite side acts as an expert-only descent back to the fire road at the base of the bluff. The entire loop covers just under 14 miles from the trailhead out and back.

To the south, the Frost Pocket Trail leads riders into the wilderness and south to the Hayward Cluster. The trail is one of the best known in the southern portion of CAMBA Trails, and one of the more difficult. It covers just under 10 miles of trails from the Silverthorn lot over doubletrack and gravel roads. The trail is named for the glacial landmarks found throughout the ride. Many of the depressions left behind by the sheer weight of the glaciers fill with cold night air produced by the shaded north woods forests. The air in these depressions stays cold year-round, supporting only hearty plant life in the form of lichens and some ferns. The pockets are also the first spots to receive frost. The ice age can also be thanked for the climbing

158

and descending found along the Frost Pocket Trail, high on the ridges and deep within the kettles.

General location: Trails depart from the north and east sides of the village of Seeley.

Technical Difficulty: Level 3.

Aerobic Level: Moderate.

Tread: Doubletrack, gravel, and pavement.

Length: Up to 50 miles.

Elevation change: The majority of the riding is done over rolling glaciated terrain, with climbs ranging from 20 to 40 feet each. The Fire Tower Trail, however, has a nasty climb to the top of the bluff which covers a good 150 feet of elevation at a sharp incline. The only thing that makes the extra effort of getting to the top worthwhile is the view . . . and the thrilling descent to follow . . . and the endorphins. When you really look at it, you come out way ahead for making the trek to the top.

Camping: See Cable Cluster. Also try the KOA campground off U.S. Highway 63 in Hayward.

Season: May to November. Fall is the most beautiful time of year to be here. Summer can sometimes be quite muggy and spring a little wet, but with the diverse mix of trails, there is something to ride in any season. In winter the trails area is used by skiers and is closed to bikers.

Fees: The CH OO/Birkie Trailhead parking costs $5 a day or $30 annually. Stop in at the Cable Area Chamber of Commerce to see how you can become a member of the Chequamegon Area Mountain Bike Association and help support the trails.

Services: Bathrooms and water are available at Silverthorn Park and at the County Highway OO parking lot. Seeley is the logical place to stop for food, gas, and bike parts.

Hazards: Watch out for the descent on the Fire Tower Trail, it's a lu-lu. On the Lake Helane route, caution should be taken when completing the descent on Boedecker Road as it meets Northern Lights Road. Loose gravel and tree falls are other hazards to watch for.

Rescue: Ride in groups whenever in an area this large in order to help your partners out in an emergency. Use the Phipps Firelane to get any injured riders back to the parking lot. Hayward to the south is the closest town and the first stop in an emergency.

Land status: Sawyer County Forest.

Maps: Available at trailheads, or through CAMBA. The CAMBA package includes an area map and five cluster maps. See Appendix A.

Finding the trail: Follow U.S. Highway 63 north from Hayward through Seeley and 0.5 mile past the intersection with County Highway OO. Turn left onto Park Road to find the Silverthorn Trailhead. To get to the CH OO trailhead lot, turn right (east) at the US 63/CH OO intersection and follow CH OO for 3.5 miles to the Birkebeiner Trailhead. The Birkebeiner is long and cuts through several trailhead parking lots. It is included in several CAMBA Clusters. You are midway through the Birkie Trail at this point.

The entire network is well marked with a numerical system, an "S" denoting that you are on the Seeley Cluster followed by a number indicating where you are on the map. Leaving the Silverthorn lot, follow the Northern Light S Trail northeast to Northern Lights Road. Turn right and go south for two miles to County Highway OO. At the T intersection, you can either continue straight to return to the lot or turn left to follow a snowmobile trail south. Marker S1 comes up within a mile on the snowmobile trail. At the S1 intersection, continuing straight leads riders onto the Frost Pocket Trail which runs in a clockwise direction onto Phipps Firelane. At the southernmost point the firelane continues on to the Hayward Cluster. By staying to the right, however, you can make the full Frost Pocket circuit. The CH OO parking lot is 0.33 mile east of the Frost Pocket Loop.

Riders turning left at the S1 intersection will follow the snowmobile trail past markers S2 and S3 to Boedecker Road and the Winding Pine Trail. This leads in a clockwise direction, leaving Boedecker Road within a mile and turning right, traversing forest and hills to marker S8. Turning right at marker S8 will take riders down the Lake Helane Trail, a counterclockwise route riding past Spider Lake, Smith Lake, and of course Lake Helane before returning to the S8 intersection. Riders turning left at S8 will be on the Fire Tower Trail, which connects to the Cable Cluster at its northernmost point. About 0.5 mile after leaving the intersection a spur to the right leads up to the former site of the Seeley fire tower. The spur is a two-way route allowing riders to return to the main loop or, for those a bit more brave, to try a quicker and more technical descent found on the opposite side. Turn right at the base of the descent to return to marker S8.

From any of the trails, return to Boedecker Road to get back to the Silverthorn Trailhead. Follow Boedecker from marker S9 through S6 and then for another mile to the intersection with Northern Lights Road. Be careful to keep your speed under control coming up to this intersection. Follow Northern Lights left to CH OO, cross the old Chicago and Northwestern railroad grade, and follow the road north to the lot.

35

Cable Cluster

The Cable Cluster is located at the heart of the CAMBA system. The name Cable is synonymous with great mountain biking, and the Telemark resort— which serves as one of the two trailheads for this cluster—is the finish for the annual Chequamegon Fat Tire Festival race. The area is densely wooded and the terrain shows the distinct markings of glaciation, with esker ridges and kettle depressions as landmarks on many trails. Just over 45 miles of trail are found here, covering a variety of terrain from singletrack to paved and gravel roads. While the riding is tough and appears to be fairly spread out in terms of distance, in comparison to some of the CAMBA riding further to the north, it is far more technical and condensed. This allows riders to open up and fly without feeling they are burning themselves out to early in the ride. The parking lot is never more than eight miles away.

The trail names for this cluster are some of the most well known in the state. The Short and Fat Trail is the actual route riders take during the annual Fat Tire Festival, covering everything from singletrack to gravel and paved roads. The riding is tough because of the distance, just over 15 miles, but several cut-offs allow riders who have had enough to cash in early. The woods fly by in a blur as the trails roll through the hills, helping to carry momentum from each descent through the next climb.

The Esker Trail and Nature Trail are the two most challenging of the five loops, both distinctly different from each other. The Esker Trail is just that, a singletrack roller coaster laid out along the back of an enormous esker left behind by glacial washout that piled up in the shape of a monstrous snake. The downhills can get out of hand at times, with riders building up a great deal of speed on fairly uneven terrain.

The Nature Trail is substantially less difficult than the Esker though still covering all single- and doubletrack, some of the best in the north woods. The riding is technical and challenging, demanding that riders use their entire body to maneuver the bike over and around obstacles and terrain variations. Together, the Esker and Nature Trails supply riders coming to the CAMBA system for the first time the excitement they dreamed they would find in this, Wisconsin's mountain bike promised land.

The Sleigh Trail and Spring Creek Trails both log in at around 10 miles and, while not technical, are tough rides forcing mountain bikers to exert themselves and test their endurance. The Sleigh Trail is aptly named, following an old logging sleigh route throughout the pines on single- and doubletrack and logging roads. The terrain is rolling and short climbs demand bursts of energy and powerful legs. The Spring Creek Trail is a gravel road tour that offers no cutoffs for tired riders. Once you've headed out on

CAMBA–CABLE CLUSTER

Ride 35

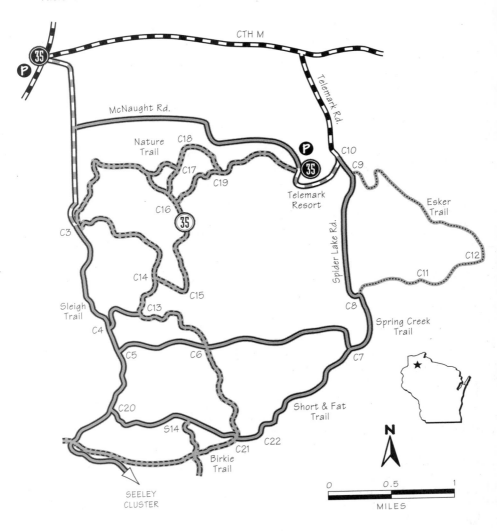

this route, you're committed. The scenery, however, is beautiful and, though ten miles of bumpy gravel roads might seem killer at the onset, the miles drift by and the mind is mesmerized by the colors of the foliage surrounding the path.

General location: The trails start on the outskirts of Cable, two blocks east of the center of town and spread out to the southeast. Many of the trails also start a bit further out of town at Telemark.

Technical Difficulty: Level 3 to 4.

162

Aerobic Level: Moderate.

Tread: Singletrack and doubletrack, paved and gravel.

Length: Up to 47 miles.

Elevation change: Climbing on the Esker Trail is at times extreme and covers 80 to 100 feet at a time. The majority of the remaining trails are ridden over rolling hills with 20- to 30-foot climbs the norm.

Camping: Namekagon Lake Campground is 12 miles northeast of Cable off County Highway D. The site has 33 units, drinking water, and a swimming area. A daily fee is required.

Season: Telemark begins catering to skiers as soon as the snow starts to fall in late October and early November. Winter in this area means snowmobiles and four-wheel drive vehicles. The riding is best in early spring just after the thaw and in fall when the trees have turned. Midsummer riding is also very pleasant, though a bit more crowded with both people and bugs.

Fees: None. Stop in at the Cable Area Chamber of Commerce to see how you can become a member of the Chequamegon Area Mountain Bike Association and help support the trails.

Services: Stop in Cable to find all necessities—food, gas, lodging, and bike repair. The Cable Chamber of Commerce is an excellent place to stop for information on the trails, as is the Telemark Resort gift shop at the Telemark Trailhead.

Hazards: Watch for high speeds on downhills; several of them have hidden dips that are not easily spotted from the top. Tree falls will occasionally block the path but because these trails lie at the heart of Cable they are well ridden and blockages are cleared out quickly. There is one water crossing that will introduce a new technique to many riders: Unless the water is clear enough to see that the bottom is comprised of rocks, it is never a good idea to ride in with the front tire and hope that the base is solid. The best technique is to pull the front tire into the air and ride through on the back tire. As the bottom starts to pull in the back tire, the front tire should slap down on the opposite bank helping to pull the bike through and out onto dry ground. Keep in mind, this works best on streams approximately 6 feet across. Use your own ingenuity for wider passes.

Rescue: For assistance, go to the village of Cable (the Chamber of Commerce is at the corner of County Highway M and Main Street). Or stop in at the desk of the Telemark Resort.

Land status: Bayfield County Forest and Telemark Resort.

Maps: Available at trailheads or through CAMBA. The CAMBA package includes an area map and five cluster maps.

Sources of more information: See Appendix A.

Finding the trail: This cluster has 2 trailheads. The Cable Trailhead is located at the center of town. After entering Cable from the south on U.S. Highway 63, turn right (east) on County Highway M. After 2 blocks turn right (south) onto Randysek Road and drive 1 block to First Street. Turn right and drive half a block to the old Cable schoolhouse. To find the Telemark Resort Trailhead you need to pass up the Cable Trailhead on CH M. Travel 2 miles east out of Cable on CH M. Turn right (south) on Telemark Road and follow it for 2 miles until you reach the parking lot of Telemark Resort.

Yet another climb on the back of the Esker in the Cable Cluster.

THE RIDE

The entire network is easily marked with a numerical system, a "C" denoting that you are on the Cable Cluster followed by a number indicating where you are on the map. Leaving the Cable Trailhead the route starts off on the Short and Fat Trail heading south. As you will find out quickly, many of the loops cover the same ground at times, overlapping one another a great deal throughout the cluster. At marker C3 the Power Line cutoff heads east and lets riders return to the trailhead early. Continuing straight, the Sleigh Trail breaks off from the route within the next mile at marker C4. The Sleigh Trail cuts across the center of the network through the hills and around the base of Mount Telemark. After passing marker C19 the trail reaches the Telemark Resort within 0.66 miles and cuts back to the west.

Back on the Short and Fat route, continuing straight at marker C4 takes riders south to the junction with the Seeley Cluster Fire Tower Trail. Stay to the left at marker C20 and follow the route to the east. Within a mile the Birkebeiner trail comes up at marker C21 and cuts across some of the more hilly terrain in the entire CAMBA network on its way to the Telemark Resort, four miles to the north. Continuing straight at marker C21 keeps riders on the Short and Fat route on Spider Lake Road. At marker C7 the trail cuts back to the west and carries riders across the center of network, onto the Birkie Trail and north past markers C13, C14, and back to C3.

To find the Esker Trail from Telemark Resort, follow Telemark Road back toward County Highway M until it meets Spider Lake Road. Follow this for

0.25 miles to the singletrack path on the left. The loop heads out along the back of an esker around the surrounding forest and meadow until it reaches marker C8 and turns back toward the resort on Spider Lake Road.

The Spring Creek Trail originates at Telemark Resort and follows CH M to Spider Lake Road. From there it heads south to Timber Trail Road at marker C7. The trail turns right and travels north for 2.5 miles to Randysek Road, where it turns right and continues on to McNaught Road. Follow McNaught to the right and back to the resort.

It should be noted that after the 1997 season the status of the Nature Trail was questionable due to erosion. Check postings and information at the Cable Area Chamber of Commerce to see if it is ridable before departing. The Sleigh Trail and Short and Fat Trail both are slated to be rerouted in 1998, also due to erosion.

36

Namakagon Cluster

The Namakagon Cluster is located due east of Cable and is one of the more diverse sections of riding found in the entire network. The trails start off from the Town Hall Trailhead on the east and Rock Lake Trailhead on the west and sprawl out to the south stemming from some of the main logging roads. This is such a wide expanse of trails, fifty people can set off at the same time from the trailheads and only cross paths once the rest of the day.

The Namakagon Trails are a system unto themselves and not connected to any of the other clusters, though a 5- to 6-mile ride down Rock Lake Road (FR 207) will take you to the Cable and Seeley clusters. There are four marked trails which intertwine into an elaborate system of routes. The Namakagon Trail is the first one riders come to after leaving the Town Hall Trailhead parking lot. The trail covers double- and singletrack on its 10- mile route and is very conducive to heavy hammering, wide open big-ring riding through the hardwoods and out to the vast birch stands.

The Patsy Lake Trail connects to the cluster at the southern end and takes riders out around Patsy Lake. The ride is certainly not for the weak or inexperienced, as the name might suggest, but instead for the more advanced rider trained in using body language to maneuver through tight, wooded singletrack. This 12.5-mile route, predominately double- and singletrack, covers some excellent technical riding. Included on this ride is one of the strangest landmarks of any of the trails. Quite a distance out on the Namakagon Trail, a 1950s-era Chevy lies rotting high up on an embankment,

CAMBA–NAMAKAGON CLUSTER

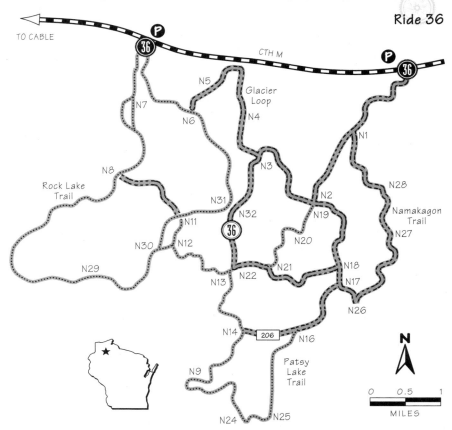

having perhaps crashed there during a late-night joyride on the fire road that runs by it.

Leaving the Rock Lake Trailhead the first path is the Rock Lake Trail, a route which covers singletrack throughout and is one of the more technically challenging in all the north woods. The climbing is at times horrendous but is always rewarded with screaming downhills. The trail is set into a series of glacial pits and valleys that make up a thin swath of land running south almost to Sawyer County. The trail skirts the edge of several lakes on its circuit.

The aptly named Glacier Trail completes the cluster and is connected to the town hall portion of the cluster at two intersections. The majority of the riding is off-road on double- and singletrack with a small section over gravel roads, consistently ducking through kettles. As with the Namakagon Trail, this is excellent for fast, open riding through glorious north woods scenery. It will take even an advanced rider a full day's riding to cover all the trails in this system.

General location: 8 miles east of Cable.

Technical Difficulty: Level 3.

Aerobic Level: Moderate.

Tread: Singletrack and doubletrack.

Length: Up to 43 miles.

Elevation Change: Both the Namakagon and Glacier Trails are primarily flat to rolling, with climbing on gentle grades. The Patsy Lake Trail has climbs in short bursts covering 20 to 30 feet of elevation at most. The Rock Lake Trail has a great deal more climbing, most of which is in the 30- to 40-foot range but at steep inclines.

Camping: See Cable Cluster. Also try Helm Point County Grounds off of County Highway M, 1 mile west of Rock Lake.

Season: May to November. Because of the concentration of hardwoods in this section the fall colors are particularly striking. The trails are also pleasant in spring and summer, with temperatures kept at bay by the shade of the forest. Spring can be a bit damp from snow melt, and the Patsy Lake Trail becomes impassable at times.

Fees: USDA Forest Service parking costs $2 per day or $8 for an annual pass at Rock Lake. Stop in at the Cable Area Chamber of Commerce to see how you can become a member of the Chequamegon Area Mountain Bike Association and help support the trails.

Services: There are toilets at the Rock Lake lot and a pay phone at the Town Hall Trailhead lot. Stop in the town of Cable for gas, food, and information.

Hazards: Watch for narrow passes between trees on the Patsy Lake Trail. Tree falls are also a possible hazard, though the trails are quite wide and most obstacles are easily avoidable. Please report locations of downed trees to CAMBA. Keep the front

The author returning from a day in the saddle on the dirt paths of the Namakagon Cluster.
Laura Hutchins Photo

tire light when going through water and use good judgment in picking a line. Stay on high ground whenever possible. Although it's fun to be muddy, dry equipment works better.

Rescue: Ride in groups and in case of emergency, get back to one of the trailheads to summon help from the passing highway.

Land status: Chequamegon National Forest.

Maps: Available at trailheads, or through CAMBA. The CAMBA package includes an area map and five cluster maps.

Sources of more information: See Appendix A.

Finding the trail: From Cable follow County Highway M east for 7 miles. The Rock Lake Trailhead is on the right side of the road. Continuing on CH M the Town Hall Parking Lot Trailhead is 3 more miles on the right.

THE RIDE

The entire network is well marked with a numerical system, an "N" denoting that you are on the Namakagon Trail followed by a number indicating where you are on the map. Departing from the town hall the Namakagon Trail heads south along a wide dirt and gravel path. At marker N2 the trail cuts back to the right and heads east to the first intersection, where it connects to the Rock Lake Trails at marker N3. Stay to the left to continue on the Namakagon Trail heading south. A mile farther at marker N22 an intersection is found with several options. To the left the Namakagon Trail continues as it starts the trek back across the network past markers N21, 17, and 26, then south for three miles to the parking lot.

Turning left at marker N22 puts riders on the Patsy Lake Trail. Immediately on the right a path (N13) leads off to the Rock Lake Trails. Continuing on singletrack past Patsy Lake, the route passes Fire Road 206 and continues south before turning back, passing marker N16, crossing the Namekagon Trail at N 17, and returning to the N2 intersection. Stay to the left here to do another loop or turn right to return to the lot.

From the Rock Lake lot the Rock Lake Trail heads south past the fork at N7 (it doesn't matter which of the two you take) and down to marker N8. Staying to the right will keep riders on the Rock Lake Trail which travels in a counterclockwise arc, while turning left will take riders on to the Glacier Trail; the two intersect again at N11. From marker N11 the Glacier Trail completes its circuit through a long series of hills, meeting with the Town Hall trails at two intersections. The Rock Lake Loop cuts across the center of the system meeting with the Glacier Loop at N6 and returning together to the trailhead.

37

Drummond Cluster

The Drummond Trails are the second farthest north of the six CAMBA clusters and are actually tethered to the Delta Trails to the north by doubletrack. The system is served by two trailheads, both located at the center of the cluster in the town of Drummond. The town is known for its logging history, and those not familiar with the timber industry may feel as if they've been dropped into another world. The trails departing Drummond Town Park pass through the center of town, and riders have a chance to see the massive logging equipment and piles of timbers strapped to the backs of flat-bed trucks, before the trails head out for wilderness.

This is one of the more relaxed areas of riding in the CAMBA network and the first that beginning riders should investigate. For scenery it is hard to beat, with beautiful wooded bluffs and quiet northern lakes edging the trail. Much of the riding is done on the paved and gravel roads surrounding the northern portion of the town and outlying areas. Trails departing from Drummond Town Park are primarily paved or gravel. Trails departing from the Drummond Ski Trails parking lot are ridden off-road on double- and singletrack.

The trails north of town cover a great deal of distance and are ideal for riders looking for the beauty of this north country. The idea behind these loops is not to turn record-setting times or find hairy technical descents but instead to enjoy the views of wildlife, wildflowers, and deep, dark lakes. The Cisco Lake Trail is the first encountered after leaving the trailhead, covering 4.5 miles on gravel and paved roads. Beyond that the Star Lake Trail at 11.5 miles, Reynard Lake trail at 15 miles, Pigeon Lake Trail at 11.5 miles, and Horse Pasture Trail at 18 miles round out the northern section of the cluster, all over gravel and paved roads.

Even on the southern routes, which cover more doubletrack, the idea remains the same, the off-road trails providing less in terms of difficult terrain and more in regards to natural beauty. The 4-mile Antler Trail and 5-mile Jack Rabbit trail are ridden on singletrack. Both provide a gentle introduction to singletrack, off-road riding, allowing beginners to ease into the skills necessary for more technical riding. The Boulevard Trail is also found in the southern portion of the cluster and covers double- and singletrack on its way out to Owen Lake and back. The riding is a bit tougher, endurance-wise, than the other two off-road trails but nothing in comparison to the rides farther south within the Drummond Cluster.

General location: Directly north and south of Drummond.

Technical Difficulty: Level 2 to 3.

Aerobic Level: Moderate.

CAMBA–DRUMMOND CLUSTER

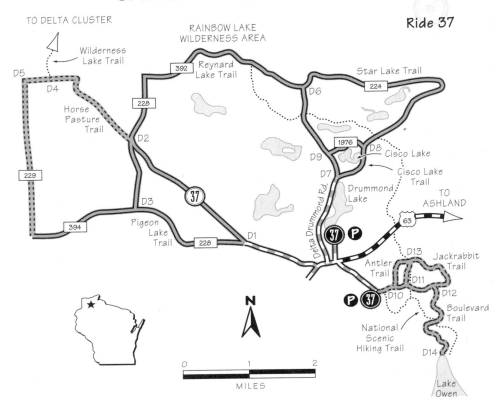

Tread: Singletrack and doubletrack, gravel and paved roads.

Length: Up to 75 miles.

Elevation change: The trails range from very flat to rolling, a good portion being over the fairly level logging roads in the area.

Camping: Two Lakes Campground is three miles southeast of Drummond off Fire Road 213. The site features 90 units (7 of which are walk-in), drinking water, and swimming. A daily fee is required. The Perch Lake Campground is 5 miles south of Delta on Delta Drummond Road, and has 16 units. Drinking water is available and a daily fee is required.

Season: May through November. The ski trails as always are the domain of the skiers after the first snowfall, and biking is prohibited.

Fees: None. Stop in at the Cable Area Chamber of Commerce to see how you can become a member of the Chequamegon Area Mountain Bike Association and help support the trails.

Services: Restrooms are found at the Town Park Trailhead. Gas, food, and water are all available in the town of Drummond. Travel south to Hayward and Seeley for bike repair.

Hazards: Watch for traffic on all paved and gravel roads. The shoulders are narrow and speeds of 45+ mph are common. A flashing amber light is a good idea on these roads, even in daylight hours, to increase visibility.

Rescue: Ride in groups and return to the town of Drummond to summon help in case of emergency.

Land status: Chequamegon National Forest.

Maps: Available at trailheads, or through CAMBA. The CAMBA package includes an area map and five cluster maps.

Sources of more information: See Appendix A.

Finding the trail: When entering Drummond from the south on U.S. Highway 63, the town park is 1 block past Delta Drummond Road on the left (north). The road to the park runs parallel to the old Chicago and Northwestern Railroad track running through town. The Drummond Ski Trails Trailhead is a block farther along US 63 on the right (south). Turn onto Lake Owen Drive and follow it for 0.75 mile to the trailhead on the left.

THE RIDE

The entire network is easily marked with a numerical system, a "D" denoting that you are on the Drummond Cluster followed by a number indicating where you are on the map. Five of the eight loops in the Drummond Cluster depart from the Town Park Trailhead. The Cisco Lake Trail is closest to the town and covers 4.5 miles on paved and gravel roads. The route is beautiful during any season and even the most advanced riders will be happy they took the time to cruise it. Travel out from the trailhead to U.S. Highway 63, turn right onto Delta Drummond Road and follow it north to marker D7. Stay to the right and at D8 turn left to follow the Cisco Lake Trail west and then back to the lot, or stay to the right to pick up the Star Lake Trail.

The Star Lake Trail starts off on the same road as the Cisco but covers 11.5 miles, and accesses several more north woods lakes. The riding is again over gravel and paved roads, but the distance makes up for what the trail lacks in technical challenge. The North County Scenic Trail cuts across this section of the cluster and, while bike access to this trail is permitted, it is not promoted or necessary with the amount of approved mountain bike trails in the area. In 3.5 miles, or three-quarters of the way around the Star Lake Loop, marker D6 approaches, connecting riders to the Reynard Lake Trail.

The Reynard Lake, Horse Pasture, and Pigeon Lake Trails make up the western half of the cluster. The Reynard Loop comes in at just under 15 miles and covers most of its ground on gravel roads. The path follows Fire Road 392 across the north end of the cluster before heading south along Fire Road 228. The riding is not technical and 15 miles blows by quickly in the midst of such vivid scenery. The north section of the trail travels through more hilly terrain than the south and offers more in the way of lakes and marshland areas. Watch for postings regarding the Rainbow Lake Wilderness area to the north, which prohibits bicycles. The trail defines the southern border of the wilderness area.

At marker D2 two options are available. Turning to the right riders will join Fire Road 396 which leads onto the Horse Pasture Trail. Two miles in at marker D4, a trail heading north connects the Drummond Cluster to the massive Delta cluster farther north. Continuing straight through the intersection at D2 takes riders onto the Pigeon Lake Trail. One mile along, the trail turns left (east) onto Fire Road 228 which merges into County Highway N within two miles and returns to the trailhead in another 1.5 miles.

38

Delta Cluster

The Delta Cluster is the farthest north of the CAMBA clusters and is by far the most widespread of all the trail networks. It was created by local trail activists who apparently got carried away and continued to push farther and farther out in their marking efforts until they created the massive expanse that exists today. The mountain biking found in this area is true north woods riding, covering a great deal of distance through rugged areas in vast wilderness. The loops in the Delta Cluster range from the small village of Delta north to the town of Iron River. The area is served by four trailheads, with six trails in all found in the cluster. The riding varies from gravel roads in and around Delta to singletrack within the pine and hardwood forest. Just as the terrain is varied, so is the forest, with everything from dense, old-growth pine, to birch stands, to recently forested lands, to desolate, rolling hills, barren of trees and filled only with stumps. The entire trail network covers just over 100 miles all together and, as mentioned earlier, is therefore the most widespread of any of the six CAMBA clusters.

The best-known path in this cluster is the Tall Pines Trail, leading riders out to the west from the Tall Pines Trailhead on a 12.5-mile loop. The trail covers singletrack and doubletrack and a short portion of logging road. The distance is tiring and a couple of good-sized climbs are included. Most CAMBA literature will tell you that this cluster, and more specifically this trail, is a great place to pick blueberries in the summer. Packing your normal supply of trail mix is still advised but spicing it up with fresh berries will add some local flavor to the mix.

The Twin Bear Trail is the largest of all the loops, coming in at nearly 20 miles. The Pine Barrens Cutoff bisects the loop allowing riders to swing in a bit early, 2 miles earlier to be exact, but not a great deal of difference in the

CAMBA–DELTA CLUSTER

Ride 38

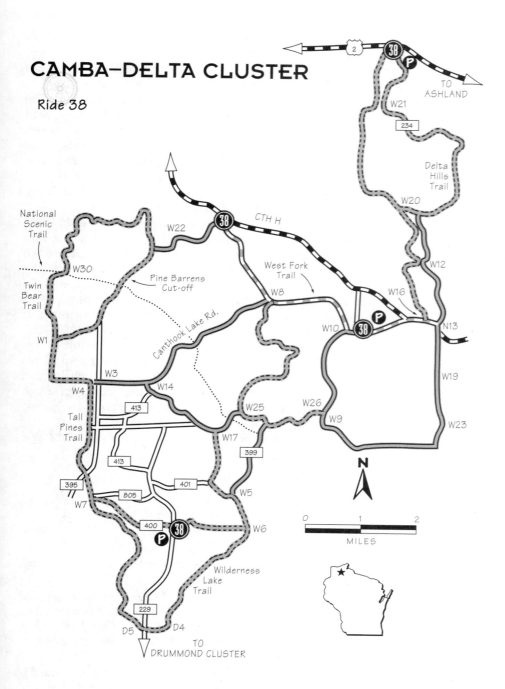

2

38
P

TO
ASHLAND

W21

234

Delta
Hills
Trail

W20

National
Scenic
Trail

W22

38

CTH H

West Fork
Trail

W12

W30

W16

W8

N13

Twin
Bear
Trail

Pine Barrens
Cut-off

W10

38
P

W1

Canthook Lake Rd.

W19

W3

W14

W25

W26

W9

W23

W4

413

Tall
Pines
Trail

W17

413

399

395

401

805

W5

W7

400

38
P

W6

229

Wilderness
Lake
Trail

D5

D4

TO
DRUMMOND CLUSTER

N

0   1   2
MILES

grand scheme of things. The Pine Barrens are just that— barren, rolling hills of stumps with a few lonely trees still standing tall on wind swept ridges. The Twin Bear Trail, on the other hand, covers the deep, dark forest of pines on a combination of singletrack, logging roads, and paved county roads.

The West and South Fork trails both depart the Delta Lake Trailhead. The two take their name from the forks of the White River which they each follow. The South Fork Trail is the easier of the two and one of the few rides suitable for beginners in this area. The entire loop is ridden on roads, some paved, some gravel, but all easier than pounding over singletrack. The West Fork covers some road riding but also gets off-road for some very cool singletrack riding. Between the towering pines and the rushing White River, this is one of the more picturesque rides in the CAMBA system.

The Wilderness Lake Trail and Delta Hills Trails round out the six loops found in the Delta Cluster. Wilderness Lake serves not only as an excellent intermediate loop but also as the connector to the Drummond trails to the south. The trail is primarily on doubletrack winding its way through the vast forest lands. The Delta Hills trail to the north is by far the hardest in the cluster in terms of endurance. The hills will get to you, no matter your condition, by the end of the 16-mile circuit. A bit of everything is found in terms of terrain from single- and doubletrack to roads.

It will take most riders a couple of days to cover all the ground in this entire system. Camping is available in the area, perfect for setting up a base camp and riding out from it to the trails each morning. Fishing in area streams and lakes is excellent, too, so remember to bring your license and pole. The fish grow freakishly large in the cold, vast north country.

General location: Trails sprawl out to the north and west of the village of Delta, extending as far as U.S. Highway 2 to the north.

Technical Difficulty: Level 2.

Aerobic Level: Moderate to strenuous.

Tread: Singletrack and doubletrack, gravel and paved roads.

Length: Up to 75 miles.

Elevation change: All of the loops involve climbing, most of which is in rolling hills with 20- to 30-foot gradual changes in elevation. A few climbs in the 50- to 75-foot range are found over gradual grades.

Camping: The Perch Lake Campground is 5 miles south of Delta on Delta Drummond Road, and has 16 units. Drinking water is available and a daily fee is required. The Wanoka Lake North Forest Campground, found at the Wanoka Lake Trailhead, is also a good bet. Campsites are also at the Twin Bear and Delta Lake campgrounds; both are county-owned and serve as trailheads for this section.

Season: This is a very good trail system for early spring, especially if the ground is too wet in the southern clusters for riding; the base of the trails drains very well. Fall is beautiful in this part of the world, with so many trees in vivid fall colors. The temperatures are crisp in the fall and very conducive to hard, long rides. Winter is brutal in this area, especially once the snow has begun to pile up. Summer is the prime season, with more bikers and bugs then the others, but more sun and open trails as well.

Fees: None. Stop in at the Cable Area Chamber of Commerce to see how you can become a member of the Chequamegon Area Mountain Bike Association and help support the trails.

Services: Water and toilets are supplied at the Twin Bear Trailhead, Delta Lake Trailhead, Wanoka Lake, and in Iron River. Bike repair is available in Delta as well as in Cable and Seeley to the south. Gas and groceries are in Drummond.

Hazards: Getting lost. Take a map, a compass and a friend. The trails in this part of the woods are often quite far from civilization and riding alone is not advised. Be certain to take along adequate water, a PowerBar in case of emergency, and the proper tools for repairing minor mechanical difficulties. The trails are well maintained, but tree falls are bound to be encountered in a system as large as this. Try to move any manageable pieces to the edge of the trail to help other riders. After rains, watch for washed-out sections on downhills.

Rescue: Always ride in a group this far into the wilderness. In case of emergency get out onto one of the logging roads and begin to make your way back to the trailhead. The roads are not well traveled but do improve your chance of being picked up from the trail.

Land status: Chequamegon National Forest, with trails managed and maintained by the Chequamegon Area Mountain Bike Association.

Maps: Available at trailheads, or through CAMBA. The CAMBA package includes an area map and five cluster maps.

Sources of more information: See Appendix A.

Finding the trail: The Delta Cluster has 4 separate trailheads. When entering the town of Drummond from the south on U.S. Highway 63, turn left (west) on County Highway N. Follow CH N for 6 miles to Beck Road (Fire Road 229). Turn right (north) and follow Beck Road for 5.5 miles to the Tall Pines Trailhead on the right.

The Delta Lake Park Trailhead is located just west of Delta on CH H. Follow CH H 0.5 mile to Scenic Drive; turn left (west) on Scenic Drive and follow it for 1.5 miles to the trailhead on the left at the entrance to the Delta Lake County Campground.

The Wanoka Lake Trailhead is most easily located from the town of Iron River. Follow US 2 out of Iron River east for 6 miles. Turn right (south) on Fire Road 241. The trailhead is in 0.13 mile. The last of the trailheads, Twin Bear Lake Park, is also easiest found from Iron River. Follow CH H south out of Iron River 6 miles to the trailhead at the Twin Bear Lake Campground.

THE RIDE

The entire network is easily marked with a numerical system, a "W" denoting that you are on the Drummond Cluster followed by a number indicating where you are on the map. From the Tall Pines Trailhead the path leads away in both directions along Fire Road 400. To the east the path travels 1.5 miles to marker W7 where it turns north. At marker W4 the trail splits. To the right the Tall Pines Trail continues on for one mile to W14, heads back south past the entrance to the northern portion of the cluster at W17, and on to W6 where it turns left and follows Fire Road 400 to the trailhead.

Turn left at W4 onto the Twin Bear Trail. The trail heads west for 0.5 mile before abruptly turning north. 0.5 mile past the turn the Pine Barrens Cutoff takes off across the network from marker W1 and climbs across several barren hills on its way to the far side. Continuing straight at W1 on the main Twin Bear Trail, the route ducks through the forest before rejoining the Pine Barren Cutoff 3 miles later and continuing east to the Twin Bear Trailhead. The trail continues on its long trek south, staying left at W8, left at W14, and then following the same return route as the Tall Pines Trail.

Departing east from the Tall Pines Trailhead, the Wilderness Lake trail travels 1 mile to marker W6, turns right and loops in a clockwise rotation to the south on FR 398 and 392. Riders can either turn back to the trailhead by turning right at the W7 marker, or continue north onto either of the two longer routes.

From the Delta Lake Park Trailhead the West Fork and South Fork trails both depart along Basswood Drive. The West Fork departs to the west and joins FR 231 at marker W26, following it west to marker W25. At this intersection the West Fork Trail continues north, meeting with the southern portion of the cluster at this intersection and again in three miles at W8 before turning east and returning to the trailhead.

The South Fork departs to the east and follows a simple fire road path in a clockwise direction around the White River Fishery area. At the W16 marker the trail diverts to the north allowing riders the option of connecting to the northern routes best served by the Wanoka Lake Trailhead. Finger Lake Road runs north from W16 and forms the bottom figure-8 portion of the Delta Hills Trail. Two miles at marker W20, riders can either use the Tub Lake Cutoff to return early or continue to the north on FR 425 on the loop running all the way to Wanoka Lake and the northernmost trailhead. The Delta Hills Trail returns south along FR 234C, reconnecting to the South Fork Trail 5.5 miles south at W13.

A word of warning: The Rainbow Lake Wilderness area to the south is strictly off-limits to mountain bikes. This shouldn't be a problem, however, as there are so many miles of trail in the Delta Cluster that no one could ever run out of trail to ride.

Northwest Wisconsin

The northwestern portion of the state is centered around the Chequamegon National Forest with the CAMBA trails at its heart. Wisconsin is lucky to have two national forests within its borders—the Nicolet to the east and Chequamegon to the west—both filled with trees, lakes, and camping, not to mention miles and miles of excellent fat-tire terrain. The famed CAMBA Trails of this part of the state are so extensive they have their own section in this guide, leaving four other north woods routes to be covered here. The riding here is not technical but instead tests endurance and offers the chance to be close to nature, out of earshot of city traffic and human voices.

The northernmost border of this corner of the state borders Lake Superior—a massive body of water both in surface area and in depth. The big ships live here and haul cargo throughout the Great Lakes and out to the ocean. In the winter, however, the lake freezes over and those who are daring enough will drive across into Canada during particularly frigid times. To the west, the St. Croix River flows to the Mississippi. The shores of this river are largely federally protected and therefore are some of the most pristine and beautiful found anywhere. The lakes and streams of the north woods are famed for trophy fish, from trout to walleye to muskellunge. All grow to frightening proportions—the musky with its hundreds of razor-like teeth and the walleye with its white, nocturnal eyes are among the most interesting.

The trees we see today are, for the most part, second generation, the first generation having been cleared in the logging boom of the 1800s. The towns of Menominee, Chippewa Falls, and Eau Claire served as the main logging towns, with old mills still edging some of the rivers. The reforestation has been successful and it is hard to imagine the land cleared so extensively at one time, when so many trees are alive today.

The four rides described in this section of the book are spread out from Eau Claire north to the shore of Superior. The Lowes Creek Trails are the tamest and easiest to reach, located just south of Eau Claire. The riding is short and simple, and best for beginners looking for practice before getting into the toughest rides farther north.

In the center of this area, the Flambeau River Trails and Blue Hills Trails take riders through seriously glaciated country. Hills too numerous to count fill both areas and the trails are long enough to challenge any rider. The Flambeau River Trails follow the edge of the river through grass-covered hills and along several flowage areas and creeks connecting the river to various lakes to the west. In contrast, the area around the Blue Hills is not as aquatic but instead is focused more on solitude. The feeling of truly being all alone in the woods is strangely reassuring and pleasant. The climbing here makes you feel as if you have accomplished something and the descending keeps your wits sharp and your reflexes jumping.

To the far north, Copper Falls State Park has startlingly dramatic views to offer as two major rivers pour through the forest and into a common pool. The trails here play second fiddle to hiking paths surrounding the falls, but for those with the drive to camp, time can be spent doing both. Bike and hike throughout the day to see the whole park and finish up with a night in the campground to round out the experience.

39

Lowes Creek Trails

The Lowes Creek Trails just south of the town of Eau Claire are an easily accessible stop-off for bikers traveling through northern Wisconsin. The trails are only 3 miles off the interstate, but once out and riding in the quiet of the forest, one would never know the road was so close. The entire system is located within a county park and, though the routes included here only make up 6 miles of trail, they provide a great deal of fun for a family outing or an easy afternoon for beginners. The park itself is built around Lowes Creek—a small, winding stream making its way north to the Chippewa River. The riding takes place under the cover of a hardwood forest that turns into a sea of reds, oranges, and yellows in autumn.

The 1.3-mile upper loop is particularly interesting for those looking for a rounded fitness program. The grass bike path follows a Parcourse, a training course with workout stations that became popular in many state and municipal parks in the 1970s. The Parcourse has a dozen workout areas designed to work all the muscles of the body with pull-ups, push-ups, sit-ups, and a variety of other exercises. The entire course is laid out alongside the bike path and provides a nice finish to a ride.

The real riding is east of the Parcourse and takes place on either side of the creek. There is only one major climb in the entire system and, as long as riders stay on top of the east bluff, it only has to be conquered once. The far east loops log in at only 3.5 miles but have a good deal of singletrack and one rather rough descent. A central trail just west of the creek is also fun to explore, taking riders on a short, one-mile loop out of the forest, through a meadow, and back to the parking lot.

The entire set, without a workout on the fitness course, should take intermediate riders less than an hour to complete. Lowes Creek isn't for everyone, but it is a good introduction to singletrack. Those interested in more

LOWES CREEK TRAILS

Ride 39

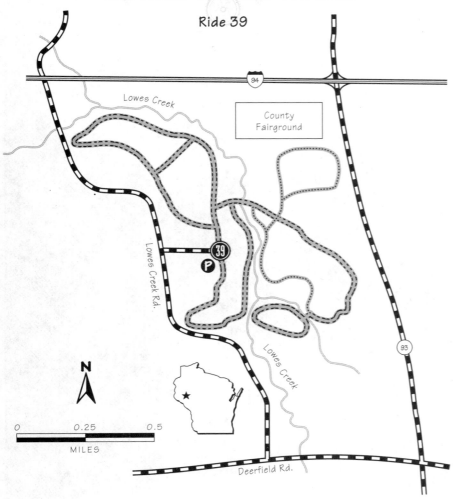

strenuous and involved riding should continue traveling north to some of the more challenging rides in the Chequamegon Forest.

General location: 3 miles southwest of the Interstate 94/Wisconsin Highway 93 intersection south of Eau Claire.

Technical Difficulty: Level 1 to 2.

Aerobic Level: Easy.

Tread: Single- and doubletrack.

Length: 5.4 miles.

Elevation change: There is one climb in the entire network worth mentioning, which takes riders to the top of the trails on the west bluff and covers approximately

A wooden bridge crosses Lowes Creek and connects the loops on either side.

50 feet of elevation. The climbs on the singletrack routes on the center section of trails are very moderate.

Camping: There is no camping available in the immediate vicinity.

Season: April to November when cross-country skiers are not able to use the route. Any time of year is pleasant, as the riding isn't strenuous enough to cause trouble on even the hottest days.

Fees: None.

Services: A water pump is located at the Parcourse entrance. Bathrooms are located in the parking lot. All other necessities including bike maintenance can be found in Eau Claire.

Hazards: There is bad erosion on the climb and descent on the west bluff. In some places the rut formed by rain water is over two feet wide and very deep. Try to avoid putting the front tire into this on the way down the hill. The small descent to the side of this climb also has some erosion problems, though erosion blocks were installed at one time but have since rotted away. Tree falls are also common throughout the forested sections.

Rescue: Though the park is seldom crowded, other park users are the first to look for in case of emergency. If no one can be found, make your way out to the road which is well used and flag down a passing car.

Land Status: County Forest.

Maps: The trail area is shown on the USGS 7.5-minute quad for Cleghorn.

Sources of more information: See Appendix A, in particular the Eau Claire Chamber of Commerce, Wisconsin Department of Tourism, and WORBA.

Finding the trail: Travel west on I-94 to the exit for WI 93 South. Drive 2 miles to Deerfield Road and turn right (west). Go 0.75 mile to Lowes Creek Road and turn right (north). Travel 1 mile to the park entrance on the right.

THE RIDE

Departing from the west side of the parking lot, the Parcourse Trail takes off in a counterclockwise direction. A cutoff bisecting the Parcourse Loop is found midway through that follows the fitness course stations. The other half of the bisected loop covers another 0.5 mile through flat meadowland.

The connector to the east loops is found at the beginning of the Parcourse Loop, 0.10 mile in. The trail descends gradually over gravel to a bridge over the creek. Just before reaching the bridge a singletrack path starts off to the right. This is the one-mile loop leading out of the forest, across a rolling meadow, and back to the parking lot. Across the bridge the trail splits. To the left the trail ends abruptly at benches from which to view the winding creek. To the right the trail leads up to the east bluff, at first on doubletrack, then on a wide gravel path that climbs abruptly to the top of the bluff and then forks. To the left the singletrack leads to the woods and makes a simple loop out to the fenceline of the neighboring County Fairgrounds and back. To the right the trail departs on another loop, this one with several cut-offs that can make for diversity on multiple passes. This trail loops around with no climbing involved. Back at the top of the bluff, riders can descend on the wide gravel path they came up on or a narrow gravel path located just south of the main loop.

There are no signs marking the way through the system, but because of its small size and simple layout, it is hard to get lost.

40

Blue Hills Trails

The Blue Hills Trails are a desolate pair of trail clusters in northern Wisconsin with just over 20 miles of mapped routes. The trails were developed in the late 1980s in the southern portion of the Rusk County Forest by the area trail association, in hopes of providing a secluded, scenic, wooded area for a variety of users. Bikers, hikers, skiers, and hunters all take advantage of the property, making it important to be aware of others on the trail at all times. Until recently, the paths were also open to horses but due to the soft terrain, the weight of the animals was tearing up the trails, and horses are no longer allowed on the east-side trails.

At press time, some trails were undergoing development and restoration—still ridable but definitely under development. The trails are soft and in some areas marsh-like, making them not only difficult to ride but susceptible to damage from even the most moderate traffic. To fight this, many bridges are currently being constructed in these areas to carry riders across the wet sections. Also, to correct the problems caused by bikers and horseback riders, tractors affixed with straight plow blades are flattening out the existing trail network to hopefully provide smoother riding in the flat stretches.

Because the area was constructed originally with skiers in mind, there is no singletrack. Instead the paths are wide enough for skate-style skiing throughout, and brush at the edges of the trails is kept at a distance. The trails are set up in two separate loops, an east and west cluster to either side of the fire lane entrance, the west being the shorter section, the east more densely intertwined within itself. The wide-track paths are mainly on grass and in some cases are doubletrack truck paths.

The system is quite extensive and once riders are used to the trail marking system—using letters and numbers to designate various loops—it is easy to find your way around. To ride the entire system would take approximately 2.5 hours for an intermediate rider, though choosing a specific route and completing it is more likely to be the plan. The east side of the trail system is more dense than the west and has a good deal more climbing. The cluster is built on top of a series of small hills and the paths roll around and over them frequently. The west side of the system is a bit more spread out and lighter on miles. The terrain is flatter and open scenic areas are more common than in the thick forest of the east side.

General location: 12 miles northwest of Bruce, off County Highway O.

Technical Difficulty: Level 2.

BLUE HILLS TRAILS

Ride 40

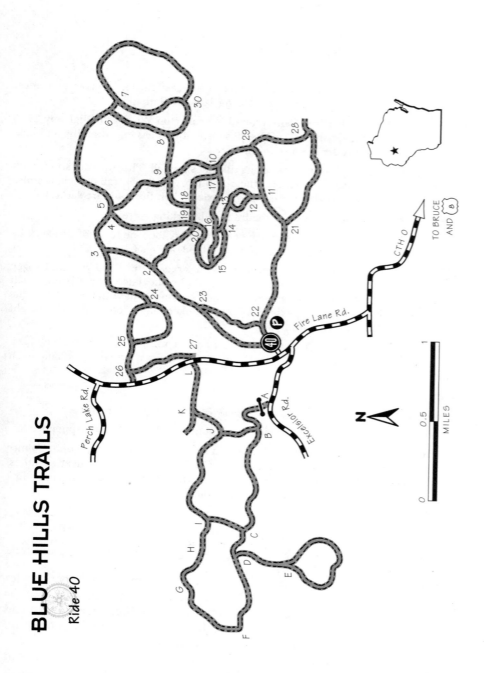

Aerobic Level: Moderate.

Tread: Wide-path grass and doubletrack.

Length: 20 miles.

Elevation change: Climbs of 40 to 50 feet in the east cluster are common, most often at rather steep grades. The west cluster is much flatter.

Camping: Thornapple River Campground is nearby on Wisconsin Highway 27, 3 miles northeast of Ladysmith. It offers 25 sites, with access to swimming and fishing. Restrooms and water are also available.

Season: Opposite ski season. Late spring till first snowfall. The trails are strictly off-limits during ski season to maintain the grooming. The local trail association also asks that riders show good judgment and not ride when the trails are saturated.

Fees: There is a self-pay station at the trailhead. Parking is free.

Services: Toilets are located just north of the parking lot. The town of Bruce is the closest location for other needs such as water, food, and gas.

Hazards: The boggy areas are hazardous, with large, water-filled ruts and soggy outcroppings of muddy earth. This hazard should be alleviated by the bridges that are being constructed. Fallen branches are fairly common but with the width of the trail seldom block the whole passage. Watch for hikers on all loops and wear bright clothing in case of hunters in the area.

Rescue: Ride in a group. The trails are set far back in the woods away from civilization, and help is not readily available. Drive into the town of Bruce to find help in an emergency.

Land status: County Forest.

Maps: The trail area is shown on the USGS 7.5-minute quad for Bruce.

Sources of more information: See Rusk County Trail Association, Appendix A.

Finding the trail: Travel north on Wisconsin Highway 40 and turn left onto County Highway O at the north end of Bruce. Follow CH O northwest for the next 7.5 miles, then turn right onto the gravel fire road marked with a Blue Hills Trails sign. Follow this for 2.5 miles to the trailhead parking lot on the right.

THE RIDE

The east-side cluster of the trail network departs from the main parking lot off the fire road. The entire trail is on a wide grass surface. The route is marked with numbers at the various intersections throughout the forest and makes it a very easy system to navigate. Just look at the number posted on the tree, find it on the map, and pinpoint your location.

The main section of trails is found at the heart of the cluster by starting at #1, going to #23 and then to #2, then turning right and entering the maze at #20. To get to the west loop via the east-side trails, take #1 to #23 to #2, then on to #3. Turn left and follow the trail from #24 to #25 to #26, south to #27 and across the fire road to the west loop.

You can also enter the west-side trails from the road. Take Excelsior Road, which is located just south of the parking lot entrance on the opposite side of the street; the trails depart in one mile from the right side of the road. No parking is available at this location. Again, it is a good idea to carry a map of the area with you, to help you pinpoint locations or plot routes through the forest.

Flambeau River State Forest

The mountain bike trails in the Flambeau River State Forest were dedicated in 1990 to David Klug and took on his name the same year. Klug was the Assistant State Forest Supervisor, instrumental in trail development and an individual as interested in the exploration of nature on cross-country skis as is any mountain biker on their bicycle. The trail system found here is quite extensive, stretching from County Highway W all the way to the small town of Oxbo and beyond along the northern fork of the Flambeau River. The Flambeau River State Forest is a gigantic range of pines and hardwoods, made even larger by the adjoining Chequamegon National Forest to the north, making the entire area a natural reserve that is largely undeveloped.

The trails were originally constructed for cross-country skiers and therefore follow wide grass paths through the entire network. The area is very swampy and water collects in the low-lying areas even in the driest part of the season, especially in trail sections that skirt along the edges of the river. The terrain is very hilly and, though no major climbs are found, it is the sheer number of climbs that will exhaust most riders. The trails are bumpy throughout, not well-ridden enough to have a singletrack path worn into them, and it is difficult to gain momentum. Riders will earn every inch of ground through pedal strokes, not speed built from downhills or previous hard cranking.

Evidence of the days of heavy foresting are still present on these trails, though it is now mostly buried beneath the forest floor. Wooden rail ties can be felt beneath the trail at times and in some places are still visible.

General location: 22 miles west of Phillips.

Technical Difficulty: Level 2.

Aerobic Level: Moderate.

Tread: Wide path, grass.

Length: 18.9 miles.

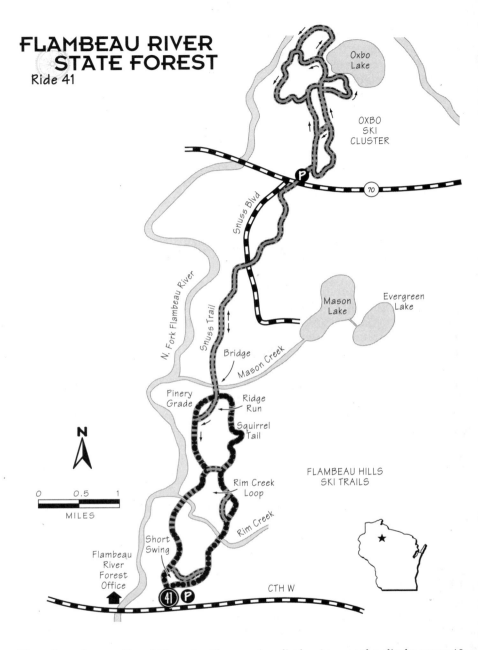

FLAMBEAU RIVER STATE FOREST
Ride 41

Oxbo Lake

OXBO SKI CLUSTER

70

Snuss Blvd

N. Fork Flambeau River

Snuss Trail

Mason Lake

Evergreen Lake

Bridge

Mason Creek

Pinery Grade

Ridge Run

Squirrel Tail

FLAMBEAU HILLS SKI TRAILS

Rim Creek Loop

Rim Creek

N

0   0.5   1

MILES

Short Swing

Flambeau River Forest Office

41 P

CTH W

Elevation change: Very hilly, yet with no major climbs. At most the climbs cover 40 feet of elevation before descending again to do it all over.

Camping: There are 60 sites at 2 different campgrounds within the forest.

Season: The trails are open to mountain bikers when snow is not present and cross-country skiers are unable to use the paths. In summer the heat can be oppressive, especially in the swampy areas and in the high grass, where the heat seems to hang around the most. Fall is the best time of year, with the driest trails, the prettiest surroundings, and the coolest temperatures.

Fees: Donations are accepted at the trailhead.

Services: There are toilets in the parking lot but no water. A single shelter is found west of the short ridge run trail. The towns of Winter and Phillips are the closest points of civilization, both approximately 20 miles to the west and east respectively. Food, gas, and water can be found in either location.

Hazards: There are a few small water crossings, that trail workers have bridged with large, rotting logs. These are probably easy enough to cross in winter when they are hard-frozen, but at other times of year the logs simply break apart as a mountain bike places its load on them—causing some rather exciting crashes into the mud. It is advisable to walk your bike across these instead. In some sections, wooden bridges have been built across small streams that cross the path. Watch for the lip of these bridges as they are about 6 inches higher than the ground and normally grown over with grass. Don't ride straight into the bridge, but instead lift the front wheel up and onto the wooden deck.

Rescue: The trails are not very well traveled and it is miles to the nearest towns. To be safe, ride in pairs, and in case of injury, make your way to a nearby road and flag down help.

Land status: Wisconsin DNR, Flambeau River State Forest.

Maps: The trail area is shown on the USGS 7.5-minute quad for Kennan NW and Oxbo.

Sources of more information: See Appendix A, in particular the Rusk County Trail Association, Flambeau River State Forest, Wisconsin Department of Tourism, and WORBA.

Finding the trail: When approaching Phillips from the south on Wisconsin Highway 13, turn left (west) onto County Highway W. Follow CH W for 22 miles to the trailhead parking lot on the right (north) side of the street. The lot is marked with a large wooden sign.

Grassy singletrack at Flambeau River State Forest.

Leaving from the County Highway W parking lot, the trail heads north on a wide grass path. The trail is consistent throughout in this respect, never getting narrower than eight feet in width. Six loops comprise the southern portion of the cluster. The Short Swing is the first path encountered and, at 1.1 total miles, it never gets very far away from the parking lot on its clockwise route. The Rim Creek Trail is the next trail, and the longest of the southern section. It crosses Rim Creek (hence the name) both on the way out and on the way back. Watch for the lips on both bridges as you approach them. Like the Short Swing, the Rim Creek Trail runs in a one-way clockwise pattern.

North of this the Squirrel Tail, Ridge Run, and Pinery Grade form a counterclockwise loop that caps off the southern cluster. The climbing and descending get a bit more intense and challenging, especially on the Squirrel Tail, which is encountered first. The subtle ruts in the trail make it difficult to keep momentum on climbs and tough to stay in the saddle on downhills.

At the farthest point north on the southern cluster, where the Squirrel Tail meets the Ridge Run, the Snuss connector trail departs to the north and covers 4.5 miles to the second cluster at Oxbo.

The Snuss Trail is easy and uneventful, yet amazingly scenic. At the end of the path are WI 70 and the north cluster parking lot. The north cluster is actually the Oxbo ski network, and the five trails are designated by number instead of name. As in the southern cluster, the trails nearer the lot are ridden over easier terrain, while the trails farther north are more difficult in the endurance department.

Trail #1 runs in a counterclockwise direction and as it cuts across the pinnacle of its route meets with #2, which takes riders north to the bulk of the trails. Routes 3, 4, and 5 all rub up against the shores of Oxbo Lake and test endurance levels with tougher climbs and descents than those found to the south. All in all, the full ride from CH W to Oxbo and back is a serious undertaking and the type of training that makes race winners.

Copper Falls State Park

For those interested in getting away from it all, why not go big and really do it? Copper Falls is as far out of the way as they come, located just 30 miles off the Lake Superior shore in the northwestern portion of the state. The park surrounds some of the most exciting whitewater action the Bad River—or any other river in the state, for that matter—has to offer. The waters of the Bad River and Tylers Fork come together in a dazzling fashion, pouring down from both sides over volcanic rock through narrow canyons, at times spilling down 30 feet before joining in a common pool and flowing off to the northeast. The waterfalls and rapids can be viewed from a series of hiking trails and observation decks constructed by the CCC (Civilian Conservation Corps). The CCC, which constructed so many of the paths in Wisconsin parks, had a way of blending the pathways into the surrounding landscape using natural materials from local sources.

As for mountain biking, 4.5 miles of off-road trails wind through the forest in two separate figure-eight loops. A third 3-mile section of riding is located south of the park entrance and covers easier terrain than the two northern loops. The trails are comparable to those at Devil's Lake, definitely worth exploring but separated by some distance from the truly breathtaking natural features the park has to offer. The majority of the riding takes place on forest floor-type terrain, an uneven path of pine needles, grass, and soil. In some places the wide path is worn down in the middle to a singletrack path. It will take intermediate riders approximately two hours to explore the three trails found within the park, though speed is definitely not the goal here. The purpose of riding at Copper Falls is to explore the forest and enjoy the natural beauty. As with Devil's Lake, the idea is to come for the hiking and camping, but to bring a mountain bike along to explore the three off-road routes and for simple transportation to and from town for supplies.

The area north of the park is worth exploring, as well. The town of Ashland is only 30 miles north on Wisconsin Highway 13, which skirts the Bad River Indian Reservation. The town is a major shipping center with enormous wooden piers extending out into Lake Superior and an exquisite old business district with many of the town's original buildings still intact. Another half hour north on WI 13 is the town of Bayfield, located just south of the Red Cliff Indian Reservation. A ferry is available from Bayfield out to Madeline Island, the largest of the twenty-two Apostle Islands in Chequamegon Bay. Riders may want to spend some time cycling the roads on the island and camping in the state campground on Big Bay.

General location: 3 miles north of Mellen.

COPPER FALLS
STATE PARK

Ride 42

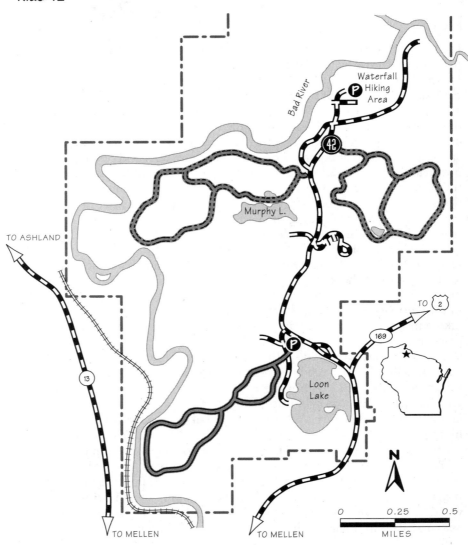

Technical Difficulty: Level 2.

Aerobic Level: Easy to moderate.

Tread: Doubletrack and gravel roads.

Length: Up to 7.5 miles.

Elevation Change: Climbing is moderate on all loops with no climbs or descents over 40 feet. The majority of the rolling terrain takes riders over 10- to 20-foot rises.

Camping: There are 56 sites located within the park. Fire pits are found in each unit, and restrooms and drinking water are within walking distance.

Season: The trails are open from May to October. The best times of year to explore Copper Falls are in fall, when the trees have changed and the air is crisp, and spring, when the river is at full speed with snow melt from the surrounding countryside.

Fees: A trail pass and vehicle admission sticker are required. Both are available as annual passes from the DNR.

Services: Water can be found throughout the North Camp Area. Toilets are located in the north picnic/parking area that serves as the trailhead. Food and gasoline are available in the town of Mellen.

Hazards: Tree falls are the main obstacles to watch for. Try to move larger debris to the side of the trail as a courtesy to other riders. The bases of some of the descents are a bit loose, being filled in with soil and gravel. Though ridable, these may cause trouble for inexperienced riders. Both loops are open to hikers; watch for them, especially on blind corners.

Rescue: The first stops for help are at the park headquarters north of the ballfield or the entrance booth at the south end of the park.

Several smaller bodies of water pour into the Bad River at Copper Falls.

Land status: Wisconsin DNR, Copper Falls State Park.

Maps: The trail area is shown on the USGS 7.5-minute quad for Mellen and High Bridge. Maps are available from the ranger station at the south entrance to the park.

Sources of more information: See Appendix A, in particular the Mellen Chamber of Commerce, Wisconsin Department of Tourism, and WORBA.

Finding the trail: Travel north on Wisconsin Highway 13, turn right (east) on WI 169. Follow WI 169 for 2 miles to a fork in the road; the park entrance is marked by a large sign on the left. After registering at the park headquarters, continue driving to the far north end of the park to the picnic area parking lot. Farther north are the falls and surrounding hiking paths. This parking lot serves as the trailhead.

THE RIDE

Departing south from the parking lot, riders should head in the direction of the North Camp Area to find the off-road trails. The western set is located at the juncture of the main park road and the south entrance to the camp area. The trailhead is marked with a bicycle icon. The trail runs one-way in a counterclockwise direction over forest floor terrain. After 0.5 mile over some minor hills, a cutoff trail approaches on the left. This cuts across the loop and offers riders who are tiring an easy way out.

Those who decide to carry on will be rewarded with a nice descent on the far side of the loop followed by a series of rolling hills. The trail ends by edging along the shore of Murphy Lake through a marshy section before returning to the trailhead. Some technical skills will be needed to negotiate these trails because of their rough, natural surface, though most experienced riders should have no trouble.

The eastern section of trail is found on the opposite side of the main road in the baseball field parking lot. The trail is again marked with a bicycle icon. This section of off-road riding starts off on doubletrack leading away from the ball park. The trail heads out on a very moderate climb, passes a "Do Not Enter" sign marking a return path, and comes to the first turn at the 0.25-mile mark. The trail breaks to the right and makes its way across a section of rolling hills to the far side of the loop. Two choices are offered, heading out in opposite directions: an easy grade to the right, or a more difficult grade to the left. Both sections bring riders back to within 100 yards of the trailhead.

The Red Granite Loop, south of the ranger station at the park entrance is now also open to mountain bikers. The trail is simple yet offers another section of riding for mountain bikers eager to explore all corners of the park. The trail offers an additional 3 miles of riding and passes near Red Granite Falls on its course.

Appendix A
Sources of Additional Information

State Departments and Organizations
Wisconsin Department of Tourism
123 W. Washington Ave.
P.O. Box 7976
Madison, WI 53707
608-266-2161

Wisconsin Off-Road Bike Association (WORBA)
P.O. Box 1681
Madison, WI 53701
608-222-5608
Several trails covered in this book are also found in the Wisconsin Department of Tourism "Wisconsin Biking Guide" available for no cost by calling 800-372-2737 or locally 608-266-2161.

Area Chambers of Commerce

Baraboo Chamber of Commerce
124 2nd St.
P.O. Box 442
Baraboo, WI 53913-0442
608-356-8533

Black River Falls Chamber of Commerce
336 N. Water St.
Black River Falls, WI 54615
715-284-4658

Boulder Junction Chamber of Commerce
5352 Hwy. M
P.O. Box 286
Boulder Junction, WI 54512-0286
boulderjct@centuryinter.net
715-385-2400

Cable Area Chamber of Commerce
P.O. Box 217
Cable, WI 54821-0217
800-533-7454

Delafield Chamber of Commerce
421 Main St.

P.O. Box 171
Delafield, WI 53018
414-646-8100

Dodgeville Chamber of Commerce
P.O. Box 141
Dodgeville, WI 53533
608-935-5993

Door County Chamber of Commerce
1015 Green Bay Rd.
P.O. Box 406
Sturgeon Bay, WI 54235-0406
414-743-4456

Eau Claire Chamber of Commerce
3625 Gateway Dr.
Eau Claire, WI 54701-8187
info@ecchamber.org
715-834-1204

Hayward Chamber of Commerce
P.O. Box 726
Hayward, WI 54843-0726
800-724-2992

Kewaskum Chamber of Commerce
P.O. Box 300
Kewaskum, WI 53040
414-626-3336

Mercer Chamber of Commerce
Hwy. 51 S.
P.O. Box 368
Mercer, WI 54547-0368
715-476-2389

Mellen Chamber of Commerce
P.O. Box 193
Mellen, WI 54546
715-274-2330

Palmyra Chamber of Commerce
P.O. Box 139
Palmyra, WI 53156-0139
414-495-2611

Prairie du Chien Chamber of Commerce
211 S. Main St.

P.O. Box 326
Prairie du Chien, WI 53821
608-326-8555

Rhinelander Chamber of Commerce
P.O. Box 795
Rhinelander, WI 54501-0795
715-385-2400

Vilas County Chamber of Commerce
P.O. Box 369
Eagle River, WI 54521-0369
715-479-3649

Waupaca Chamber of Commerce
221 Main St.
P.O. Box 262
Waupaca, WI 54981
discoverwaupaca@waupacaareachamber.com
715-258-7343

Wausau Chamber of Commerce
300 3rd Street #200
P.O. Box 442
Wausau, WI 53913-0442
608-356-8333

State Parks and Forests

Black River State Forest
910 Hwy. 54 E.
Black River Falls, WI 54615-9276
715-284-4103

Blue Mound State Park
P.O. Box 98
Blue Mounds, WI 53517
608-437-5711

Devil's Lake State Park
S. 5975 Park Rd.
Baraboo, WI 53913-9299
608-356-6618

Flambeau River State Forest
715-332-5271

Governor Dodge State Park
4175 Hwy. 23
Dodgeville, WI 53533-9506
608-935-2315

Hartman Creek State Park
N. 2480 Hartman Creek Rd.
Waupaca, WI 54981-9727

High Cliff State Park

N. 7475 High Cliff Rd.
Menasha, WI 54952
414-989-1106

Mirror Lake State Park
E. 10320 Fern Dell Rd.
Baraboo, WI 53913
608-254-2333

Newport State Park
414-854-2500

Peninsula State Park
Box 218
Fish Creek, WI 54212-0218
414-868-3258

Perrot State Park
608-534-6409

Point Beach State Forest
9400 County Truck O.
Two Rivers, WI 54241
414-794-7480

Potawatomi State Park
3740 Park Dr.
Sturgeon Bay, WI 54235
414-746-2890

Wyalusing State Park
13342 County Hwy. C
Bagley, WI 53801
608-996-2261

Trail Associations

Chequamegon Area Mountain Bike Association (CAMBA)
P.O. Box 141
Cable, WI 54821
www.cable 4fun.com/camba
800-533-7454

Nine-Mile Forest Office
500 Forest St.
Wausau, WI 54403
715-847-5267

Rusk County Trail Association
P.O. Box 251
Bruce, WI 54819

County Forests

Clark County Forestry and Park Department
517 Court St.
Neillsville, WI 54456
715-743-5140

Appendix B
Further Reading

Judd, Mary K. *Wisconsin Wildlife Viewing Guide*. Falcon Publishing, 1995.

Risjord, Norman K. *Wisconsin: The Story of the Badger State*. Wisconsin Trails, 1995.

Valkenberg, Phil, and Jack McHugh. *The Mountain Biker's Guide to the Great Lakes State*. Falcon Press-Menasha Ridge Publishing, 1995.

Will, Tracy. *Wisconsin: Compass American Guides*. Fodor's Travel Publications, Inc., 1997.

About the author

Colby Waller lives in Cedarburg, Wisconsin, with anthropologist Laura Hutchins and their German shepherd, Caesar. When not riding the trails in his area, Waller spends his time restoring old bicycles and other antiquities. A 1990 graduate of Marquette University's advertising program, he has worked for the Milwaukee Chamber Orchestra and Astronomy Magazine, as well as the Olympic Supply Company. While working at Olympic he came in contact with his first mountain bike and learned how to true wheels and perform bike maintenance from an old master, Alphonse Goniu.

What lies ahead? Perhaps international biking in the Scandinavian lands that were home to his ancestors.

Index

MOUNTAIN BIKING GUIDES

Mountain Biking Arizona
Mountain Biking Colorado
Mountain Biking New Mexico
Mountain Biking New York
Mountain Biking Northern New England
Mountain Biking Southern New England
Mountain Biking Utah

Local Cycling Series

Fat Trax Bozeman
Fat Trax Colorado Springs
Mountain Biking Bend
Mountain Biking Boise
Mountain Biking Chequamegon
Mountain Biking Denver/Boulder
Mountain Biking Durango
Mountain Biking Helena
Mountain Biking Moab

FALCON®

■ *To order any of these books, check with your local bookseller
or call FALCON® at **1-800-582-2665**.
Visit us on the world wide web at:*
www.falconguide.com

get FALCON GUIDED

FALCON®

■ *To order any of these books, check with your local bookseller
or call FALCON® at* **1-800-582-2665**.
Visit us on the world wide web at:
www.falconguide.com

SCENIC DRIVING GUIDES

Scenic Driving Alaska and the Yukon
Scenic Driving Arizona
Scenic Driving the Beartooth Highway
Scenic Driving California
Scenic Driving Colorado
Scenic Driving Florida
Scenic Driving Georgia
Scenic Driving Hawaii
Scenic Driving Idaho
Scenic Driving Michigan
Scenic Driving Minnesota
Scenic Driving Montana
Scenic Driving New England
Scenic Driving New Mexico
Scenic Driving North Carolina
Scenic Driving Oregon
Scenic Driving the Ozarks including the
   Ouchita Mountains
Scenic Driving Texas
Scenic Driving Utah
Scenic Driving Washington
Scenic Driving Wisconsin
Scenic Driving Wyoming
Back Country Byways
National Forest Scenic Byways
National Forest Scenic Byways II

HISTORIC TRAIL GUIDES

Traveling California's Gold Rush Country
Traveler's Guide to the Lewis & Clark Trail
Traveling the Oregon Trail
Traveler's Guide to the Pony Express Trail

WILDLIFE VIEWING GUIDES

Alaska Wildlife Viewing Guide
Arizona Wildlife Viewing Guide
California Wildlife Viewing Guide
Colorado Wildlife Viewing Guide
Florida Wildlife Viewing Guide
Idaho Wildlife Viewing Guide
Indiana Wildlife Vewing Guide
Iowa Wildlife Viewing Guide
Kentucky Wildlife Viewing Guide
Massachusetts Wildlife Viewing Guide
Montana Wildlife Viewing Guide
Nebraska Wildlife Viewing Guide
Nevada Wildlife Viewing Guide
New Hampshire Wildlife Viewing Guide
New Jersey Wildlife Viewing Guide
New Mexico Wildlife Viewing Guide
New York Wildlife Viewing Guide
North Carolina Wildlife Viewing Guide
North Dakota Wildlife Viewing Guide
Ohio Wildlife Viewing Guide
Oregon Wildlife Viewing Guide
Tennessee Wildlife Viewing Guide
Texas Wildlife Viewing Guide
Utah Wildlife Viewing Guide
Vermont Wildlife Viewing Guide
Virginia Wildlife Viewing Guide
Washington Wildlife Viewing Guide
West Virginia Wildlife Viewing Guide
Wisconsin Wildlife Viewing Guide

FALCON®

■ *To order any of these books, check with your local bookseller*
*or call FALCON® at **1-800-582-2665**.*
Visit us on the world wide web at:
www.falconguide.com

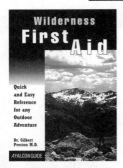

WILDERNESS FIRST AID

By Dr. Gilbert Preston M.D.
Enjoy the outdoors and face the inherent risks with confidence. By reading this easy-to-follow first-aid text, all outdoor enthusiasts can pack a little extra peace of mind on their next adventure. *Wilderness First Aid* offers expert medical advice for dealing with outdoor emergencies beyond the reach of 911. It easily fits in most backcountry first-aid kits.

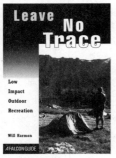

LEAVE NO TRACE

By Will Harmon
The concept of "leave no trace" seems simple, but it actually gets fairly complicated. This handy quick-reference guidebook includes all the newest information on this growing and all-important subjec This book is written to help the outdoor enthusiast make the hundreds of decisions necessary to protect the natural landscape at still have an enjoyable wilderness experience. Part of the proceeds from the sale of this book go to continue leave-no-trace education efforts. The Official Manual of American Hiking Society.

BEAR AWARE

By Bill Schneider
Hiking in bear country can be very safe if hikers follow the guidelines summarized in this small, "packable" book. Extensively reviewed by bear experts, the book contains the latest information on the intriguing science of bear-human interactions. *Bear Aware* can not only make your hike safer, but it can help you avoid the fear of bears that can take the edge off your trip.

MOUNTAIN LION ALERT

By Steve Torres
Recent mountain lion attacks have received national attention. Although infrequent, lion attacks raise concern for public safety. *Mountain Lion Alert* contains helpful advice for mountain bikers, trail runners, horse riders, pet owners, and suburban landowners on how to reduce the chances of mountain lion-human conflicts.

Also Available
• *Wilderness Survival* • *Reading Weather* • *Backpacking Tips*
• *Climbing Safely* • *Avalanche Aware*
To order check with your local bookseller or
call FALCON® at **1-800-582-2665.**
www.falconguide.com